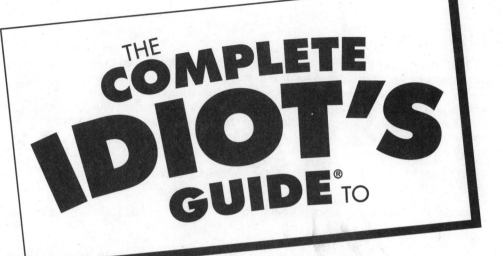

THE

COMPLETE IDIOT'S GUIDE® TO

PCs,

Sixth Edition

by Joe Kraynak

alpha books

A Division of Macmillan General Reference
A Simon & Schuster Macmillan Company
1633 Broadway, New York, NY 10019-6785

To Bob Dylan, for keeping me sane.

©1998 by Alpha

THE COMPLETE IDIOT'S GUIDE TO & Design is a registered trademark of Prentice-Hall, Inc.

Library of Congress Catalog No.: 98-84056

ISBN: 0-7897-1631-3

01 00 99 98   6 5 4

Interpretation of the printing code: the rightmost double-digit number is the year of the book's printing; the rightmost single-digit number, the number of the book's printing. For example, a printing code of 98-1 shows that the first printing of the book occurred in 1998.

Printed in the United States of America

Credits

Executive Editor
Angela Wethington

Acquisitions Editor
Stephanie J. McComb

Development Editor
Lorna Gentry

Technical Editor
Kyle Bryant

Illustrator
Judd Winick

Managing Editor
Thomas F. Hayes

Production Editor
Heather E. Butler

Copy Editors
Kate Givens
Tom Stevens
Kate Talbot

Indexer
Chris Wilcox

Production Team
Jeanne Clark
Christy M. Lemasters
Sossity Smith
Heather Stephenson

Composed in **Stone Serif** *and* **Revue** *by Alpha.*

Contents at a Glance

Contents

Introduction: Keeping Up with the Jetsons

The computer revolution is in high gear. Almost all of us have a computer, and if we don't have one, we're figuring out a way to get one, or get a better one. We want to save time. We want to waste time. We want to play games, make our own greeting cards, design our own homes, quickly balance our checkbooks, and fill out our own tax returns. We want to cruise the World Wide Web, send and receive email, and hang out in Internet chat rooms. We want to understand all the inside computer jokes on *Good Morning America!*

If you want to keep up in this fast-paced world of technology and communications, you had better get your own computer and learn how to use it. The trouble is that using a computer is not as simple as experienced users make it sound. It's not "just like flipping on a TV set" or "programming your VCR." Your TV set and VCR don't have a keyboard and mouse connected to them, they don't have software you have to install and maintain, and they don't have files you have painstakingly created and can delete with a single click of a mouse button.

You need help, you need it fast, and you need it in a way that teaches you, in plain and simple terms, just what you need to know—no more, no less.

Welcome to The Complete Idiot's Guide to PCs

The Complete Idiot's Guide to PCs, Sixth Edition works on the premise that you don't need to be a computer technician in order to run a program. In this book, I won't pack your head with high-tech fluff. I'm not going to explain how a computer chip works, how a monitor displays pretty pictures, or how a printer prints. I promise.

Instead, you'll learn practical, hands-on stuff such as

➤ How to kick-start your computer (and restart it when all else fails).

➤ How to get around in Microsoft Windows 95, and what to expect from Windows 98.

➤ How to install and uninstall programs.

➤ How to find, copy, delete, and undelete files.

➤ How to print your creations, and what to do when your printer goes on strike.

➤ How to connect to the Internet, surf the World Wide Web, and send and receive email.

➤ How to buy a computer that's not obsolete.

➤ How to get out of trouble.

You'll be surprised at how little you *need* to know in order to use a computer, and at how much you *can* know to use it more effectively.

How Do You Use This Book?

You don't have to read this book from cover to cover (although you may miss something funny if you skip around). If you're going computer shopping, skip to Chapter 26, "Savvy Consumer Guide to Buying a Computer." If you want a quick lesson in using Windows, skip to Chapter 4, "Windows Survival Guide." Each chapter is a self-contained unit that includes the information you need to survive one aspect of the computer world. However, to provide some structure to this book, I divided it into the following six parts:

➤ **Part 1**, **"Basic Training,"** deals with the bare minimum: the parts of a computer, how to turn on your computer, how to work with a keyboard and mouse, how to insert and remove floppy disks and CDs, and how to get around in Windows.

➤ **Part 2**, **"Get with the Program(s),"** focuses on applications (the programs you use to perform tasks such as writing letters and creating graphs). Here, you'll learn how to install and run programs, enter commands, save and open document files, and print your documents.

➤ **Part 3, "Get Organized! (Managing Disks, Folders, and Files),"** teaches you everything you need to know about disks, directories (*folders*), and files. Here, you'll learn how to prepare disks for storing data, copy and delete files, organize files with directories, and find misplaced files.

➤ **Part 4, "Going Global with Modems, Online Services, and the Internet,"** launches you into the world of telecommunications. In this part, you'll learn how to select and install a modem, connect to an online service, surf the Internet, send and receive email, and much more.

➤ **Part 5, "Guerrilla Computing,"** shows you how to survive in the real world. In these chapters, you will learn how to shop for a new computer, work on the run with a notebook (or laptop) PC, upgrade your old computer, and tune up your computer to enhance its performance.

➤ **Part 6, "Houston, We've Got a Problem,"** shows you how to prevent disasters and recover from the disasters you cannot prevent. Here you will learn preventive maintenance, how to back up the files on your hard disk, how to fix common computer problems, and how to find professional help for the problems you can't fix yourself.

How We Do Things in This Part of the Country

I used several conventions in this book to make the book easier to use. For example, when you need to type something, here's how it will appear:

type this

Just type what it says. It's as simple as that.

If you want to understand more about the command you're typing, you'll find some background information in boxes. You can quickly skip over the information I put in the boxes if you want to avoid the gory details.

You'll see two kinds of boxes in this book. They're distinguished by special icons that help you learn just what you need:

Techno Talk

Skip this background fodder (technical twaddle) unless you're truly interested.

Check This Out...

In these boxes, you'll find a hodgepodge of information including easy-to-understand definitions, time-saving tips, hints for staying out of trouble, and amusing anecdotes from yours truly.

Acknowledgments

Several people had to don hard hats and get their hands dirty to build a better book. I owe special thanks to Lorna Gentry for guiding the content of this book and keeping it focused on new users. And thanks to Kyle Bryant for making sure the information in this book is accurate and timely. Heather Butler deserves a free trip to the Bahamas for shepherding the manuscript (and art) through production. And our production team merits a round of applause for transforming a collection of electronic files into such an attractive, bound book.

Trademarks

All terms mentioned in this book that are known to be, or are suspected of being, trademarks or service marks are appropriately capitalized. Macmillan Computer Publishing cannot attest to the accuracy of this information. Use of a term in this book should not be regarded as affecting the validity of any trademark or service mark.

Part 1
Basic Training

This is war! From the time you flip the power switch on your computer to the time you beat it into submission, your computer is trying to defeat you. Its tactics are irrational and overwhelming. You enter a command, and your computer displays "Bad command or filename." You click on a button, and the manuscript you've been working on for hours disappears in a flash of light. You try to open a file you created and saved, and you find that it has apparently gone AWOL. With this constant barrage of illogical assaults, the computer hopes to wear you down, to force you into unconditional surrender.

To win the war (or at least put up a good fight), you need to learn about the enemy: what it's made up of, how it thinks, and how you can tell it what to do. In this part, you'll get the basic training you need to survive that first encounter with your computer.

Kick-Starting Your Computer

Computers have come a long way. Back in the early '80s, you had to perform a little ceremony to start your computer: insert a startup disk, search for hidden power switches, and even swap floppy disks in and out of your computer as you ran it. Nowadays, turning on a computer is about as simple as turning on a television set (although the computer takes a little longer to warm up). You just press a couple of buttons and watch your computer leap into action.

In this chapter, you'll learn how to set up your computer and turn on all the computer parts in the proper order. As an added bonus, I'll tell you the proper names of all the parts, just in case you encounter one in your next crossword puzzle.

Naming the Parts of Your Computer

When you're sitting at the computer, you really don't need to know the names of all the parts to explain your frustration when something doesn't work the way *you* think it should. You can simply point and say, "That thing there started grinding, so I pressed this button, and now I can't find anything." Or, "I stuck one of these flat things in this here hole, and now I can't get it out." However, when people start talking about computers at a cocktail party or you need to set up a new computer, you better know your part names. Carry this figure with you, if you have trouble.

A personal computer consists of a few basic parts.

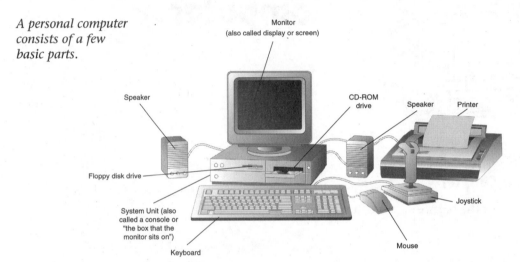

Monitor (also called display or screen)

Speaker

CD-ROM drive

Speaker   Printer

Floppy disk drive

Joystick

System Unit (also called a console or "the box that the monitor sits on")

Keyboard

Mouse

What's a PC?

Before it was hip to be politically correct, PC stood for *personal computer* and was used specifically for IBM personal computers, as opposed to Apples, Macintoshes, and Commodores (excluding Lionel Ritchie). Although many people use the term "personal computer" to describe any computer that can stand on its own two feet, I use the term specifically for IBM and compatible computers (Compaqs, Packard Bells, Gateways, and so on).

The System Unit: Brains in a Box

Although the system unit doesn't look any more impressive than a big shoe box, it contains the following components that enable your computer to carry out the most complex operations:

➤ **Memory Chips**   Also called RAM (random-access memory), these chips electronically store program instructions and data, so your computer can grab the information in a hurry.

➤ **Central Processing Unit**   CPU, pronounced "sea-pea-you," is your computer's brain. If it's real smart, it's called a *Pentium* and it has MMX tacked to the end of it. (MMX doesn't stand for anything, but it gives the chip increased capabilities for playing multimedia.) Older chips are known by their numbers: 486, 386, 286, and so on.

➤ **Input and Output Ports**   Located at the back of the system unit are several outlets into which you can plug your keyboard, mouse, monitor, printer, modem, and other devices. I'll tell you more about ports in Chapter 26, "Savvy Consumer Guide to Buying a Computer."

➤ **Floppy Disk Drives**   Appearing as slots on the front of the system unit, these devices read from and write to diskettes (those square plastic things you stick in the slots). Most new computers have only one floppy disk drive.

➤ **Hard Disk Drives**   A hard disk drive usually hides inside the system unit, so you can't see it or stick anything in it. The hard disk itself acts as a giant floppy disk, storing hundreds of times more information than any floppy disk can swallow.

➤ **CD-ROM Drive**   Most new computers come with a CD-ROM drive that acts a lot like a CD player. This CD player, however, can play programs, games, video clips, sound, and music. New DVD (Digital Video Disc) players do the same thing, but they're faster and they hold truckloads of data (see Chapter 26 for details).

➤ **Other Goodies**   The system unit might also contain a modem (for connecting to other computers using the phone), a sound card (for playing audio), and other electronic gadgets.

Check This Out...

Which Chip Do You Have?   In Windows 95 or later, you can figure out which chip you have by holding down the Alt key while double-clicking the **My Computer** icon (found in the upper-left corner of the screen). The System Properties dialog box also displays the Windows version number and the amount of memory installed in your computer.

Check This Out...

Peripherals   The system unit is the central part of the computer. Any devices that are attached to the system unit are considered *peripherals*. Peripheral devices include the monitor, printer, keyboard, mouse, modem, and joystick.

The Monitor: That TV Thing

The monitor is your computer's windshield. As you drive your computer, the monitor lets you see where you're going. It even collects about as much dirt as your car's windshield—everything from tiny bits of dust to globs of unidentifiable gunk.

You'll run into all sorts of monitors, including the standard 15-inch variety and monitors that look like big-screen TVs. These big monitors are designed mostly for people who do page layout and require a screen that can show an entire page or two-page spread. They're also useful if you're pulling up pages on the Internet.

If you already started your computer, you may notice that the picture doesn't completely fill the screen, as it does on a TV set. Don't worry, your monitor isn't defective. The picture size is typically adjusted by the manufacturer to make the picture as clear as possible. If you make the picture bigger, the edges of the picture can become a little blurry.

Speaking of picture quality, your monitor has several controls, typically located on the front or back of the monitor, which enable you to adjust the brightness, contrast, position, and size of the display. These controls might be tiny knobs, push buttons, or little dials that you need a screwdriver to turn, and they may be hidden behind a panel. (If you have the screwdriver dials, don't use a metal screwdriver: Get a special plastic screwdriver from your neighborhood electronics store.)

Before you fiddle with the controls on the monitor itself, you should check the display settings in Windows. The cause of most display problems resides in a software issue, not in the monitor. To change your display settings in Windows, see "My Screen Is Flickering" in Chapter 32 for instructions. If you need to adjust the monitor itself, make changes in small increments, especially if you are changing the position of the display on the screen: Otherwise, you might move the display right off the screen.

Do I Need a Screen Saver?

A screen saver is a program that displays a moving picture on the screen when you are not using your computer. You may have seen screen savers that display swimming fish, flying objects, or animated geometrical shapes. On old monitors, screen savers helped prevent the monitor from burning a static image into the monitor. Although newer monitors are not as susceptible to burn-in, screen savers do prevent people from snooping at your screen when you're away from your computer, and they offer some security by enabling you to protect your computer with a password. See "Turning on a Screen Saver" in Chapter 5 for details on how to use a screen saver.

The Keyboard (Yes, You Have to Type)

The keyboard has more keys than a high school custodian (another product of the human penchant to overcomplicate). In addition to providing keys for typing text, numbers, and punctuation, a computer keyboard contains special function keys (labeled F1–F12), cursor-movement keys (the arrow keys, plus Home, End, Page Up, and Page Down), and a few other funky keys.

Now, you might think that all keyboards are created equal. The fact is that some keyboards are more equal than others. You'll find ergonomic keyboards whose shape follows the contours of your hands, keyboards that split in half enabling you to raise or lower each half separately, and keyboards with a built-in Windows shortcut key. You may even encounter infrared (wireless) keyboards, which connect to a special infrared port on the computer and transmit signals via light! You'll learn all about the keyboard in Chapter 2, "Taking Control with Your Keyboard and Mouse."

The Mouse: A Rodent You Must Live With

The mouse, also called a "Mexican hairless," is a critter that sits next to the keyboard. You slide the mouse over your desktop or mouse pad to move a pointer around on the monitor. The buttons on the mouse let you select commands and other objects that appear on the monitor.

Like keyboards, mice come in several flavors. The plain-vanilla mouse has two buttons, but you'll see mice with three buttons or two buttons and a little wheel you can spin, and even mice that look like miniature keyboards. And, if you happen to be a lefty, you'll be happy to know that you can easily switch the functions of the left and right mouse buttons, as explained in "Using the Windows Control Panel," in Chapter 5. For details on mouse basics, see Chapter 2.

Your Modem: Calling Other Computers

If you plan on being hip, your computer should have a modem, so you can connect to the Internet and go to places such as **www.cool.com**, send email messages to your friends and relatives, chat with complete strangers, and explore other ways to reduce your productivity at work.

The modem sits inside or outside the computer, and connects to your phone jack. (If you're not sure whether your computer has an internal modem, check the back of the system unit: If there's a phone jack, you have an internal modem.) It can dial numbers for you and connect to remote computers all over the world. I would go into more detail about the wonders of modems and telecommunications, but I've saved that for Part 4, "Going Global with Modems, Online Services, and the Internet."

The Printer: Getting It on Paper

The printer's job is to transform the electric burps and beeps in your computer into something that normal human-type people can read. Printers range from inexpensive dot-matrix types, which print each character as a series of dots, to expensive laser printers, which operate like copy machines. In between are inkjet printers, which spray ink on the page (sounds messy, but it's not). For more information about the various types of printers, see Chapter 26.

The Peripheral Grab Bag: Other Computer Accessories

Although the previous sections introduced the most common parts that make up a computer, many computer dealers offer additional toys that you might not be able to pass up. Here's a list of the most common add-on devices:

➤ **Audio**   Rarely do you see an ad for a computer without a stereo sound card, speakers, and a microphone. If you want to listen to audio CDs, explore a multimedia encyclopedia, hear robots blow up in a video game, or listen to audio clips on the Internet, your computer needs a sound card. And if you want to record sounds or use your computer as an overpriced telephone, it had better be equipped with a microphone, as well. Although most microphones plug into the same sound card you use for your speakers, the microphone might clip onto your lapel, hang on your monitor, or sit on your desktop.

➤ **Joystick**   If you plan on playing Mech Warrior or some other video game, you'll need a joystick. Don't go cheap, because lousy joysticks provide little control for the latest games. Get a Microsoft SideWinder or comparable joystick.

➤ **Scanner**   A scanner can copy text or images from paper copy and transfer the data to your computer so you can use it in your documents. Before you run out and buy a scanner, consider purchasing a combination printer, scanner, copy, fax machine. You can usually find one of these inexpensive combo machines for about $300 more than the price of a comparable printer, and you won't clutter your desk with individual units.

➤ **Zip and Backup Drives**   A Zip or backup drive is a high-capacity drive that uses removable storage disks, cartridges, or tapes. This enables you to transfer data from one computer to another, take it on the road, or back up files from your hard disk.

➤ **Digital Cameras**   One of the hottest new computer toys, the digital camera allows you to take photos or record video clips and then store and play them on your computer. Many of these cameras come with enough memory to store hundreds of snapshots or several minutes of full-motion video, and you don't have to take your film to PhotoMat to have it developed! In addition, because the photos are digitized, you can plop the pictures into letters, cards, and other documents you create.

➤ **TV Converters**   Your monitor looks like a TV, so it may as well act like one, too. With a special display card that plugs in to your system unit, you can watch your favorite TV shows on your computer.

Zip Drive Buyer Beware

Before you shell out extra money for a Zip or backup drive, consider the size of your hard disk. If you get a 100MB Zip drive, you're going to need 10 Zip cartridges to store 1 gigabyte of data. Try to get a Zip or backup drive that is at least half the capacity of your hard disk drive. This ensures that you can back up everything on your hard disk (in a compressed format) onto a single cartridge or tape, and you won't have to sit there swapping disks in and out of the drive during the backup. See Chapter 31, "Backing Up for the Inevitable Crash," for details on backing up your hard disk.

Some Assembly Required: Setting Up Your New Computer

Chances are you didn't wait to read this book before you set up your computer. You've probably ripped open the boxes and pieced the thing together on your own or with a knowledgeable friend. However, if you just purchased your computer (or it arrived at your front door), read the following cautions and tips before you do anything:

➤ Set all the boxes on the *floor* in the room that will be your computer's new "home," so nothing will fall and break.

➤ Don't cut into boxes with a knife. You might scratch something or hack through a cable.

➤ If your computer was delivered to you on a cold day, let it warm up to room temperature. Any condensation needs to dissipate before you turn on the power.

➤ Clear all drinks from the work area. You don't want to spill anything on your computer.

➤ Don't force anything. Plugs should slide easily into outlets. If you have to force something, the prongs are probably not aligned with the holes they're supposed to go in. Forcing the plug will break the prongs.

➤ Pick a location next to a phone jack and a grounded outlet. If you're in an old house and you're not sure whether the outlet is grounded, go to the hardware store and buy an outlet tester; it has indicator lights that show if the outlet is properly grounded.

➤ Don't plug the computer into an outlet that's on the same circuit as an energy hog, such as a dryer or air conditioner. Power fluctuations can hurt your computer and destroy files.

➤ Place your computer in an environment that is clean, dry, and cool. Don't place it near a radiator, next to a hot lamp, or in your new tanning bed.

➤ Don't shove any part of the computer up against a wall, or stack books or other things on top, under, or around any part of the computer. The computer has fans and vents to keep it cool. If you block the vents, the computer might overheat. You don't want a two-thousand dollar piece of toast.

➤ Keep the computer away from magnetic fields created by fans, radios, large speakers, air conditioners, microwave ovens, and other appliances.

➤ Don't turn anything on until everything is connected.

To figure out where to plug things in, look for words or pictures on the back (and front) of the system unit; most receptacles are marked. If you don't see any pictures next to the receptacles, try to match the plugs with their outlets. Look at the overall shape of the outlet and see if it has pins or holes. Count the pins and holes and make sure there are at least as many holes as there are pins. As a last resort, look for the documentation that came with the computer.

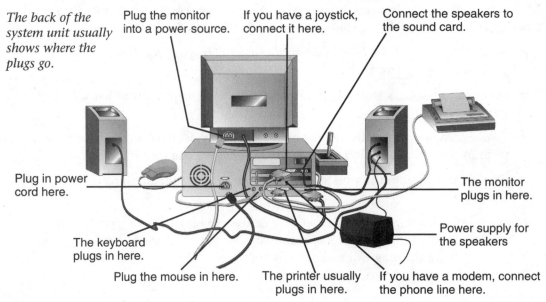

The back of the system unit usually shows where the plugs go.

Plug the monitor into a power source.

If you have a joystick, connect it here.

Connect the speakers to the sound card.

Plug in power cord here.

The monitor plugs in here.

The keyboard plugs in here.

Power supply for the speakers

Plug the mouse in here.

The printer usually plugs in here.

If you have a modem, connect the phone line here.

Software: Instructions on a Disk

Before your computer can do anything useful, it needs an education—some instructions that tell it what to do. In the computer world, these instructions are called *software*. I could bore you with a complete explanation of software, but all you need to know are the following facts:

➤ Computers need a special type of software called *operating system software* to start. Common operating systems are DOS, Windows 3.1, Windows 95, and Windows 98. Chapters 4 and 5 focus on Windows 95 and Windows 98 (prereleased version).

➤ If you just purchased a computer, it has the operating system software on its hard disk. When you turn on your computer, the operating system runs automatically. You probably also received the operating system on a CD, just in case you have to reinstall it.

➤ Once the computer starts, you can run other software *applications* or *programs*. Applications include word processors, spreadsheets, games, backup programs, Web browsers (for the Internet), email programs, and any other program that lets you do something specific. Most computers come with several games and other applications preinstalled, to give you immediate gratification without having to install a bunch of programs. See Part 2, "Get with the Program(s)," to learn how to install and use applications.

Okay, Start 'Er Up

You've probably started your computer a hundred times already. You don't need a book to tell you how to do it, right? Well, maybe you're not turning it on *properly*. Run through the following procedure to make sure you're turning on all the parts in the right order:

1. All your equipment (system unit, monitor, printer, external modem—anything with a power supply cord) should be plugged into a surge-protector power strip. The power strip prevents any sudden spikes in the electrical current from zapping sensitive components in your computer. Make sure the power strip is on.

Check This Out...

Don't Skimp on the Surge Protector

Make sure your surge-protector (surge-suppressor) has a UL rating of 400 or less and an energy-absorption rating of 400 or more. The UL rating represents the maximum voltage that the surge-protector will let pass through it. The energy-absorption rating represents the amount of energy the suppressor can absorb before it's toasted. For better protection, get a line conditioner or UPS (Uninterruptible Power Supply). A UPS has a built-in battery that can supply power to your computer in the event of a blackout or brownout.

2. Press the button on the monitor or flip its switch to turn it on. Computer manufacturers recommend that you turn on the monitor *first*. This enables you to see the
   startup messages, and it prevents the monitor's power surge from passing through
   the system unit's components. The monitor will remain blank until you turn on the
   system unit. (On many newer PCs, the monitor comes on automatically when you
   turn on the system unit.)

3. If you plan on printing, turn on the printer. Otherwise, leave it off. The printer
   consumes a lot of power; you can turn it on later, just before you decide to print.

4. When you turn on the printer, make sure its On Line light is lit (not blinking). If the
   light is blinking, make sure the printer has paper, and then press the **On Line**
   button (if the printer has an online button).

5. If you have speakers or other devices connected to your computer, turn them on.

6. Make sure your floppy disk drive is empty. If the drive has a floppy disk in it, press
   the eject button on the drive and then gently remove the disk. (Don't worry about
   removing any CDs from the CD-ROM drive.)

7. Press the power button or flip the switch on the system unit.

8. Ahhh, this is where the fun starts. Stuff appears onscreen; lights flash; disk drives
   grind. You'll hear beeps, burps, gurgles, and grunts. Eventually, your system settles
   down, and you see something useful on your screen.

If you hear some rude grinding and you see a message onscreen telling you to insert a
system disk in drive A or that you have an invalid system disk, don't worry. You (or
someone else) may have left a disk in drive A (the computer's floppy disk drive) when you
turned off the computer. The computer can't find the system information it needs to
wake up. No biggy; remove the disk from drive A and press **Enter**.

Do You Have Windows 3.1, Windows 95, Windows 98, or DOS?

Before I can tell you what to do next, you have to figure out which operating system you
have (if you don't know already). Most new computers are set up to run Windows 95 or
98 automatically, in which case you'll see a Start button in the lower-left corner of your
screen. If you have an older system, you'll see Windows 3.1 (which displays a bunch of
tiny icons) or the DOS prompt, which looks like C:\> (or something similar).

Telling the difference between Windows 3.1 and Windows 95 is child's play, but telling
the difference between various versions of Windows 95 and between Windows 95 and the

upcoming Windows 98 is tricky. During its illustrious history, the *new and improved* Windows has gone through several changes:

➤ **Windows 95 OEM Service Release 1** (OSR 1, for short) came with several bug fixes for Windows, but didn't change the way Windows 95 looked or acted. (OEM stands for Original Equipment Manufacturer, meaning that this version was intended to be installed only on new computers.)

➤ **Window 95 OSR 2** included more bug fixes, increased support for newer hardware devices, improved power management tools, and some nifty utilities (tools) for improving the performance of your computer's hard disk drive. Again, this version did not look or act much differently from the original Windows 95. You couldn't buy this new version; it came only with new computers. (Microsoft labeled this version Windows 95 4.00.950 B.)

➤ **Windows 95 OSR 2.5** is the latest (and possibly the last) version of Windows 95. This version includes Internet Explorer 4, a Web browser you'll learn more about in later chapters. Internet Explorer 4 changes the look of the opening Windows screen, displaying a channel bar and Quick Launch toolbar, as shown in the following figure. The big difference you will notice is that you can single-click icons in this version of Windows instead of double-clicking them as you would in previous versions.

➤ **Windows 98** looks like Windows 95 OSR 2.5, and is also fully integrated with Internet Explorer. You can single-click icons instead of double-clicking them. You'll learn more about this new Windows in Chapter 5, "Windows Tips, Tricks, and Traps."

The easiest way to determine which version you have is to hold down the **Alt** key while double-clicking the **My Computer** icon (the small picture of a computer) in the upper-left corner of the opening screen. Windows displays the version number under **System**. Click the X in the upper-right corner of the window to close it. The following figure can also help you determine which version of Windows you have.

Responsible Disclaimer or Shameless Cop-out? At the time I was writing this book, Windows 98 had not been released. The figure of the Windows 98 screen shows a pre-released (beta) version of the product. You now have the option of condemning me and my publisher for not waiting for the released version or thanking us for giving you a sneak peek at what's on the horizon.

*Which operating
system do you have?*

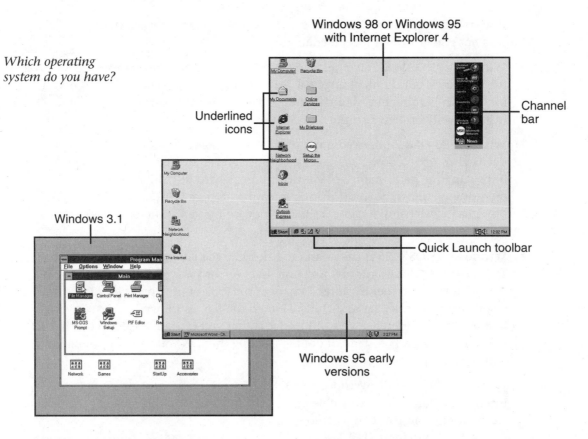

If you have Windows 95 or 98, you're in luck; Chapters 4 and 5 provide a tour of the Windows opening screen and show you how to expertly navigate Windows.

Giving Your Old Windows 95 a New Look

If you recently purchased a new computer, you're lucky—it probably came with Windows 95 OSR 2.5 or Windows 98. If you have an older version of Windows 95, you can at least make it *look* like one of these later versions by installing Internet Explorer 4.0. You can purchase it dirt cheap at most computer stores or get a free copy from Microsoft's Internet site. See Chapter 21, "Whipping Around the World Wide Web," to learn how to get a free copy of Internet Explorer 4 from Microsoft's Web site.

If you have Windows 3.1 or DOS, you probably purchased your computer at a garage sale. You should look for some old books to go with your old computer. With DOS, you must type commands at the DOS prompt (C:\>) to run programs and perform DOS-related tasks, such as copying files. You have to know what you're doing.

Windows 3.1 is a little more helpful. It provides a screenful of icons you can click to run your programs and to use the applications that come with Windows. If your computer displays the DOS prompt at startup and you know Windows is installed, type **cd\windows**, press **Enter**, type **win**, and press **Enter**. This starts Windows 3.1, so you won't have to deal with DOS.

> **Blank Screen?** If your computer starts with a blank screen, you probably forgot to turn on the monitor. Make sure the monitor is plugged into a power source and connected to the system unit and try turning it on again. If it's still blank, crank up the brightness control. The control should be on the front or back of the monitor.

Restarting Your Computer When It Locks Up

Sometimes you may find that your computer has locked up, refusing to do any more work. You press **Esc**, click the mouse everywhere, press the **F1** key (usually used for getting help), and press all the other keys, and it gives you the same blank stare.

When this happens, you will be tempted to turn the computer off and then on. Resist the temptation. Try to *warm boot* the computer first. Warm booting forces the computer to reread its startup instructions without turning the power off and on. To warm boot the computer, hold down the **Ctrl** key and the **Alt** key while pressing the **Del** key. This key combination, **Ctrl+Alt+Del**, is commonly referred to as the "three-key salute." Warm booting is preferred to cold booting, because it doesn't jolt your computer with another startup surge.

If you try to warm boot from Windows, you see a warning screen that explains the potential risks and your options. Read the entire screen before proceeding. In most cases, your computer is busy performing some task, or one of the applications you're running is conflicting with Windows. You can probably regain control without rebooting, simply by exiting the program that caused your computer to lock up. If you press **Ctrl+Alt+Del** and you see the Close Program dialog box, Windows may display [not responding] next to the name of the program that's causing problems. Click the program's name and click the **End Task** button.

Check This Out...

Avoid Rebooting
Reboot (warm or cold boot) your computer only as a last resort. If you are working on a project and you have to reboot, you will lose everything you did since the last time you saved

If Ctrl+Alt+Del Doesn't Work...

Sometimes, the **Ctrl+Alt+Del** key combination doesn't work. You press the combination, and nothing happens. What next? If your computer has a Reset button, try pressing the **Reset** button to reboot your computer. Like **Ctrl+Alt+Del**, the Reset button reboots your computer without turning the power off and on.

The Cold Boot Restart: The Last Resort

If **Ctrl+Alt+Del** doesn't work and your computer doesn't have a Reset button, you will have to cold boot your computer. To cold boot your computer, start by flipping the system unit power switch to the Off position. (Don't turn off the monitor or any other devices, just the system unit.)

Wait 30 to 60 seconds for the system to come to a complete rest and to allow the system to clear everything from memory. Listen to your computer carefully, and you'll be able to hear it "power down" for a few seconds. You may also hear the hard disk drive spin to a stop. This is important, because if you flip the power back on before the hard disk drive stops spinning, the "needle" (read/write head) in the drive might crash down on the disk and destroy data stored on that part of the disk. After the sound of powering down ends, flip the system unit power switch to the On position.

After you have rebooted, you should run a utility called ScanDisk to check your disk for file fragments that may be causing your computer to crash, and may continue to cause crashes. In Windows 95 OSR 2 and later, Windows automatically runs ScanDisk when you start your computer after an improper shutdown. See Chapter 28, "Do-It-Yourself Computer Tune-Ups," for instructions on running ScanDisk.

Turning Everything Off

Although your computer may look like nothing more than a fancy TV, you can't just turn it off when you're finished working. Doing so could destroy data and foul up your programs. Here's the right way to turn off your computer:

1. Save any files you have open on a disk. When you have a file open, your work is stored in RAM, which is like brain cells that require electricity to work. If you turn off the electricity without saving your work on a disk, your computer forgets your work. See Chapter 9, "Making, Saving, and Naming Documents," for instructions on how to save your work.

2. Quit any programs you are currently using. When you close a program, it makes sure you've saved all your work to disk, and then it shuts itself down properly. To exit most programs, you click the **Close** button (an X in the upper-right corner of the program's window), or you open the program's **File** menu and select **Exit**.

3. Click the **Start** button in the lower-left corner of the Windows screen and choose **Shut Down**. A dialog box appears asking whether you want to shut down the computer or reboot it.

4. Click **Shut Down** and then click the **OK** button.

5. Wait until Windows tells you that it is now safe to shut down your computer.

6. Put your floppy disks away. Floppy disks can become damaged if you leave them in the disk drives. First, make sure that the floppy drive light goes off. Then, remove the floppy disk from the disk drive and put it away.

7. Make sure the hard disk drive light is off, and then turn off the system unit.

8. Turn off the monitor and any other devices that are connected to the system unit. (On laptop computers and some newer desktop models, the system may shut down the monitor or place it in sleep mode automatically when you shut down Windows or turn off the system unit.)

9. Pour libations to the computer gods. Without divine intervention, no computer task is possible.

Tech Check

Before you start playing with your keyboard and mouse in the next chapter, make sure you can do the following:

➤ Point to the parts of your computer and call out their names.

➤ Figure out which processing chip is installed in your computer.

➤ Name at least three peripheral devices connected to your computer.

➤ Turn on your computer the right way.

➤ Figure out whether your computer runs DOS, Windows 3.1, Windows 95, or Windows 98 on startup.

➤ Name two ways to safely restart your computer when it locks up.

➤ Turn off your computer without losing any work.

THIS ONE'S FOR ALL THOSE PROGRAMMERS OUT THERE.

Chapter 2

Taking Control with Your Keyboard and Mouse

In This Chapter

➤ Ctrl, Alt, F1, and other funky keys

➤ Point, click, drag, and other mouse moves

➤ Alternative pointing devices for rodentphobes

➤ Voice-activated computing—"I talk, it types."

If you believe all the techno-hype, in the not-so-distant future we will all be wired to computers and have mini hard drives implanted in our brains to aid our memories. Instead of clicking little pictures, selecting items from onscreen menus, and typing commands, we'll be wrapped in virtual suits and work in three-dimensional programs, computing and getting a cardiovascular workout at the same time.

Until then, we have to communicate with our computers and programs using the standard low-tech tools—the mouse and the keyboard. In this chapter, you'll learn how to use these standard tools along with a few other technologies that help you talk to your computer.

Pecking Away at the Keyboard

The keyboard and printer are pretty much all that is left of the old manual typewriter, and the keyboard hasn't changed much in its computer adaptation. It still has the letter and number keys, but a few keys have been added to manage specialized computer operations:

➤ **Function keys**   The 10 or 12 F keys at the top or left side of the keyboard (F1, F2, F3, and so on) were frequently used in old DOS programs to enter commands quickly. F1 is still used to display help in Windows and most Windows programs, and you can assign function keys to perform specific tasks in most programs.

➤ **Arrow keys, Page Up, Page Down, Home, and End**   Also known as cursor-movement keys, these keys move the cursor (the blinking line or box) around onscreen.

➤ **Numeric keypad**   A group of number keys positioned like the keys on an adding machine. You use these keys to type numbers or to move around onscreen. Press the **Num Lock** key to use the keys for entering numbers. With Num Lock off, the keys act as arrow or cursor-movement keys. Most computers turn on Num Lock on startup.

➤ **Ctrl and Alt keys**   The Ctrl (Control) and Alt (Alternate) keys make the other keys on the keyboard act different from the way they normally act. For example, in Windows, you can press Ctrl+A (hold down the Ctrl key while pressing A) to select all the text or objects displayed in the current window.

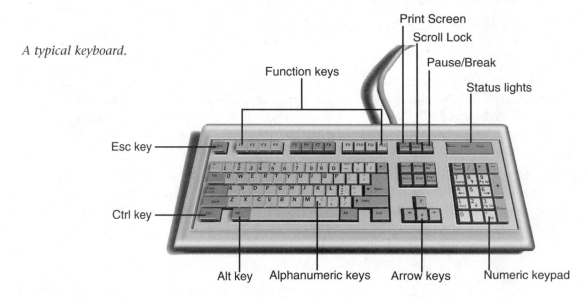

A typical keyboard.

➤ **Esc key**   You can use the Esc (Escape) key in most programs to back out of or quit whatever you are currently doing.

➤ **Print Screen/SysRq**   This key is used to actually send a copy of your screen to your printer, so you can have a printout of whatever funky-looking thing your computer is doing. In Windows, this sends the screen image to the Windows Clipboard, a temporary storage area for data. To learn more about the Clipboard, see "Cutting, Copying, and Pasting Stuff" in Chapter 10, "Giving Your Documents the Editorial Eye."

➤ **Scroll Lock**   Another fairly useless key, in some programs, Scroll Lock makes the arrow keys push text up and down on the screen one line at a time instead of moving the insertion point.

➤ **Pause/Break**   The king of all useless keys, Pause/Break used to stop your computer from performing the same task over and over again, something that DOS and DOS programs were apt to do.

➤ **More Keys?**   Some manufacturers have "improved" keyboards that offer many additional keys. Gateway computers, for instance, come with a keyboard called AnyKey, which contains keys for recording and playing back *macros*. (A macro is a recorded series of keystrokes or commands that you can play back by pressing a single key or key combination.) The AnyKey keyboard also has a Remap key, which can get you in all sorts of trouble by enabling you to reassign one key, say Tab, to another key, say K. You press Tab, and you get a K. Sounds like a sick practical joke, doesn't it?

A Special Key, Just for Windows

Many newer keyboards have an extra key that has the Windows logo on it. You can use this Windows key to quickly enter commands in Windows 95 or 98, as shown in the following table.

Windows Key Shortcuts

Press	To
Windows	Open the Start menu.
Windows+Tab	Cycle through running programs.
Windows+F	Find a file.
Ctrl+Windows+F	Find a computer on a network.

continues

21

Windows Key Shortcuts Continued

Press	To
Windows+F1	Display the Windows Help window.
Windows+R	Display the Run dialog box (for running programs).
Windows+Break	Display the System Properties dialog box.
Windows+E	Run Windows Explorer for managing folders and files.
Windows+D	Minimize or restore all program windows.
Shift+Windows+M	Undo minimize all program windows.

Cramped Keys on Notebook PCs

Portable computers, including notebook and laptop PCs, typically don't have the space for a full set of keys to spread out. To fit all the keys in a limited amount of space, many keys have to do double-duty. For example, some of the keys may be used to adjust the brightness and contrast of the display.

In most cases, the keyboard includes a key labeled Fn, which is a different color (for instance, blue). Keys that perform double-duty have their primary function displayed in black or white, and their secondary function displayed in the same color used for the Fn key. To take advantage of the secondary function of the key, you hold down the Fn key while pressing the key that's labeled with the desired secondary function.

Pointing, Clicking, and Dragging with Your Mouse

Unless you've been living in an abandoned mine shaft, you've seen the standard two-button computer mouse. It fits in the palm of your hand and has a cable that attaches it to the system unit. You roll the mouse around on your desk or a designer mouse pad to move the onscreen pointer over the desired object. To use a mouse, you have to master a few basic moves:

➤ **Point** Roll the mouse around till the tip of the onscreen arrow is over the item you want. Easy stuff.

➤ **Click** Point to something (usually an icon or menu command) and then press and release the left mouse button. Be careful not to move the mouse when you click, or you might click the wrong thing.

➤ **Right-click** Same as click but use the right mouse button. A couple of years ago, the right mouse button was pretty useless. Now it is used mainly to display *context menus,* which contain commands that apply only to the currently selected object.

➤ **Double-click**   Same as click but you press and release the mouse button twice real fast without moving the mouse. This is kind of tough for new computer users to master.

➤ **Drag**   Click an object and then hold down the left mouse button while moving the mouse. You typically drag to move an object, draw (in a drawing or paint program), or select text (in a word-processing program). In some cases, you can drag with the right mouse button; when you release the mouse button, a context menu typically appears, asking what you want to do.

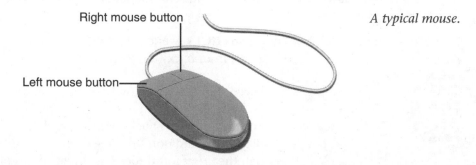

Right mouse button

Left mouse button

A typical mouse.

Mouse with No Tail?

Most keyboards and mice have cables that attach them to the system unit. However, wireless versions are becoming more available. You can now purchase wireless mice and keyboards that connect to a special infrared port via light, sort of like a TV control. However, for an infrared mouse to work, you must have an infrared port on your computer and there must be a direct line of sight between the mouse and the infrared port. See Chapter 26, "Savvy Consumer Guide to Buying a Computer," for details.

Building a Smarter Mouse (Microsoft's IntelliMouse)

Similar in shape to the standard two-button Microsoft mouse, the IntelliMouse has a small gray wheel between the left and right buttons. Although it feels like a lump on an otherwise smooth mouse, the wheel gives you more control over scrolling and entering commands, and it is fairly easy to use.

The left and right mouse buttons work as they always have, but in applications that support the IntelliMouse (including most new Microsoft applications), you can do two things with the wheel: spin it and click it. What spinning and clicking do depend on the application. For example, in Microsoft Word, you can use the wheel to scroll more accurately, as described here:

➤ Rotate the wheel forward to scroll text up; rotate backward to scroll down.

➤ To pan up or down, click and hold the wheel while moving the mouse pointer in the direction of the text that you want to bring into view. (Panning is sort of like scrolling, but it's smoother.)

➤ To autoscroll up or down, click the wheel, and then move the mouse pointer up (to scroll up) or down (to scroll down). Autoscrolling remains on until you click the wheel again.

➤ To zoom in or out, hold down the **Ctrl** key and rotate the wheel. Rotate forward to zoom in or backward to zoom out.

> **Techno Talk**
>
> **What's a Driver?** A driver is special software that tells the computer how to use a particular device. Each device that is connected to your computer (the printer, monitor, mouse, sound card, joystick, and so on) requires its own driver.

If you don't have an IntelliMouse, don't run out and buy one. It's not an essential toy. However, if you have an extra hundred bucks lying around, it is kind of fun to play with. And don't rip one off from work unless you nab the *driver* for it, too. The driver comes on a floppy disk, and you have to install it before you can take advantage of the wheel. See Chapter 27, "Upgrading Your Computer to Make It the Best It Can Be," for instructions on installing drivers.

Other Devices for Poking Around on Your Computer

In search of the perfect pointing device, computer manufacturers have toyed with other ideas: trackballs, joysticks, touchpads, light-sensitive pens, and little gear shifts stuck in the middle of keyboards. I've even seen two foot pedals set up to act like a mouse! The following sections introduce you to some of the more popular navigational devices.

On Track with Trackballs

The trackball is basically an upside-down mouse. Instead of sliding the mouse to roll the ball inside the mouse, you roll the ball yourself. The good thing about a trackball is that it doesn't require much desk space and it doesn't get gunked up from dust and hair on your desk. The bad thing about trackballs is that they haven't figured out a good place to put the buttons. You almost need two hands to drag with a trackball: one to hold down the button and the other to roll the ball. Stick with a mouse.

If you have a laptop or notebook computer that has a built-in trackball (which is pretty common), I take back all those negative comments about the trackball. But seriously, if you don't like your laptop's trackball, you can usually disable it and connect a mouse to the computer's serial port.

A trackball is sort of like an upside-down mouse.

Getting in Touch with Touchpads

A touchpad is a pressure-sensitive square that you slide your finger across to move the pointer (very popular in the touchy-feely '90s). A typical touchpad has two buttons next to it that act like mouse buttons: you click or double-click the buttons or hold down a button to drag. With most touchpads, you can also tap the touchpad itself to click or double-click.

Sound cool? I thought so, too, until I purchased a notebook computer with a touchpad. Touchpads have two big drawbacks:

➤ If your finger is slightly damp (fingers have been known to perspire), there's no telling where your pointer is going to end up. It follows the hot spot, which just might be where your finger was resting before you moved it.

➤ The touchpad on portable computers is positioned right where your thumbs rest. Move your thumb or tap it against the touchpad, and your pointer and insertion point follow your thumbs. Although you can adjust the sensitivity of the touchpad to help alleviate this problem, the adjustments don't help much.

Fortunately, most notebook computers allow you to disable the touchpad and use a mouse, instead.

> *Check This Out...*
>
> **IBM's Little Red Button** You've probably seen portable computers with a little red lever smack in the middle of the keyboard. The lever acts sort of like a joystick; you push the lever in the direction you want to move the mouse pointer. You use buttons next to the keyboard to click and drag. Although the lever gives you fairly good control and has none of the problems associated with touchpads, it takes some getting used to.

Joysticks: A Must-Have for Computer Games

If you plan on playing any arcade games on your computer, you need a joystick. A standard joystick looks like a flight stick or one of those controls you've seen on video arcade games. It has a base with a lever sticking out of it. The lever usually has a few buttons for firing weapons and accelerating.

To use a joystick, you plug it into a special joystick port on the back of the system unit or on your sound card (near the jacks where you plug in your speakers). You then have to install a driver for the joystick, which is usually included on a floppy disk. Windows comes with its own drivers for popular joysticks. To install a driver in Windows, see Chapter 27.

Poking Around with Light Pens

You probably have seen light pens in doctors' offices and hospitals, where people need to input a great deal of data. A light pen looks a lot like a pen light with a cable attaching it to the system unit. Instead of moving the pen around on a pad or desktop, you point the pen directly at objects on the screen and then press the pen tip against the screen to click or drag. A receptor inside the pen tip can determine the tip's position based on the glow of the tiny dots that make up the screen image.

Check This Out...

Light Pens for Seniors A study by Kelley and Charness (1995) shows that older folks have a much easier time navigating with light pens than with mice.

Although light pens function as nice mouse substitutes, there are other pen technologies that offer additional advantages. For instance, pen-based input devices allow you to write and draw on a pressure-sensitive pad or light-sensitive grid to transform handwritten messages and drawings to your computer. You may have seen such devices built into hand-held computers, but the technology is also available for desktop computers.

Voice-Activated Computing for the Truly Lazy

When you start talking to your computer, it can mean one of two things: either you have voice recognition software, or you've been spending way too much time with your computer. Voice recognition software allows you to enter commands and "type" by speaking into a microphone connected to your computer.

The most basic voice recognition software allows you to train your computer to accept certain voice commands, such as "Save File" or "Delete." More sophisticated software, such as IBM's ViaVoice and Kurzweil's VoicePad, provide you with your own secretary, who can transform your spoken words into typed documents.

The problem with voice and speech recognition is that for it to work properly, you need a good sound card, a great microphone, and several free hours to assign voice commands to specific tasks and train the program to recognize the variations in your voice. Even then, if you wake up with a gravelly voice or talk a little too fast, the program might not quite understand you.

"Smart" Homes

Many newer "homes of the future" have voice recognition systems that have been proven to be so far ahead of their time that they don't work. Owners of these homes complain that their water comes on when the dog barks, that the oven confuses words like "bake" and "broil," and that their security systems lock them out. Expect the same from your voice recognition software until the technology is perfected.

Tech Check

The input devices on your computer provide the only way for you to talk to your computer. Before moving on to the next chapter, you should be able to do the following:

➤ Locate the 12 function keys on your keyboard.

➤ Point to the Ctrl and Alt keys.

➤ Find the cursor movement keys.

➤ Name the five basic mouse moves.

➤ Use the wheel on an IntelliMouse, if you have to.

➤ Name three other ways to talk to your computer.

Chapter 3

Whicka. Whicka. Whicka.

Playing Disk Jockey with Hard Disks, Floppy Disks, and CDs

In This Chapter

➤ Point to your floppy disk drive

➤ Label your disk drives A, B, C, and D

➤ Touch a floppy disk without violating its integrity

➤ Insert a disk into a disk drive (and coax one out)

If you can stick a videotape into your VCR, you have all the technical expertise you need to insert floppy disks and CDs into your computer's floppy and CD-ROM drives. However, the computer complicates matters by assigning names to your drives that you may not recognize. For instance, instead of calling your floppy drive "Floppy," your computer refers to it as A or B. Your CD-ROM drive is D, usually, but it can be named anything from D to Z. In addition, disk drives are not all created equal. A floppy drive lets you insert and remove disks, whereas a hard disk is hermetically sealed inside the drive.

In this chapter, you'll learn everything you need to know about disks and drives, including how to insert and remove disks, recognize a drive by its letter, and keep your disks and CDs in good condition.

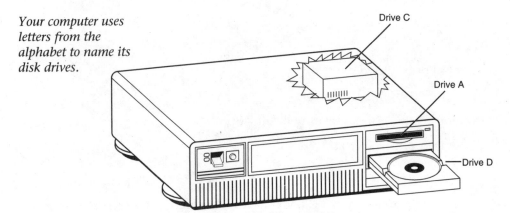

What's a Disk?

A disk is a circular piece of plastic that's covered with microscopic magnetic particles. (A floppy disk is circular on the inside, but is covered with a square plastic case, so you never really see the disk part.) A disk drive inside the computer can "read" the charges of the magnetic particles and convert them to electrical charges that are stored in the computer's memory. The drive can also write information from memory (RAM) to the disk the same way a cassette recorder can record sounds on a tape.

Disk Drives: Easy as A-B-C

Most computers have three disk drives, as shown here. DOS refers to the drives as A, C, and D. If you're wondering what happened to B, it's used only if the computer has a second floppy disk drive.

Your computer uses letters from the alphabet to name its disk drives.

Drive C

Drive A

Drive D

The Floppy Disk Drives: A (and Sometimes B)

Your computer's system unit has one or more slots or openings on the front, into which you can shove a floppy disk, a CD, or a tape, depending on the type of drive. For now, look for a narrow slot that might be horizontal or vertical. This is your computer's floppy disk drive. The drive is not floppy, the disk is; and even the disk isn't very floppy, as you will soon learn.

The Hard Disk Drive: C

The drive shown inside the computer is the *internal hard disk drive*, usually called drive C. Some computers have an *external* hard drive, which sits outside the computer and is connected to the system unit by a cable (it's still drive C). With hard drives, you don't handle the disk; it's hermetically sealed inside the drive.

The CD-ROM Drive: D?

If you're lucky, your computer has a CD-ROM drive. If it's an internal CD-ROM drive, it will be near the floppy drives, although the CD-ROM drive is larger and is *rarely* vertical. If it's an external drive, it will stand alone, connected with a cable to your system unit. Either way, the CD-ROM drive is usually drive D. These drives are very similar to audio CD players; most can even play audio CDs.

You may have seen people place the system unit on its side. Hey, it saves space and looks cool. However, if your system unit has a CD-ROM drive, you may have to sacrifice cool for functional. Although there are some CD-ROM drives that can function if positioned vertically, most CD-ROM drives can't even hold a disc when set on their sides.

Two, Two, Two Disks in One A hard disk drive can be *partitioned* (or divided) into one or more drives, which the computer refers to as drive C, drive D, drive E, and so on. The actual hard disk drive is called the *physical* drive; each partition is called a *logical* drive. If you encounter a computer that displays letters for more than one hard drive, the computer may have multiple hard drives or a partitioned hard drive.

Zip and Tape Backup Drives

If you were to cross a hard drive with a floppy drive, you'd end up with a Zip or tape backup drive—these drives use removable storage media (disks, tapes, or cartridges), like a floppy drive, but store gobs of data on a single disk, like a hard drive. Why do you need one of these special drives? Because everyone, including me, is going to tell you that you should back up the files on your hard disk regularly just in case your hard disk goes bad. And if you do the math, you'll realize that backing up a 1 gigabyte hard drive on a set of 1.44 megabyte floppy disks is no way to spend a Friday night.

If you have a backup drive that can store half as much as your hard disk can hold, you can back up everything on your hard disk to a single disk or tape (the backup program will squish the files so they fit in half the space). In other words, you can start the backup and go play while your computer works. You can even schedule your backup program to run at a specific time every day, so you don't even have to start it!

Buyer Beware

Not to knock market-savvy computer manufacturers, but I've seen several ads lately for computers that come with 4 gigabyte drives and a 100 megabyte Zip drive. If the hard drive were full, you would still need about 20 Zip disks to back it up. Make sure you get a backup drive that can store at least half of the capacity of your hard disk. You'll save enough money on disks or tapes to pay for the more expensive backup drive.

What's on My Disks?

So, how can you figure out what's on a disk? You must use a file management utility to display the contents of the disk. Windows comes with two such utilities: My Computer and Windows Explorer. When you run My Computer, it displays icons for every disk drive on your computer. You simply click the icon for the disk whose contents you want to view (or double-click if the icon names are not underlined). My Computer then displays the names of all of the files and folder on the disk. See Chapter 4, "Windows Survival Guide," for details.

The following figure shows the drive icons displayed in My Computer running on Windows with Internet Explorer 4 installed. If Internet Explorer 4 is not installed on your computer, the icons will not appear underlined, you'll see a different toolbar, and there will be no graphic on the left side of the window.

In Windows, My Computer displays an icon for each disk drive on your computer.

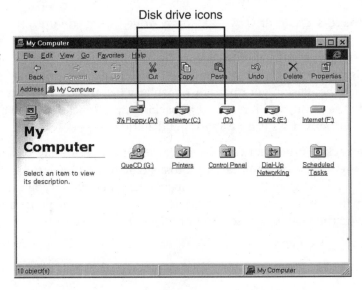

Disk drive icons

Serving Information to the Computer on Floppy Disks

Think of a floppy disk as a serving tray. Whenever you want to get information into the computer, you must deliver the information on a floppy disk. Likewise, if there is something in your computer that you want to store for safekeeping or share with another user, you can copy the information from the computer to a floppy disk.

Two characteristics describe floppy disks: *size* and *capacity*. Size you can measure with a ruler. The size tells you which floppy drive the disk will fit in. You can get 3 1/2" disks (which are not floppy) or 5 1/4" disks (which are floppy), as shown here.

Floppy disks come in two sizes.

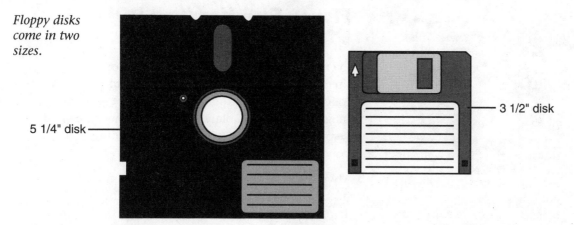

5 1/4" disk

3 1/2" disk

Capacity refers to the amount of information the disk can hold; it's sort of like pints, quarts, and gallons. Capacity is measured in *kilobytes (K or KB)* and *megabytes (MB)*. Each *byte* consists of eight *bits* and is used to store a single character—A, B, C, 1, 2, 3, and so on. (For example, 01000001 is a byte that represents an uppercase A; each 1 or 0 is a *bit*.) A kilobyte is 1,024 bytes—1,024 characters. A megabyte is a little over a million bytes. A gigabyte is a little over 1000 megabytes. Grababyte means to go get lunch.

The following table shows the four basic types of floppy disks and how much information each type can hold. These are standard floppy disks. You might also encounter less standard disks and drives, such as the Iomega Zip Drive, which can store about 100 megabytes of data on a special disk, and tape or cartridge drives that can store from 40 megabytes to more than 3 gigabytes!

Four Basic Types of Floppy Disks

Disk Size	Disk Type	Disk Capacity
5 1/4"	Double-sided Double-density (DS/DD)	360KB
5 1/4"	Double-sided High-density (DS/HD)	1.2MB
3 1/2"	Double-sided Double-density (DS/DD)	720KB
3 1/2"	Double-sided High-density (DS/HD)	1.44MB

Can My Drive Read This Disk? In general, a disk drive can read disks that are equal to or less than its own capacity. A high-capacity disk drive can read low-capacity disks, but the reverse will not work; a low-capacity disk drive cannot read high-capacity disks. Fortunately, manufacturers have stopped making and using low-capacity drives and 5.25-inch floppy drives.

Floppy Disk Handling DOs and DON'Ts

Every beginning computer book contains a list of precautions telling you what *not* to do to a disk. Don't touch it here, don't touch it there, don't get it near any magnets, blah blah blah…. Although these are good warnings, by the time you get done reading them, you're too afraid to even pick up a disk.

My recommendation is to chill out when it comes to disks. They're pretty sturdy, especially the 3 1/2" variety. Throw a disk across the room; it'll survive. Touch the exposed part (God forbid), and your data will probably remain intact. The best advice I can give you is to treat a disk as if it is your favorite CD or cassette tape. However, if you really want to ruin a disk, perform the following acts of destruction:

➤ Chew on it like a pen cap.

➤ Use a disk as a coaster to keep those ugly rings off your desk.

➤ Take a refrigerator magnet and rub it all over the disk in tiny circles. (Usually, if you just rest the magnet on the disk it won't do anything.)

➤ Press the eject button on the floppy disk drive when the light is still on. The disk drive will spit out the disk and nibble on it as you yank it out.

Sticking It In, Pulling It Out

A disk will fit into a floppy drive in any number of ways—upside-down, sideways, even backward. But a disk drive is like one of those dollar changer machines; if you don't insert the disk the right way, the drive won't be able to read it. To insert the disk properly,

1. Hold the disk by its label, with the label facing up.

2. Insert the disk into the drive, as shown in the following figure. (If the disk slot is vertical, hold the disk so the label faces away from the eject button.)

3. If the floppy drive has a lever or a door, close the door or flip the lever so it covers the slot.

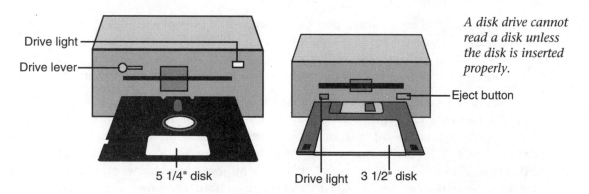

Drive light

Drive lever

5 1/4" disk

A disk drive cannot read a disk unless the disk is inserted properly.

Eject button

Drive light   3 1/2" disk

Now that you have the disk in the drive, how do you get it out? Here's what you do:

1. Make sure the drive light is off.

2. If the drive has an eject button, press the button and the disk will pop out like a piece of toast. If the drive has a lever or door, flip the lever or open the door, and the disk will partially pop out.

3. Gently pull the disk from the drive. Insert the disk into its pouch so the label faces out.

Check This Out...

It Won't Eject!

If your disk refuses to come out of the drive, don't try to fish it out with a letter opener or pliers. If the leading edge of the disk is caught on the drive, gently push the disk down and in to free it. If the disk label is causing the problem, gently push the label back down on the disk without pushing the disk farther into the drive; you don't want the label coming completely off in the drive. If you are certain that the label is stuck securely to the disk, try pushing the disk all the way in and then pressing the eject button again.

Loading and Unloading CDs

You can't just slide a CD into your computer like a quarter in a slot machine. You have to serve it to your computer on a tray, just as if you were placing an audio CD in your CD player. And you have to be just as careful handling these CD-ROM CDs. Hold the CD only by its edges, so you don't get any gooey fingerprints on the surface that the CD-ROM player reads.

Some CD-ROM drives come with a removable *carriage*. You remove the CD from its jewel case, place the CD into the carriage, and then insert the carriage into the drive. Other drives have built-in carriages, sort of like a dresser drawer. You press a button to open the drawer, and then you place the CD in the drawer and press the **Load/Eject** button.

If you ever have trouble playing a CD in your CD-ROM drive, it might be because the CD is dirty. To clean the CD, wipe it off with a soft, lint-free cloth from the center of the CD out to its edges. (Wipe the side without the picture or printing on it, because this is the side that the CD-ROM player reads.) Don't wipe in little circles, no matter what your mother says. If something sticky gets on it, spray a little window cleaner on it, and then wipe from the center out. Let the CD dry thoroughly before inserting it in the drive.

Can I Play My Zeppelin CD? (Going Multimedia with CDs)

The newest breed of CD-ROM players can play audio CDs, as well as computer CDs, so you can rock to your favorite tunes while balancing your budget. With Windows, you simply load the audio CD, and Windows starts to play it. If your computer has a sound card, the audio will play through the speakers. If not, you must plug a set of headphones into the headphone jack on the CD-ROM drive.

If you can't hear your CD, and you know that the speakers are turned on, chances are that the volume is turned down. Right-click the speaker icon in the lower-right corner of your screen and click **Open Volume Controls**. Under Volume Control and CD Audio, make sure the Mute box is *not* checked (if it is checked, click the box to remove the check mark). Hold down the mouse button and drag the Volume slider (the little gray box) below the Volume Control and CD Audio Volume up. The volume control on your CD-ROM drive controls the volume for the headphones only. If your sound card (where your speakers are plugged in) has a volume control on it, you can adjust the volume using that control, as well. If you still don't get sound, see "I Can't Hear My Speakers!" in Chapter 32, "Do-It-Yourself Fixes for Common Ailments."

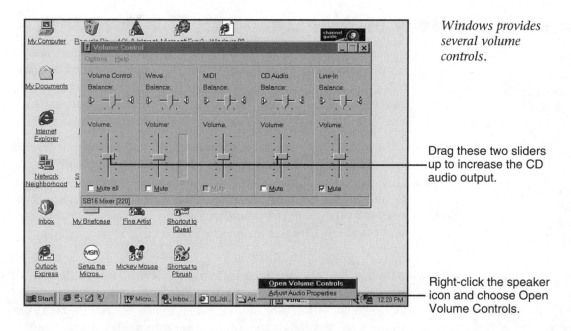

Windows provides several volume controls.

Drag these two sliders up to increase the CD audio output.

Right-click the speaker icon and choose Open Volume Controls.

Your CD-ROM drive can also play *multimedia* CDs, CDs that contain text, pictures, video clips, and audio clips. The most common interactive, multimedia CDs are encyclopedias. To play a multimedia CD, you must first install it, as explained in Chapter 6, "Do-It-Yourself Program Installation Guide." You can then play the CD as you would play any program; see Chapter 7, "Running and Juggling Programs," for details.

Check This Out...

No AutoPlay?

With Auto Insert Notification on, Windows should start to play the audio CD as soon as you insert it. If Windows does not start to play the CD, click the Windows **Start** button (on the lower-left corner of the screen), point to **Settings**, and click **Control Panel**. Double-click the icon labeled **System** and then click the **Device Manager** tab. Click the plus sign next to CD-ROM, and then double-click the name of your CD-ROM. Click the **Settings** tab and make sure there is a check mark in the **Auto Insert Notification** box. Click **OK** to save your changes and click **OK** again to close the System Settings dialog box.

Inside the Belly of Your Computer: The Hard Disk

As I said earlier, floppy disks are bite-sized morsels—mere finger-food for a computer. Any computer worth its salt can gobble up a handful of floppy disks in a matter of seconds and still be grumbling for more. To prevent the computer from always asking for more disks, computer engineers have given modern computers the equivalent of stomachs. The stomachs are called *hard disk drives*, and these hard disks can store lots of information.

The hard disk drive is like a big floppy disk drive complete with disk (you don't take the disk out, it stays in the drive forever). A medium-sized hard disk drive can store more than 500 megabytes, the equivalent of about 350 3 1/2-inch, high-density floppy disks. Many new computers come with a hard drive that can store over three gigabytes—3000 megabytes! Sound excessive? When you consider that Microsoft Windows 95 consumes about 80 megabytes and Microsoft Office consumes nearly 100 megabytes, a gigabyte doesn't look all that big.

To get information to the hard disk, you copy information to it from floppy disks or CDs, or you save the files you create directly to the hard disk. The information stays on the hard disk until you choose to erase the information. When the computer needs information, it goes directly to the hard disk, reads the information into memory, and continues working.

Don't Feed the Animals: Diskless Computers

If your computer is part of a network, or if you purchased one of those newfangled network computers (NCs), it may not have a disk drive. If that's the case, forget all this babble about floppy disks and hard disks. Your network probably has a *server* with a disk drive as big as an elephant that stores all the information and programs you will ever need. A person called the *network administrator* acts as the zookeeper, feeding the server, making sure all the information you need is on hand, and keeping the server happy.

Techno Talk

blah blah
blah bla
h b
b

Network Computers (NCs)

You may have heard the buzz about the new NCs (network computers) that come without a hard disk drive. Supposedly, before the year 2000, we'll all be using remote storage facilities on the Internet, so we won't need hard disk space. (Several major companies, including IBM, are betting on it, anyway.) IBM and a couple other companies are creating inexpensive computers that basically connect to the Internet and use its resources instead of the resources of the computer itself. These computers sell for about 800 bucks. Personally, I'd rather shell out another grand, and get a PC that has some memory and local storage, so I can use it for personal computing as well as an access to the Internet.

The Food on the Disks: Files

Information doesn't just slosh around on a disk like slop in a bucket. Each packet of information is stored as a separate file that has its own name.

Your computer uses two types of files: *data files* and *program files*. Data files are the files you create and save—your business letters, reports, the pictures you draw, the results of any games you save. Program files are the files you get when you purchase a program. These files contain the instructions that tell your computer how to perform a task. A program may consist of a hundred or more interrelated files.

To manage all these files, you can store the files in separate *folders* (also known as *directories*). Whenever you install a program, the installation utility (which places the program on your hard disk) automatically creates a folder for the program. To manage the files you create, you can create and name your own folders. See Chapter 16, "Copying, Moving, and Nuking Folders and Files," for more information.

Tech Check

In this chapter, I've given you a lot to chew on, so don't chew on your disks. Before moving on to Windows in the next chapter, you should be able to do the following:

➤ Label each disk drive on your computer with the correct letter from the alphabet.

➤ Insert and remove a floppy disk from your computer's floppy disk drive.

➤ Name three sure ways to destroy a floppy disk.

➤ Insert and remove a CD from your computer's CD-ROM drive.

➤ Play a music CD.

➤ Draw a picture showing how files are organized on a hard disk drive.

Chapter 4

Windows Survival Guide

In This Chapter

➤ Run at least five Windows programs

➤ Find out what's on your hard disk

➤ Dump stuff in the Recycle Bin

➤ Make your own shortcut icons on the Windows desktop

➤ Check out what's new in Windows 98

If you took Mick Jagger's advice to "Start it up!" (or if the manufacturer of your new computer installed Windows on your hard disk without asking your permission), you're now facing the opening Windows screen, a Spartan screen with a lowly Start button that lets you run all your programs. But how do you start? And how do you navigate this brave, new operating system? In this chapter, you'll find the answers you need and specific instructions on how to perform the most basic Windows tasks.

We Now Have Control of Your TV

There's no starting Windows; there's no stopping it, either. Once it's installed, it comes up whenever you turn on your computer. After an interim screen that welcomes you to

Windows, you'll find yourself on the Windows desktop, as shown here. The icons (little pictures) you see on your desktop may differ, depending on how you or the dealer installed Windows and whether you have additional programs.

If your icons are underlined, if the taskbar contains a mini-toolbar to the right of it, and if there's a thick bar in the upper-right corner of the screen, you have Windows 98 or Windows 95 with Internet Explorer 4. See "What's New with Windows?" near the end of this chapter, to learn how to deal with the new Windows desktop. To hold you over till then, here's a tip: If the icon name is *not* underlined, click to select it, double-click to activate it; if the icon name is underlined, point to it to select it, click to activate it.

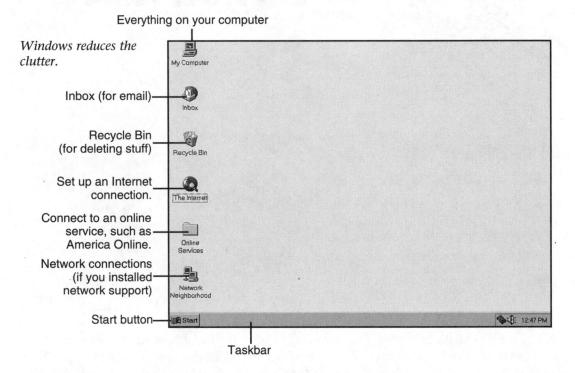

Windows reduces the clutter.

Everything on your computer

Inbox (for email)

Recycle Bin (for deleting stuff)

Set up an Internet connection.

Connect to an online service, such as America Online.

Network connections (if you installed network support)

Start button

Taskbar

Windows may prompt you to *log on* at startup. You may have to log on to Windows or to your network, if your computer is on a network. The Logon dialog box prompts you to enter your name and password. If you work on a network, ask your company's network administrator for your password. If your computer is not on a network, you can type any password; if you leave the Password text box blank, Windows will not prompt you for a password next time. Click **OK**.

Taking Off with the Start Button

Granted, the Windows screen looks about as barren as the Bonneville Salt Flats. It does, however, contain the one item you need to start working: a Start button. You click the big **Start** button, and a menu with nine or more options appears. Slide the mouse pointer up to the word **Programs** (you don't have to click it), and another menu appears listing all the programs you can run. Move the mouse pointer so that it rests on the program you want to run, and then click the icon to run the desired program.

Although the Start menu is designed to make your computer easier to use, it can be a bit difficult to navigate at first. Here are a few tips to help you through your first encounter:

Don't Forget Your Password! If you enter a password, write it down somewhere and hide it. If you forget your password, click **Cancel** when asked for your logon name. In My Computer, change to the Windows folder on drive C, find the file whose name matches your logon name and ends in .pwl, and delete it. Restart Windows and enter your logon name and a new password.

➤ If you rest the mouse pointer on an option that's followed by a right arrow, a submenu appears, listing additional options. You might have to go through several layers of submenus before you see the name of a program you want to run. (Programs commonly install themselves in separate *program groups* that appear as submenus on the Programs menu.)

➤ Options that are followed by three dots (...) open a dialog box, which allows you to carry out an operation. For example, the Shut Down... option displays a dialog box that lets you shut down or restart Windows. In early versions of Windows, you can use Shut Down... to log off so another person can log on.

➤ If you select an option that has no dots or arrow after it, you run a program. For example, if you open the Start menu and click Help, Windows opens the Help window, offering a list of help topics.

➤ Whenever you install a program, its name is added to the Start, Programs menu, or one of its submenus. To run the program, you simply click its name. See Chapter 7, "Running and Juggling Programs," for details.

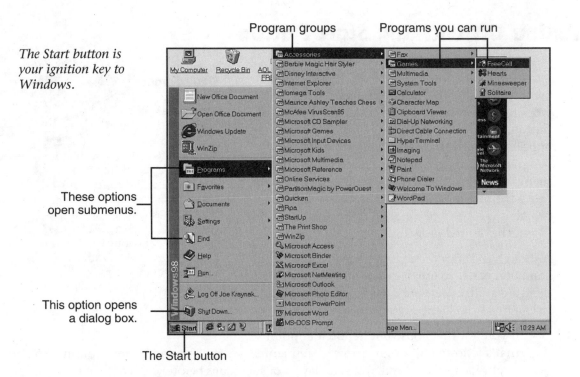

Program groups   Programs you can run

The Start button is your ignition key to Windows.

These options open submenus.

This option opens a dialog box.

The Start button

Use the Programs That Come with Windows

Chances are that your computer came loaded with all sorts of software. If you purchased a family PC, it probably came with Microsoft Office or Lotus SmartSuite and a couple of computer games. But even if your computer wasn't garnished with additional programs, Windows has several programs you can use to write letters, draw pictures, play games, and perform other tasks.

To run any of these programs, click the **Start** button, point to **Programs**, point to **Accessories**, and then click the program you want to run (your Accessories menu may contain slightly different programs and program groups):

Fax   A group of programs that enable your computer and modem to send and receive faxes over the phone lines.

Games   A group of simple computer games, including Solitaire.

Multimedia   A group of programs that enable you to play audio CDs and video clips, and adjust the speaker volume.

System Tools   A collection of programs that help you maintain your system. These tools include a backup program, a program for fixing your hard disk, and a hard disk defragmenter, which can increase the speed of your disk. See Chapter 28, "Do-It-Yourself Computer Tune-Ups," for details.

Calculator   Displays an onscreen calculator that you can use to perform addition, subtraction, division, and multiplication.

 Character Map   Allows you to copy and insert special characters and symbols, such as the registered trademark symbol, into your documents.

 Clipboard Viewer   Displays the contents of any text or other objects you cut from a document. The Clipboard acts as a temporary holding area for the last piece of data you cut or copied in a document. You can then use the Paste command to insert the contents of the Clipboard somewhere else in the document or in a different document. See Chapter 10, "Giving Your Documents the Editorial Eye," for details.

 Dial-Up Networking   Helps you connect your computer to a remote computer. See Part 4, "Going Global with Modems, Online Services, and the Internet."

 Direct Cable Connection   Allows you to connect two computers (for example, a portable and desktop computer) with a cable, so you can exchange files between the two computers.

 HyperTerminal   A telecommunications program you can use (with a modem) to connect to other computers. HyperTerminal is not very useful for connecting to online services or the Internet. You'll learn better ways to establish these connections in Part 4.

 Imaging   A more advanced graphics program created in conjunction with Kodak. It allows you to view graphics saved in various file formats, scan images (if you have a scanner), resize, and enhance images.

 Notepad   A text editing program that is useful for typing notes and other brief documents.

 Paint   A graphics program for creating and printing pictures.

 Phone Dialer   Works with a modem and a phone to create a programmable phone. You can enter and store phone numbers in Phone Dialer, and have Phone Dialer place calls for you.

 Welcome to Windows   (Included in the Windows 98 prerelease) runs an online tutorial to help you get up to speed in Windows. (In earlier versions of Windows, you can run the tutorial from the Windows help system: choose **Start**, **Help**.)

 WordPad   A more advanced word processing program that enables you to create fancier, longer documents.

Dealing with Windows

Working in Windows is like being the dealer in a card game. Whenever you start a program or maximize an icon, a new window appears onscreen in front of the other windows, and a button for that program appears in the taskbar. Open enough windows, and pretty soon, your screen looks like you've just dealt a hand of 52-card pickup. To switch to a window or reorganize the windows on the desktop, use any of the following tricks:

➤ To quickly change to a window, click its button in the taskbar (the bar at the bottom of the Windows desktop). See "Juggling Programs with the Taskbar" in Chapter 7 for details.

➤ In Windows 95 with Internet Explorer 4 or Windows 98, clicking a program button in the taskbar when the program's window is in front minimizes the window. You can click the program's button again to redisplay the program window.

➤ If you can see any part of the window, click it to move it to the front of the stack.

➤ To quickly arrange the windows, right-click on a blank area of the taskbar, and, from the shortcut menu that appears, choose one of the following options: **Tile Horizontally**, **Tile Vertically**, or **Cascade**. With Cascade, you can see the title bar (at the top) of each window. Click inside a title bar to move the window to the front.

➤ To close a window (and exit the program), click the **Close** button (the one with the X on it), located in the upper-right corner of the window (see the next figure).

➤ To make a window take up the whole screen, click the **Maximize** button (just to the left of the Close button). The Maximize button then turns into a **Restore** button, which allows you to return the window to its previous size.

➤ To shrink a window, click the **Minimize** button (the second button to the left of the Close button). The minimized window appears as a button on the taskbar. Click the button on the taskbar to reopen the window.

➤ To resize or reshape a window, place your mouse pointer in the lower-right corner of the window, and when the pointer turns to a double-headed arrow, drag the corner of the window.

➤ To move a window, drag its title bar. (You can't move a maximized window, because it takes up the whole screen.)

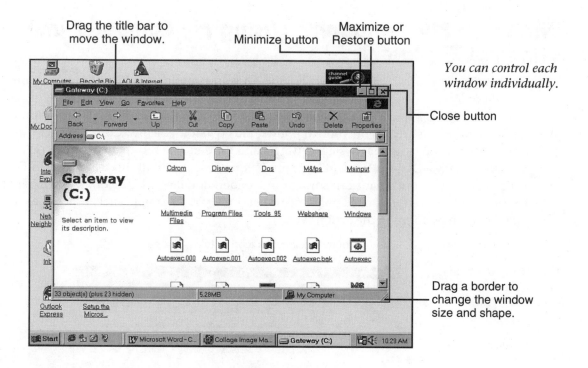

Drag the title bar to move the window.

Minimize button

Maximize or Restore button

You can control each window individually.

Close button

Drag a border to change the window size and shape.

Seeing More with Scroll Bars

Think of a window as ... well, a window. When you look through a window, you don't see everything that's on the other side of the window. You see only a portion of it.

A Windows window is the same way. If a window cannot display everything it contains, a scroll bar appears along the right side or bottom of the window. You can use the scroll bar to bring the hidden contents of the window into view, as follows:

Scroll box Move the mouse pointer over the scroll box, hold down the mouse button, and then drag the box to the area of the window you want to view. For example, to move to the middle of the window's contents, drag the scroll box to the middle of the bar.

Scroll bar Click once inside the scroll bar, on either side of the scroll box, to move the view one window at a time. For example, if you click once below the scroll box, you will see the next window of information.

Scroll arrows Click once on an arrow to scroll incrementally (typically one line at a time) in the direction of the arrow. Hold down the mouse button to scroll continuously in that direction.

47

What's on My Computer? (Using My Computer and Windows Explorer)

Windows gives you two ways to poke around on your computer and find out what's on your disks. You can double-click the **My Computer** icon (located on the desktop), or you can use Windows Explorer. If you double-click the **My Computer** icon, Windows displays icons for all the disk drives on your computer, plus two folder icons: Control Panel (which allows you to change system settings) and Printers (for setting up a printer). You might also have a Dial-Up Networking icon, if you chose to install this feature for Internet access. To find out what's on a disk or in a folder, double-click its icon. (Remember, if your icons are underlined, click only once when I tell you to double-click; otherwise, you might end up performing the action twice.)

Double-click a disk icon or folder to open it.

Use My Computer to browse the contents of a disk or folder.

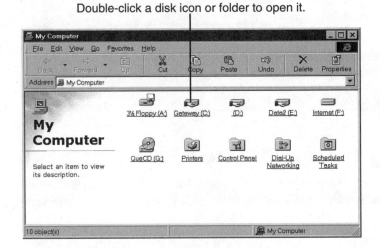

Poking Around with Windows Explorer

Windows Explorer is My Computer's superior twin. It allows you to perform the same basic tasks that you perform in My Computer, but provides better tools for managing disks, folders, and files. To run Explorer, open the **Start** menu, point to **Programs**, and select **Windows Explorer**. You see a two-pane window, with a directory tree on the left and a file list on the right. This two-paned layout allows you to easily copy and move files and folders from one disk or folder to another by dragging them from one pane to the other. See Chapter 16, "Copying, Moving, and Nuking Folders and Files," for details.

Customizing My Computer and Windows Explorer

My Computer and Windows Explorer can seem a little unwieldy at times. The files may not be listed in the best order, the icons may seem too big or small, and there must be a faster way to enter commands. To take control of My Computer or Windows Explorer, try the following:

➤ To change the look of the icons in My Computer or Windows Explorer, open the **View** menu, and select **Large Icons**, **Small Icons** (small icons with folders on the left), **List** (small icons with folders in the upper left), or **Details** (to display additional information such as the date and time files were created).

➤ To rearrange the icons, open the **View** menu, point to **Arrange Icons**, and select **By Name** (list alphabetically by filename), **By Type** (list alphabetically by file extension), **By Size**, or **By Date**. You can also choose **Auto Arrange** to have the icons rearranged automatically whenever you drag an icon. (*Extensions* consist of three or fewer characters tacked on at the end of a filename. They indicate the file type—for example, .DOC for document. Windows may not display extensions for all files.)

➤ To display a toolbar that allows you to quickly enter commands, in either My Computer or Windows Explorer, open the **View** menu and select **Toolbar**. The following figure shows how to use the toolbar to perform basic tasks. (Your toolbar may look much different, depending on the Windows version you are using.)

Check This Out...

How Much Disk Space Is Left? To find out how much disk space you have left on a particular disk, right-click the icon for the disk drive and choose **Properties**. The Properties dialog box displays the total storage capacity of the disk, the amount in use, and the amount of free space. It is useful to check the free space before installing another program on the disk or saving documents to that disk.

Check This Out...

Additional Customization Options

You can further customize My Computer or Windows Explorer by opening the **View** menu and choosing **Options** or **Folder Options** (depending on the Windows version you are using). View/Options allows you to have My Computer display filename extensions (the last three letters following the period in a file's name) or have a separate window open whenever you click a folder icon. View/Folder Options allows you to enter similar preferences but also allows you to view your computer, disks, folders, and files as Web objects that you can single-click (see "From Desktop to Webtop: Internet Integration" later in this chapter).

Cut, copy, and paste files or folders.

Undo the previous action.

Delete the selected file or folder.

Arrange the icons.

Turn on the toolbar for pushbutton commands.

Move up to the previous folder.

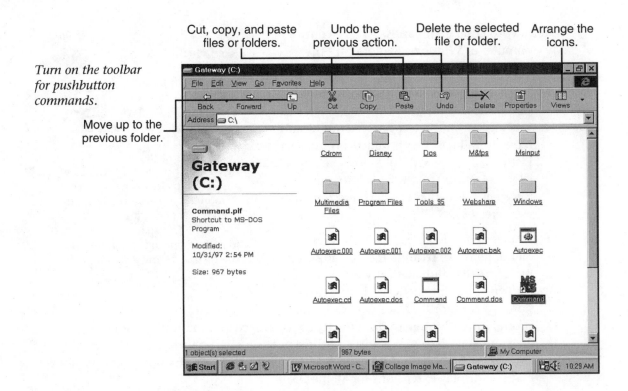

Trashing Files in the Recycle Bin

Windows 95 has an onscreen trash can into which you can dump the files and icons you no longer need. Simply drag an icon from the Windows desktop or from My Computer or Windows Explorer over the Recycle Bin icon, and release the mouse button. The file is moved to the Recycle Bin. The file is not really deleted, though, until you *empty* the Recycle Bin. Until you empty the Recycle Bin, you can still recover a file, if you deleted it by mistake, even if you have turned off the computer after deleting the file. There are other ways to send files to the Recycle Bin:

➤ Right-click a file or folder, and select **Delete** from the context menu.

➤ Select the file or folder, and then click the **Delete** button in the toolbar (the button with the **X** on it).

➤ Select the file or folder, and then press the **Del** key on your keyboard.

Recovering Deleted Files

Pulling things out of the Recycle Bin is as easy as dragging them into it. Double-click the **Recycle Bin** icon to display its contents. Click on the item you want to restore (**Ctrl+click** to select additional items). Then, perform one of the following steps:

➤ To restore the selected items to their original locations, open the **File** menu and select **Restore**.

➤ Drag the selected item onto the Windows desktop or into a folder displayed in My Computer or Windows Explorer.

Emptying the Recycle Bin

The Recycle Bin can consume a good chunk of your hard disk space with the files you pitch in there. To reclaim this disk space, you can empty the Recycle Bin, but be careful—you may not be able to recover the files after emptying the Bin. If you're sure that the Recycle Bin does not contain any files you might need, follow these steps to empty it:

1. Double-click the **Recycle Bin** icon, located on the desktop. (Single-click if "Recycle Bin" is underlined.)

2. Make sure you will never ever need any of the files in the Recycle Bin. After emptying the Recycle Bin, retrieving files is nearly impossible, and I don't tell you anywhere in this book how to do it.

3. Open the **File** menu, and select **Empty Recycle Bin**.

Out of Disk Space? If you get an error message saying you are out of disk space, before you begin deleting programs and files that you still may need, check the Recycle Bin to make sure it's empty.

Changing the Recycle Bin's Properties

As I mentioned, the Recycle Bin is set up to use a good portion (typically ten percent) of your hard disk space to store deleted files. When the ten percent is used up, the Recycle Bin automatically deletes the oldest deleted files, so you can't restore them. You can increase the amount of disk space Recycle Bin uses, to play it safe, or, if you're running low on hard disk space, you can reduce the percentage. You can adjust other settings as well:

➤ To change the Recycle Bin's properties, right-click the **Recycle Bin** icon, and click **Properties**.

Bypass the Recycle Bin To permanently delete a file or folder without sending it to the Recycle Bin, select the file or folder and press **Shift+Delete**. Be careful with this one.

➤ If you have more than one hard drive, you can click **Configure Drives Independently**, and then use the drive tabs to set Recycle Bin options for each drive.

➤ To change the amount of disk space that the Recycle Bin uses, drag the **Maximum Size of Recycle Bin** slider to the left or right to change the percentage of disk space it uses.

➤ If you don't want the safety of the Recycle Bin, you can disable it by selecting **Do Not Move Files to the Recycle Bin**. However, if you turn on this option, you won't be able to recover accidentally deleted files later.

Help Is on Its Way

If you get stuck in Windows, you don't have to flip through a book looking for help. Instead, open the **Start** menu and click **Help**. The Help window appears, offering a table of contents and an index. The following figure shows the Help window from the Windows 98 pre-release. Click the **Contents** tab if you're searching for general information about how to perform a task or use Windows. Double-click a book icon to view additional subtopics and then double-click the desired topic. In Windows 98, a single click does the trick.

The Windows Help system teaches you the basics.

Double-click a book icon to view a list of subtopics.

Double-click the desired subtopic.

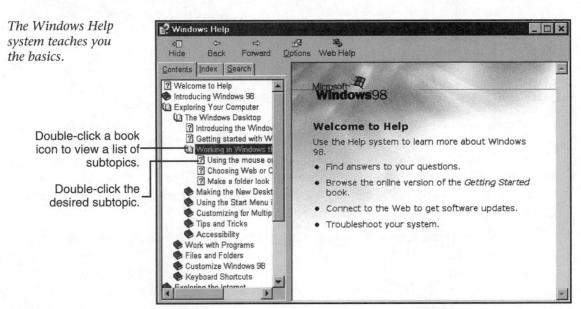

For specific help, click the **Index** tab. This tab provides an alphabetical listing of help topics that would make the most ambitious librarian cringe. The easiest way to find a topic in this list is to click inside the text box at the top, and then start typing the name of the feature, command, or procedure for which you need help. As you type, the list scrolls to show the name of the topic that matches your entry.

The **Find** or **Search** tab offers a more extensive search tool. Instead of searching only through the index of topics, Find searches the contents of the Help system. If you're having trouble tracking down the information you need, click the **Find** tab and start searching.

> **Take the Windows Guided Tour** In Windows 95, click the Contents tab and double-click **Tour: Ten Minutes to Using Windows**. In the Windows 98 pre-release version, the Welcome to Windows screen appears the first time you start Windows. Click **Begin** to start the tour. If the Welcome to Windows screen does not appear, click the **Start** button, point to **Programs**, point to **Accessories**, and click **Welcome to Windows**.

What's New with Windows?

You perform most of the basic Windows tasks covered in this chapter the same way no matter which version of Windows 95 or Windows 98 you are using. So, what's the difference? With the release of Windows 95 OSR 2.5 and the Windows 98 pre-release version, Microsoft integrated Internet Explorer 4 (its Web browser) with Windows. A *Web browser* is a program that you use to open multimedia pages (with text, pictures, video, and so on) on the Internet. This integration makes your Windows desktop act as a Web page and makes your icons act as links (graphics or underlined text that you click to access).

> **Early Versions of Windows 95** If you have an earlier version of Windows 95, you can install Internet Explorer 4 to make it look and act like Windows 95 OSR 2.5. See Chapter 21, "Whipping Around the World Wide Web," for details.

Windows 98 is also a little faster than Windows 95 and includes a few utilities to help improve your computer's performance. The following sections explain the biggest changes you'll find in Windows 98.

From Desktop to Webtop: Internet Integration

One of the greatest improvements that Internet Explorer 4 has brought to Windows is the Active Desktop, a feature that transforms your Windows desktop into an automated information center. With the Active Desktop and an Internet connection, you can place objects such as stock tickers and weather maps right on your Windows desktop and have them automatically updated via the Internet. The Channel Guide bar on the Windows desktop is a desktop component.

The Active Desktop also offers a new, improved interface for accessing your programs and documents. With the Active Desktop, the Windows desktop functions as a Web page, allowing you to run programs and open documents with a single click of the mouse.

The new desktop allows you to work in the following three modes:

➤ **Web Style (or View as Web Page)** Treats the Windows desktop and My Computer like Web pages, providing single-click access to files and programs. You can tell that Web Style is on if the names of files, folders, disks, and shortcuts appear underlined.

➤ **Classic Style** Makes Windows 98 act like Windows 95. Folders in My Computer do not appear as Web pages, and you must double-click icons to run programs or open documents.

➤ **Custom** Allows you to enter preferences that control the appearance and behavior of Windows. For example, you can keep the Web page backgrounds for My Computer but turn double-click access on.

Navigating the Web with Windows Explorer
Windows and Internet Explorer 4 work together to allow you to open Web pages (from the Internet) right inside Windows Explorer. In the left pane in Windows Explorer, click **Internet Explorer**. Web pages appear in the right pane. For details on navigating the Web, see Chapter 21.

To change modes, run **My Computer** and then open the **View** menu and choose **Folder Options**. Choose the desired mode and click **OK**. If you choose Web Style and a particular folder does not appear in Web view, open the **View** menu and choose **As Web Page**. The selected mode also affects the Windows desktop. If the desktop does not appear as a Web page, right-click a blank area of the desktop, point to **Active Desktop**, and choose **View as Web Page**. For more information about using and configuring the Active Desktop, see "Mastering the Active Desktop" in the next chapter.

New Quick Launch Toolbar

Windows with Internet Explorer 4 has a new toolbar called the Quick Launch toolbar that provides single-click access to several Internet programs and to the Windows desktop. The Quick Launch toolbar contains the following buttons:

➤ **Launch Internet Explorer Browser** Runs Internet Explorer, which allows you to open Web pages on the Internet.

➤ **Launch Outlook Express**   Runs Outlook Express, Microsoft's email program.

➤ **Show Desktop**   Quickly minimizes all open windows and returns you to the Windows desktop.

➤ **View Channels**   Displays Microsoft's channel changer, which allows you to quickly tune in to specific Web sites as easily as flipping channels on your TV.

Icon names appear underlined,
like links on Web pages.

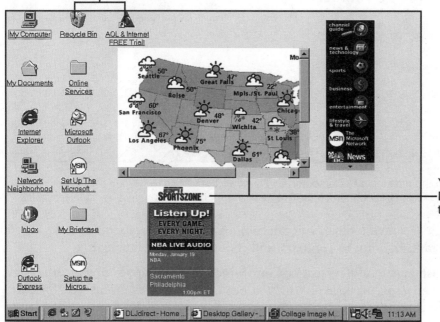

With View As Web Page on, you have single-click access to disks, folders, files, and programs.

You can add Active Desktop Components to the desktop.

You can add a button for any program, folder, or document to the Quick Launch toolbar to make it easily accessible. Simply drag the icon from the Windows desktop, My Computer, or Windows Explorer over a blank area of the Quick Launch toolbar and release the mouse button. To remove a button, right-click it and choose **Delete**.

You can add a button for any file, folder, or program to the Quick Launch toolbar.

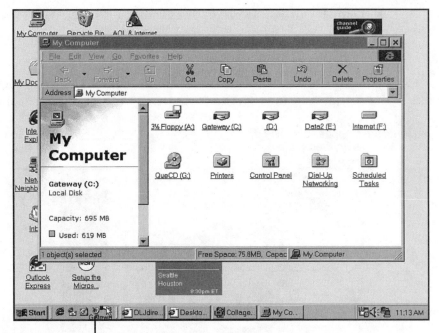

Drag an icon from the desktop, My Computer, or Windows Explorer over a blank area of the Quick Launch toolbar and release the mouse button.

If you like the Quick Launch toolbar, you can turn on additional toolbars. Right-click a blank area of the taskbar, point to **Toolbars**, and choose the desired toolbar:

➤ **Address**   Displays an Address text box into which you can type Web page addresses to quickly open a specific page on the Web. See Chapter 21 for information on how to enter Web page addresses.

➤ **Links**   Displays buttons for popular Web pages. These buttons correspond to Quick Link buttons in Internet Explorer.

➤ **Desktop**   Displays buttons for all the icons currently on your Windows desktop.

➤ **New Toolbar**   Allows you to transform any folder into a toolbar. The toolbar will contain buttons for all the files and programs in the selected folder.

To turn off a toolbar, right-click a blank area of the taskbar, point to **Toolbars**, and choose the toolbar you want to hide.

Additional Hardware Support

Whenever a new operating system comes out, people resist the change, claiming that the current operating system works just fine. That's an acceptable approach assuming that you don't need to take advantage of the latest technology. For example, you could probably stick with Windows 3.1 if you simply type documents. However, if you want to access the Internet or play the latest Windows games, you have no choice but to move up to Windows 95.

Likewise, if you want to take advantage of upcoming technologies, you really have no choice but to move up to the latest version of Windows. Recent releases of Windows offer support for the latest monitors, video cards, and printers. In addition, these new Windows releases include enhanced support for cutting-edge technologies, such as *infrared ports*, which enable wireless connections; *Universal Serial Bus (USB)*, which allows you to connect up to 127 devices to your computer through a single port without turning off your computer; and support for *TV cards*, which allow you to view television signals on your monitor.

Optimizing Your System in the New Windows

Early versions of Windows 95 have several system optimization utilities, including *ScanDisk*, which checks for and repairs disk errors; *Disk Defragmenter*, for arranging files more efficiently on your hard disk; and *DriveSpace*, for compressing files so they take up less storage space on your disks. Later Windows releases offer additional tools to help automate these tasks and keep your system operating at its peak performance:

➤ **Tune-Up Wizard** Automatically checks for and repairs disk errors, deletes temporary files, defragments files, and rearranges program files so your programs will run faster. You simply run the wizard and answer a few questions to tell it what to do and when to perform the scheduled optimizations.

➤ **Disk Cleanup** Finds and deletes useless files. Disk Cleanup removes files from the Recycle Bin, deletes temporary Internet files, and removes programs you no longer use (assuming you okay the removal, of course).

➤ **Disk Converter (FAT32)** Can increase the amount of storage space on a hard disk by restructuring the disk to use smaller storage units.

Tech Check

Until you have mastered the Windows basics, you will flounder trying to perform any other computer task. Before moving on to the fancy Windows moves in Chapter 5, you should be able to do the following:

➤ Log on to Windows when prompted.

➤ Open the Start menu and navigate its submenus.

➤ Locate the games and programs that are included with Windows.

➤ Open, close, and resize windows.

➤ Use My Computer and Windows Explorer to check out what's on your computer.

➤ Navigate the Windows Help system.

➤ Name three new features of the latest Windows releases and find them on your computer, assuming you have one of the newer Windows releases.

Chapter 5

Windows Tips, Tricks, and Traps

In This Chapter

➤ Create your own desktop (shortcut) icons

➤ Change the appearance of the Windows desktop

➤ Turn on a screen saver

➤ Run programs automatically on startup

After you've poked around on the Windows desktop, flipped through a few submenus on the Start menu, and played around with the taskbar, you know just about everything you need to know to use Windows.

However, natural curiosity leads most users to experiment with Windows to customize its look, improve performance, and take advantage of some of the time-saving features built into Windows. In this chapter, you'll get some hands-on training as you whip Windows into shape.

Installing and Uninstalling Windows Components

The first step in taking control of Windows is figuring out which Windows components are installed on your computer. The Windows setup program performs a typical installation, meaning that it installs the components that it thinks you want. You can run the setup program again (assuming you have the Windows CD) to install additional components or remove components that you don't use. To run Windows setup, take the following steps:

1. Insert the Windows CD into your CD-ROM drive. If the Windows setup window appears, close it.

2. Click the **Start** program, point to **Settings**, and click **Control Panel**. The Windows Control Panel appears, which you'll meet again later in this chapter.

3. Double-click the **Add/Remove Programs** icon. The Add/Remove Programs Properties dialog box appears.

4. Click the **Windows Setup** tab. Windows Setup checks to determine which components are installed on your computer. The Components list displays groups of related components; for example, Accessories includes Paint and WordPad. The check boxes indicate the following:

> **Clear box** (no gray, no check mark) indicates that none of the components in this group is installed.

> **Clear box with check** (check mark but no gray) indicates that all the components in this group are installed.

> **Gray box with check** (gray and check mark) indicates that some of the components in this group are installed.

You can easily determine which Windows components are installed.

No components are installed.

All components in the group are installed.

Some components are installed.

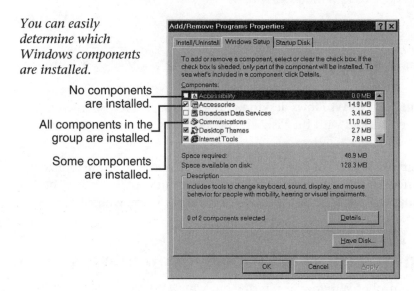

5. To view a list of components in a group, double-click the group's name or click the name and click the **Details** button. (Some groups may have only one component, in which case no additional list is displayed.)

6. To install or remove a component, click its check box to add or remove a check mark. A check mark indicates that the component will be installed or is already installed.

7. Click **OK**. This returns you to the original list of component groups. Repeat steps 5–7 to add or remove other Windows components.

8. Click **OK**. Windows Setup copies the necessary files from the Windows CD or prompts you to insert one or more of the Windows floppy disks. You may be prompted to restart your computer after Windows copies the necessary files. Follow the onscreen instructions.

Do-It-Yourself Shortcut Icons

Look closely at the icons on your Windows desktop, and you'll see that some icons have a tiny box with an arrow inside it. These are shortcut icons; they point to the original file on a disk or CD. You can place these cloned icons in any of several locations for convenient access to programs, folders, and files. For example, you might place a shortcut icon for a folder you commonly use right on the Windows desktop. That way, you don't have to run My Computer or Windows Explorer to open the folder.

To create a shortcut icon for a file, folder, or program, use the right mouse button to drag the folder, file, or program icon from My Computer or Windows Explorer over a blank area on the Windows desktop and release the mouse button. From the context menu that appears, choose **Create Shortcut(s) Here**. Presto: instant shortcut icon. (To bypass the context menu, **Ctrl+Shift+drag** the icon with the *left* mouse button.)

After creating your first shortcut icon, check out these cool tricks:

➤ Drag an icon from the desktop, My Computer, or Windows Explorer over the **Start** button and release the mouse button. A shortcut is placed at the top of the Start menu.

➤ Right-click the Windows desktop, point to **New**, and choose **Folder**. Type a name for the folder and press **Enter**. Create shortcut icons for all the programs, folders, and files you commonly use and place them in this folder. You can then double-click the folder for quick access to the programs and files you use most often.

➤ If you have a folder in which you store all the files you create, place a shortcut icon for that folder on the Windows desktop.

➤ You can create shortcut icons for your disk drives, too. Double-click My Computer and then right-drag the disk icons to the Windows desktop and choose **Create Shortcut(s) Here.**

Shortcuts, easy as 1–2–3.

1. Point to the program, folder, disk, or file icon and hold down the right mouse button.

2. Keep holding down the mouse button and drag the icon to a blank area of the Windows desktop.

3. Release the mouse button and choose Create Shortcut(s) Here.

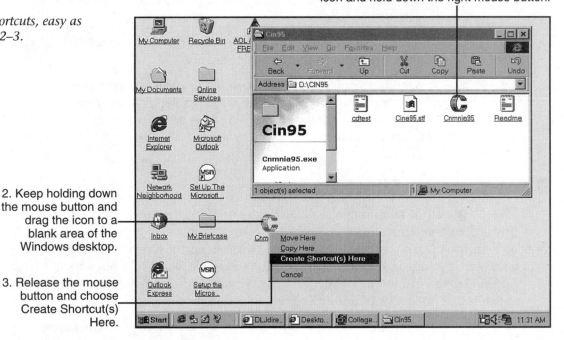

Giving Windows a Makeover

Your colleague down the hall has a neat screen saver playing on his computer. And your pal across the street has icons for all her favorite programs right on the Windows desktop! You want to do all this; you want to be cool, too. But where do you start? In the following sections, you'll find tips and tricks for taking control of Windows 95 and making your life easier.

Going Wild with Desktop Themes

Admit it: The Windows desktop is functional, but bland. Fortunately, if you have Windows with Plus! (a Windows add-on), you can choose from a selection of *desktop themes* to breathe some life into Windows. Each desktop theme contains a graphical desktop background, and specialized icons, mouse pointers, and sounds. For example, the Jungle theme places a jungle scene on the Windows background and plays animal sounds when certain events appear, such as Windows startup.

To use a desktop theme, first check the Windows Components list, as explained in the previous section, to determine whether desktop themes are installed. (If Desktop Themes is not listed, your version of Windows may not have Plus! installed.) Then, take the following steps to turn on a desktop theme:

1. Click the **Start** button, point to **Settings**, and click **Control Panel**.

2. In the Control Panel, double-click the **Desktop Themes** icon.

3. Open the **Theme** drop-down list and choose the desired desktop theme.

4. The selected theme appears in the preview area. To preview the screen saver, click the **Screen Saver** button. (See the following section for more information about screen savers.)

5. Windows plays the screen saver. Move the mouse pointer or press a key to turn it off.

6. To preview mouse pointers, sounds, and icons, click the **Pointers**, **Sounds**, etc. button.

7. The Preview window appears. Click the tab for the type of object you want to preview: **Pointers**, **Sounds**, or **Visuals**. Double-click an item in the list to display it in the preview area or play a sound. When you're done, click the **Close** button.

8. You can disable individual components of the desktop theme by clicking the name of each component to remove the check from its box. Click **OK** to save your settings.

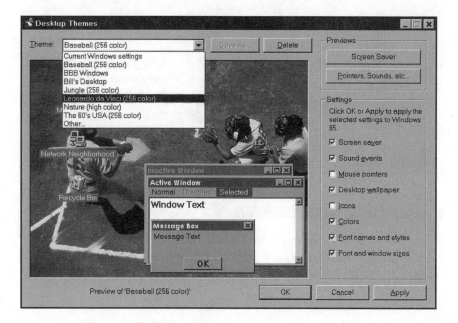

Select the desired desktop theme.

Turning on a Screen Saver

You've probably seen the winged toasters flying across somebody's screen at work, or the flying Windows, or maybe crawling cockroaches. These *screen savers* were originally developed to prevent stagnant images from being permanently *burned in* to the screen. Newer monitors don't really benefit from screen savers anymore, but they do prevent people from snooping at your screen when you're away from your desk.

To turn on a screen saver, right-click on a blank area of the Windows desktop, and select **Properties**. In the Display Properties dialog box, click the **Screen Saver** tab. Open the **Screen Saver** drop-down list, and click the desired screen saver (you can click **Preview** to see what it will look like). Click on the arrows to the right of the **Wait __ Minutes** spin box to specify how long your system must remain inactive (no typing, no mouse movement) before the screen saver kicks in. (You can also assign a password to the screen saver to prevent unauthorized access to your computer when you are away from your desk.) Click **OK**.

When your computer remains inactive for the specified amount of time, the screen saver kicks in. To turn off the screen saver, simply move your mouse or press a key.

Turn on a screen saver.

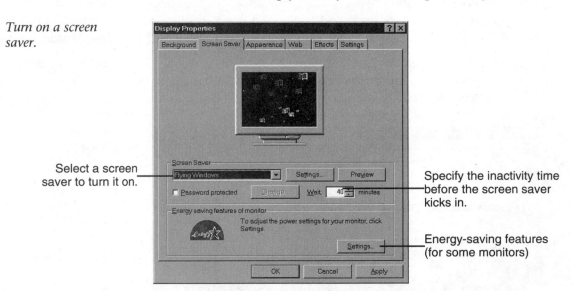

Select a screen saver to turn it on.

Specify the inactivity time before the screen saver kicks in.

Energy-saving features (for some monitors)

Changing the Appearance of Windows 95

Computers are personal, and people enjoy customizing their displays by turning on background graphics, changing the screen colors, and changing other display properties to give their screens a unique look.

To change the appearance of your Windows desktop, right-click on a blank area of the desktop, and click **Properties** to display the Display Properties dialog box. Then experiment with the following (if you have a more recent version of Windows 95, your options may differ slightly):

➤ Click the **Background** tab; select an item from the **Pattern** or **Wallpaper** list to change the look of the Windows desktop.

➤ Click the **Appearance** tab, and try selecting different color schemes from the **Scheme** drop-down list.

➤ If you don't like any of the color schemes, assign colors to various items on the desktop. Open the **Item** list, and pick the item whose appearance you want to change. Use the Size, Color, and Font options to change the look of the selected item.

➤ Click the **Settings** tab. Make sure the **Color Palette** option is set to 256 or greater. You can drag the Desktop Area slider to the left to make items appear bigger onscreen, or to the right to make them smaller (and fit more objects on the screen). (If the slider is not available, you may have a standard VGA monitor, which does not allow resizing the desktop.)

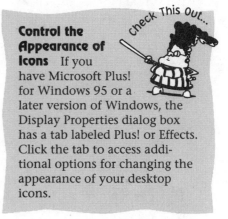

Control the Appearance of Icons If you have Microsoft Plus! for Windows 95 or a later version of Windows, the Display Properties dialog box has a tab labeled Plus! or Effects. Click the tab to access additional options for changing the appearance of your desktop icons.

If you like the way your desktop looks in the preview area of the dialog box, click **OK**. If you really messed up the desktop, click **Cancel**.

Making Windows Sound Off

All computers have some way of making sounds. New computers, equipped with a sound card and speakers, can play any sound that's been recorded and saved as a file—everything from the patented Homer Simpson belch to a snippet from Beethoven's Fifth. Older computers are equipped with a built-in speaker designed to emit only an occasional beep.

If your computer is capable of emitting sounds when you start Windows, run a program, close a window, or perform other actions, you can take advantage of all the sounds that come with Windows. You can turn on jungle sounds to make Windows sound like an old Tarzan movie, or turn on Robotz for a futuristic effect. When you select a sound scheme, Windows assigns a specific sound to each window action, such as opening a menu or closing a dialog box.

To pick a sound scheme for Windows, click the **Start** button, point to **Settings**, and click **Control Panel**. Double-click the **Sounds** icon. Open the **Schemes** drop-down list, and select the sound scheme you want to use. (If you see only one or two sound schemes, you can install additional schemes from your Windows 95 CD, as explained earlier in this chapter. Be careful—the schemes consume over 5 megabytes of hard disk space.)

Preventing Others from Messing with Your Desktop

Check This Out...

Customized Sound Schemes You can assign any sound to any Windows activity. In the Events list, click the activity to which you want to assign a sound, such as Menu Command. Then, click the **Browse** button, and select the sound you want to assign to this activity. Click **OK**.

If you share your computer with a colleague at work or with other family members at home, you don't want the other people reconfiguring Windows after you have painstakingly entered your preferences. To prevent others from messing up your desktop, you can set up Windows for multiple users. Take the following steps:

1. Click the **Start** button, point to **Settings**, and click **Control Panel**.

2. Double-click the **Passwords** icon.

3. Click the **User Profiles** tab.

4. Make sure **Users Can Customize Their Preferences and Desktop Settings** is selected.

5. Make sure both options under **User Profile Settings** are checked.

6. Click **OK**.

When you start Windows, a dialog box prompts you to enter your name and password. Instruct each person who uses your computer to enter a unique name and password when prompted to log on. Any preferences or desktop settings the user enters will then be stored under that person's name, without affecting settings that the other users enter.

When a user is done using the computer, he or she should log off. To log off, click the **Start** button and choose **Log Off [*yourname*]**. When the confirmation dialog box appears, click **Yes**. (In earlier versions of Windows, you must choose **Start**, **Shut Down** to display the option for logging off.) Windows restarts without restarting your computer and displays a dialog box prompting the next user for his or her name and password.

Using the Windows Control Panel

I could write a whole book on how to use the Windows Control Panel to customize Windows. But I'm not going to do that to you. I will, however, give you a quick way to open the Control Panel: Double-click **My Computer**, and double-click **Control Panel**.

And I will give you a list and brief descriptions of what you'll find in the Control Panel (your Control Panel may be missing some of these icons or may have additional icons, depending on which Windows components are installed and on your hardware):

Accessibility Options   If you have some hearing loss, vision impairment, or have difficulty moving the mouse or using the keyboard, double-click this icon. Windows offers some helpful customization options.

Add New Hardware   If you connected a new device to your system, run the **Add New Hardware Wizard**. The wizard leads you step by step through the process of setting up the new device.

Add/Remove Programs   Double-click this icon to install a new program. See Chapter 6, "Do-It-Yourself Program Installation Guide," for details.

Date/Time   Double-click this icon to change the system date and time. (It's quicker to just double-click on the time in the taskbar.)

Desktop Themes   Contains sets of graphics backgrounds, icons, mouse pointers, and sound schemes to decorate your Windows desktop. (You've already seen this one. Keep in mind that you'll have this icon only if Microsoft Plus! is installed.)

Display   These are the same options you get when you right-click on the Windows desktop and select Properties.

Find Fast   Indexes the files on your computer, so when you search for a file, Windows can quickly locate it. See "Tracking Down Lost Files in Windows," in Chapter 9 for details. You can use your computer a long time without ever clicking this icon.

Fonts   This icon opens a dialog box that allows you to add or remove fonts (type styles and sizes) from your computer. See "Installing Additional Fonts," in Chapter 11, for details.

Game Controllers   If you have a joystick connected to your computer, this icon lets you set up, configure, calibrate, and test the joystick. (This icon may appear as Joystick in your version of Windows.)

Internet   Prompts you to enter settings for connecting to the Internet. See Chapter 20, "Doing the Internet Shuffle," for details.

Keyboard   Double-click this icon to set the speed at which characters (or spaces) repeat when you hold down a key, and to set the amount of time you have to hold down a key before it starts repeating.

Mail and Fax   Provides the email and fax support for Windows. (Skip this one.)

Microsoft Mail Postoffice   Manages your email post office, assuming you use Microsoft Mail on a network. (It's likely that you'll never have to mess with this icon.)

 Modems   If you have a modem, you can double-click this icon to set it up and change any modem settings that might be giving you problems. See Chapter 18, "First You Need a Modem," for details.

 Mouse   Change how fast or slow your mouse pointer travels across the screen, and control how fast you have to click twice for a double-click. You can also set up your mouse to swap the functions of the left and right mouse buttons.

 Multimedia   This icon displays a dialog box that lets you enter settings for the audio, visual, MIDI, and CD devices installed on your system. (Great way to crank up your speaker volume.)

 Network   Prompts you to enter settings for connecting your computer to other computers on a network. If your computer is not networked, you can avoid this icon.

 Passwords   To prevent unauthorized use of your computer, double-click this icon and enter a password. (Just be sure you remember your password.)

 Personal Web Server   Allows you to set up your computer to act as a mock Web server, so you can test Web pages you create. This is pretty advanced, so ignore it for now.

 Power Management (or Power)   Allows you to enter settings to conserve power on your computer. You can have Windows automatically shut down your monitor and disk drives if they have not been used for a specified amount of time. This is very useful for portable computers that may be running on batteries.

 Printers   Allows you to install a printer and enter preferences for installed printers. See Chapter 13, "Okay, Now You Can Print It!" for more information.

 Regional Settings   Lets you control how numbers, currencies, dates, and times are displayed for your geographical region.

 Sounds   Allows you to assign sounds to specific events in Windows, as you saw earlier in this chapter.

 System   This icon gives you a peek at what's on your system, and allows you to change system settings. The dialog box this icon calls up contains several settings for optimizing your computer. See Chapter 28, "Do-It-Yourself Computer Tune-Ups," for details.

Telephony Allows you to enter dialing preferences for your modem. For example, if you have to dial 1 for long distance, you can enter it here to have your modem dial it automatically.

 Users Allows you to set up Windows for two or more users. Each user can then configure Windows according to his or her needs without affecting settings entered by the other users.

When you double-click most of these icons, you get a dialog box that lets you enter your preferences. Remember, if you don't understand an option in a dialog box, right-click the option, and then select **What's This?**

Mastering the Active Desktop

In the preceding chapter, you learned a little bit about the Active Desktop, a feature added to Windows by Internet Explorer 4. The Active Desktop provides single-click access to disks, folders, programs, and files. In addition, with an Internet connection, you can place components (called *active desktop components*) on the desktop that automatically download updated information from the Internet and display it right on the desktop. For example, you can place stock tickers, sports updates, and weather maps right on the Windows desktop!

Now, we're getting a little ahead of ourselves here, so if you don't have an Internet connection, or you're not sure, read Part 4, "Going Global with Modems, Online Services, and the Internet." You can then add active components to your desktop by doing the following:

1. Right-click a blank area of the Windows Desktop, point to **Active Desktop**, and click **Customize My Desktop**. The Display Properties dialog box appears.

2. Click the **Web** tab. The Web options allow you to view the desktop as a Web page and add components.

3. Click **New**. The New Active Desktop Item dialog box appears, asking if you want to go to the Active Desktop Gallery.

4. Click **Yes**. This runs Internet Explorer and connects you to the Internet, if you are not already connected. Internet Explorer loads the Active Desktop Gallery Web page.

5. Follow the trail of links to the desktop component you want. A page appears, describing the component and displaying a link or button for downloading it.

*Active Desktop
Components are
readily available on
the Web.*

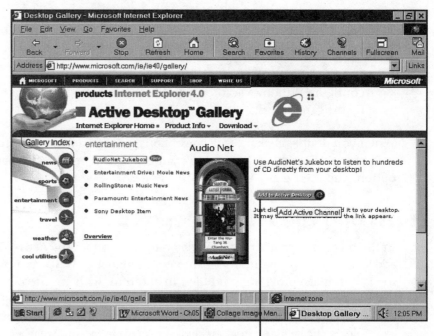

Click the link for adding the active
component to your desktop.

**Turning Off
Active
Components**
The Web tab
displays a list
of installed
desktop components. To turn off
a component, remove the check
from its box. To completely
remove it, click the component's
name and click the **Delete**
button.

6. Click the link or button to download it and place
   it on your desktop. Internet Explorer displays a
   dialog box, asking for your confirmation.

7. Click **Yes**.

8. A second dialog box appears, indicating that
   Windows will set up a subscription for this component. Click **OK**. Internet Explorer downloads
   the component and places it on the desktop.

9. To move a component, point to its title bar to
   display a gray bar at the top of the window; drag
   the gray bar to move the component.

10. To resize a component, drag one of the corners of its frame and release the mouse
    button.

10 Windows Productivity Tips

Everybody wants to be more productive, and a computer can help you do just that. However, to become truly productive in Windows, you need a few professional tips. The following list reveals ten secrets to becoming more productive in Windows:

1. **Bypass the Windows startup logo.** Turn on your computer and press **Esc** when you see the Windows logo screen. This bypasses the startup screen, shaving a couple of seconds off the time it takes the desktop to appear.

2. **Quickly restart Windows.** Whenever you choose to restart Windows, it completely restarts your computer, reloading all the startup commands. To have Windows restart more quickly, click the **Start** button, choose **Shut Down**, click **Restart**, and then hold down the **Shift** key while clicking the **OK** button.

3. **Open files quickly.** To quickly open a file, double-click the file's icon in My Computer or Windows Explorer. When you install a program, Windows associates the program to types of files that it can create. When you double-click a document file's name or icon, Windows runs the associated program, which then opens the file.

4. **Scrap it!** Drag over text in a document or click a graphical image to select it. Then drag the selection to the Windows desktop to create a *scrap*. You can then drag the scrap into another document to insert the text or graphic in that document.

5. **Alt+click properties.** You can display the properties of a disk, folder, or file by right-clicking it and choosing **Properties**. A quicker way is to hold down the **Alt** key while clicking the icon.

6. **Bypass the Recycle Bin.** To permanently delete files without placing them in the Recycle Bin, hold down the **Shift** key while choosing the **Delete** command or pressing the **Delete** key.

7. **Ctrl+Esc to the Start menu.** This allows you to keep your fingers on the keyboard. Use the arrow keys to select the desired command or submenu and press **Enter**. If your keyboard has a Windows key, you can press the **Windows** key instead of pressing **Ctrl+Esc**.

8. **Drag and drop printing.** Open My Computer and double-click the **Printers** icon. **Ctrl+Shift+drag** the icon for your printer to a blank area of the Windows desktop to create a shortcut for it. To quickly print a document file, drag the file from My Computer or Windows Explorer over the printer icon and release the mouse button. See Chapter 13 for details.

9. **Run programs on startup.** If you always use a program, you can have Windows run the program automatically when you start your computer. Simply create a shortcut for the program in the StartUp folder (C:\WINDOWS\Start Menu\Programs\StartUp). Or, simply move the program's icon to the StartUp menu as explained in "Customizing Your Start Menu," in Chapter 7. (The location of the StartUp folder may differ on your computer.)

10. **Drag-and-Drop Start Menu.** In Windows 98, you can rearrange the items on the Windows Start menu and its submenus simply by dragging them from one place to another. See "Customizing Your Start Menu," in Chapter 7, for more information on rearranging your Start menu.

Tech Check

Whew! This chapter covered some pretty advanced tasks. Before you start patting yourself on the back, make sure you can do the following:

➤ Determine which Windows components are installed on your computer.

➤ Place a shortcut icon for a program, file, folder, or disk on your Windows desktop.

➤ Turn on a desktop theme, if you have Windows 95 with Microsoft Plus! or Windows 98.

➤ Turn on a Windows screen saver.

➤ Change the Windows sound scheme.

➤ Name five icons in the Windows Control Panel.

➤ Make your Windows desktop act like a Web page.

➤ Perform five tasks that make you more productive in Windows 98, not including playing less Solitaire.

Part 2
Get with the Program(s)

You didn't buy a computer so you could watch the pretty pictures or drag icons across the screen. You got a computer so you could do some work... or play a few games. Although this part can't possibly cover all the programs you can run on your computer, these chapters teach you everything you need to know to survive in just about any program.

In this part, you'll learn how to install and run programs, quickly switch from one program to another in Windows, enter commands using menus and buttons, copy and paste data between documents, and print the documents you create. In addition, you'll learn how to access online help in most programs, so you won't have to shuffle through stacks of papers looking for the documentation. By the end of this part, you'll know how to take any application out of its box and put it to work.

WELCOME TO "THIS OLD HARD DRIVE."

Chapter 6

Do-It-Yourself Program Installation Guide

In This Chapter

➤ Preinstallation: Can your computer run the program?

➤ Installing CD-ROM programs

➤ Installing programs from floppy disks

➤ Removing programs later

If you ran out and bought your computer without thinking much about what you were going to do with it, you are probably beginning to realize that your computer doesn't have all the programs you want to use. Maybe you want to use Quicken to manage your finances, or you have read about a new computer game that you want to play.

The problem is that you don't know where to start. In fact, you don't even know whether your computer is equipped to run the program. This chapter can help. Here, you'll learn how to pick a program designed for your computer, check that your computer has enough disk space for the program, and then successfully install the program on your computer. You'll even learn how to get your old DOS games up and running in Windows.

Does Your Computer Have What It Takes?

You can't run all programs on all computers. Before you buy any program, make sure your computer can run it. The minimum hardware and software requirements are printed on every software package. Look for the following information, and use it to draw up a checklist before you go shopping:

Computer type Typically, you can't run a Macintosh application on an IBM-compatible computer. If you have a PC, make sure the application is for an IBM PC or compatible computer. (Some programs include both the Macintosh and PC versions.)

Operating system Try to find applications designed specifically for the operating system you use. Although Windows 98 can run applications designed for Windows 95, Windows 95 may not be able to run some Windows 98 programs. If your computer is still running Windows 3.1, it probably won't be able to run programs designed for Windows 95.

CPU requirements CPU stands for *central processing unit*. This is the brain of the computer. If the application requires at least a Pentium chip and you have a 486 chip, your computer won't be able to run the application effectively. The name or number of the chip inside your computer should appear on the front of your system unit. If the chip type is not displayed, Alt+double-click My Computer to display the System Properties dialog box. (Note: A Pentium is a step up from a 486.) Some newer programs require Pentium with MMX, a technology designed to increase performance for multimedia programs.

Type of monitor Here are the monitor types, from best to worst:

➤ SVGA (Super VGA)

➤ VGA (video graphics adapter)

➤ EGA (enhanced graphics adapter), not even good enough to run Windows 95

➤ CGA (color graphics adapter), obsolete

If an application requires a VGA monitor and you have an SVGA, no problem. If the application requires an SVGA and you have VGA, EGA, or CGA, you'll have problems.

Mouse If you use Windows, you need a mouse (or some other pointing device). A standard Microsoft two-button mouse is sufficient.

Joystick   Although most computer games enable you to use your keyboard, games are usually more fun if you have a joystick. Digital joysticks are the current trend. See "Game Cards and Joysticks" in Chapter 27, "Upgrading Your Computer to Make It the Best It Can Be," for tips on picking a good joystick.

CD-ROM drive   If you have a CD-ROM drive, it usually pays to get the CD-ROM version of the application. This makes it easier to install, and the CD-ROM version might come with a few extras. Check for the required speed of the drive, as well.

Sound card   Most new applications require sound cards. If you plan on running any games, using a multimedia encyclopedia, or even exploring the Internet, you'll need a sound card. Some applications can use the old 8-bit sound card, but newer applications require a 16-bit-or-better sound card, which enables stereo output.

Amount of memory (RAM)   If your computer doesn't have the required memory, it may not be able to run the application, or the application may cause the computer to crash (freeze up).

Hard disk requirements   Before using most applications, you must install (copy) the program files to your hard disk from the floppy disks or CD-ROM you bought. Make sure you have enough space on your hard disk to accommodate the new application. The next section shows you how to check disk space.

How Crowded Is Your Hard Disk?

A hard disk is like a refrigerator. You keep putting stuff in it until it's completely packed and you can't find anything. The problem with packing your disk drive full of programs is not only that it makes it difficult to find the programs and files you use most often, but also a crowded disk starts to negatively affect the overall performance of your computer and can make it impossible for you to save the documents you create.

Before installing a program, you should make sure that you have enough free disk space for the program with an additional 30MB for Windows to use as its workspace.

To check disk space, simply right-click the icon for your hard disk drive in My Computer or Windows Explorer and choose **Properties**. The Properties dialog box displays the total disk space, the amount in use, and the amount that's free, as shown in the following figure.

Windows displays the total disk space, free space, and space being used.

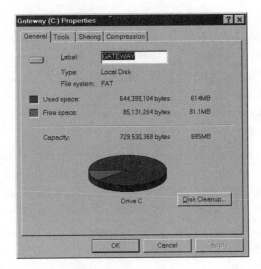

If your hard disk doesn't have sufficient free space for installing the program, you can free up some disk space by taking the following steps:

➤ Display the disk's Properties dialog box. On the General tab, click the **Disk Cleanup** button and follow the onscreen instructions to clear unnecessary files from the disk. If you have an older version of Windows, the Disk Cleanup button is unavailable.

➤ If you don't have a Disk Cleanup button, skip to "Cleaning Your Hard Disk" in Chapter 28, "Do-It-Yourself Computer Tune-Ups," to learn how to manually remove unnecessary files from your hard disk.

➤ Uninstall any programs that you no longer use. See "Uninstalling Programs You Don't Use" later in this chapter.

➤ Make sure the Recycle Bin doesn't contain any files you might need, and then empty it (open the **File** menu and choose **Empty Recycle Bin**).

➤ Run Windows Setup again, as explained in Chapter 5, "Windows Tips, Tricks, and Traps," and remove any Windows components that you don't use.

How Much Memory Does Your Computer Have?

If you're not sure how much memory (RAM) your computer has, take the following steps:

1. In Windows 95 or 98, double-click the **My Computer** icon on the Windows desktop.

2. Double-click the **Control Panel** icon.

3. Double-click the **System** icon. The System Properties dialog box appears.

4. Click the **Performance** tab. The Performance status area displays the total physical memory (RAM) installed in your computer.

5. Click the **Virtual Memory** button. Windows displays the amount of disk space available for use as memory (don't change any settings here). This number should never be less than 30MB. (Most programs specify the amount of physical memory that your system requires to run the program. Virtual memory helps when you are running several programs, but it is no replacement for physical memory.)

6. Click **Cancel** to close the Virtual Memory dialog box, and click **Close** to close the System Properties dialog box.

Total physical memory installed

Click the Virtual Memory button to find out how much disk space is available for use as memory.

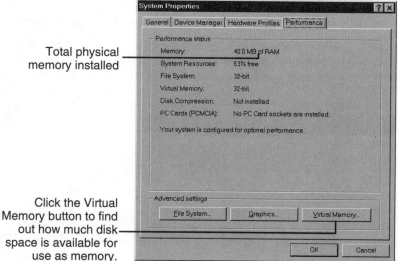

Windows displays useful information about your system.

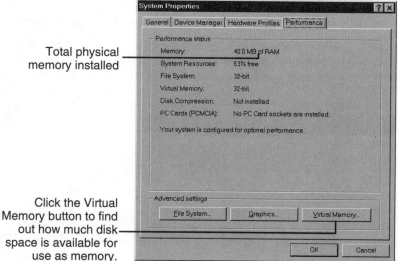

Memory Types

Most new computers use three types of memory: conventional, extended, and virtual. *Conventional* memory is what most programs use; it is the first 640KB of memory. *Extended* memory consists of additional RAM beyond the first 640KB. *Virtual* memory is disk space that Windows can use as memory. However, because a disk drive transfers information more slowly than RAM transfers information, virtual memory is relatively slow.

You can increase the amount of virtual memory by clearing files from the hard disk drive that Windows uses as virtual memory. See "Making the Most of Your Computer's Memory" in Chapter 28 for additional tips.

What Kind of Monitor Do You Have?

Monitor and Display Card Your monitor works with the display card (video card) in your system unit to render images onscreen. The display settings rely as much on your display card as on your monitor. If you have a hi-tech display card, you may have additional display options.

If you bought your monitor in the past two years, you can be sure that it's an SVGA monitor that supports at least 256 colors and a resolution of 800×600. To make sure, right-click a blank area of the Windows desktop and click **Properties**. Click the **Settings** tab. Open the **Colors** drop-down list and choose **256 Colors** or a higher color setting. If the available color settings go up to only 16, you have VGA, not SVGA. Drag the slider under Screen Area to a 640×480 or 800×600 setting or higher. (Higher settings display smaller objects, fitting more of them on the screen.) If you can't change the setting to 640×480 or higher, you don't have SVGA. Click **OK** and restart your computer when prompted.

Check your display settings.

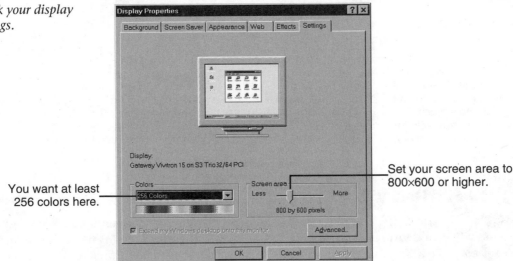

You want at least 256 colors here.

Set your screen area to 800×600 or higher.

If you know that you have an SVGA monitor and display card, but you can't enter the display settings recommended in the previous paragraph, you may not have the proper display driver installed in Windows. The display driver tells Windows how to control the image on your monitor. See "Updating Software for Your Hardware" in Chapter 32, "Do-It-Yourself Fixes for Common Ailments," to learn how to obtain and install an updated driver.

Installing a Windows Program

Although installing an application sounds about as complicated as installing central air conditioning, it's more like installing a toaster. Most applications come with an installation program (called *Setup* or *Install*) that does everything for you. You just relax, eat donuts, swap disks in and out of a drive, and answer a few questions along the way.

Windows offers a convoluted procedure for installing programs that I suspect was designed for chimps. Because you're no chimp, I'll show you an easier way:

Lousy Graphics If your monitor is set up to use only 16 colors, your graphics are going to look fuzzy. If your screen area is set to 640 by 480, not much will fit on your screen, and graphics will look blocky.

1. Insert the program CD-ROM or first floppy disk into the disk drive. (Some CD-ROM programs automatically start the installation at this point; follow the onscreen instructions.)

2. Double-click **My Computer** on the Windows desktop.

3. Double-click the icon for your CD-ROM or floppy drive. This displays a list of files and folders on the disk or CD-ROM.

4. Double-click the file named **Setup**, **Install**, or its equivalent (refer to the program's installation instructions, if necessary). This starts the installation utility.

5. Follow the onscreen instructions to complete the installation.

No Install or Setup File?

Of the programs you encounter, 99.9% have an Install or Setup file, so you shouldn't have any problem. However, if the program doesn't have its own setup utility, installation is still easy. Just use My Computer or Windows Explorer to copy the files from the CD-ROM or floppy disk to a separate folder on your hard disk. See Chapter 16, "Copying, Moving, and Nuking Folders and Files," for details. To add the program to the Windows Start menu, see Chapter 5.

*Most programs come
with their own
installation utility.*

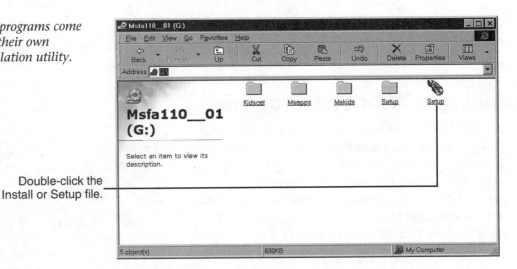

Double-click the
Install or Setup file.

Special Considerations for Installing CD-ROM Programs

**Chimps
Only** If you are
a chimp and
you had trouble
finding the
Setup or Install
file, here's how Microsoft wants
you to install programs: Open
the **Start** menu, point to
Settings, and click **Control
Panel**. Double-click the **Add/
Remove Programs** icon. Click
the **Install** button and follow
the onscreen instructions.

When you install a CD-ROM program, you might
encounter a few variations on the installation process.
First, many CD-ROMs are set up to play automatically
when you load them into the CD-ROM drive. In such a
case, the program will ask whether you want to install it.
Answer accordingly.

Second, the CD-ROM installation program usually gives
you the option of installing the entire application or
only the startup files. By installing only the startup files,
you use little space on your hard disk (typically 1–2MB),
and the application runs from the CD-ROM (though
much more slowly). If your disk is strapped for space, go
with the minimal installation.

Does Anyone Use Floppy Disks Anymore?

Floppy disks are fast becoming extinct, but you might still receive small programs on
floppy disks. Before installing a program from floppy disks, it's a good idea to write-
protect the disks, if they are not already write-protected. If you hold the disk with the
label facing up and away from you, the write-protect tab is in the disk's upper-left corner.
Slide the tab up so that you can see through the hole in the disk.

Where Else Can I Get Some Programs?

You walk into Best Buy, CompUSA, or your other favorite computer store, pull a program box off the shelf, and hand over your Visa card. The box contains a CD-ROM or some floppy disks, a registration card, and a skimpy manual. That's the way you usually purchase software.

However, more and more companies are choosing to distribute their software over the Internet. Thousands of software developers have made their software available on the Internet, as freeware, shareware (try now, pay later), and commercial software. You simply download (copy) a file to your computer and then run it. See Chapter 21, "Whipping Around the World Wide Web," to learn more about downloading files.

> **Write-Protect Prohibited**
> Some programs allow only a certain number of installations or require you to enter a password or registration number during installation. The installation utility then records this information on the floppy disk. In such cases, you may not be able to write-protect the disk.

This method of distributing software introduces some variations to the installation procedure. To make the file smaller, so it transfers to your computer faster, the creator typically stores the program as a compressed file. To install the program, you must decompress it. In most cases, the file you download is self-extracting and self-installing. You simply place the file in a folder of its own and double-click the file. It decompresses itself and then runs the installation utility, which leads you through the setup.

In other cases, the file may decompress itself but not run the installation. After the file is decompressed, look in its folder to see whether it has an Install or Setup file. If it does, double-click the file to run the installation utility. If no Install or Setup file is present, look for the file/icon for running the program and double-click it.

Many files on the Internet are packaged as compressed files that don't extract themselves. Most compressed PC files are stored in the ZIP format (the file's name ends in **.zip**). To decompress ZIP files, you need a special *shareware* (try before you buy) program called WinZip, which you can download from **www.winzip.com**. WinZip comes as a self-extracting, self-installing file. After installing WinZip, double-click the ZIP file you downloaded. WinZip displays a list of files in the ZIP file. If a **Setup** or **Install** file is in the list, double-click it. Otherwise, click the **Extract** button to decompress the files.

Registering Your Program

After you have installed your program, you should register it. I know, you want to play with the program first, but if you do that, you'll never get around to registering the program, so do it now.

Why should you register? There are several reasons. By registering, you let the manufacturer know that you have a legal copy of the program (not a copy you pirated from Uncle Fred). If you run into trouble later, the manufacturer will know that you paid for the program and will more likely help you solve the problem (assuming you can get through to their tech support department). In addition, if the manufacturer develops a newer version of the program, registered users can usually acquire the program at a reduced price.

Uninstalling Programs You Don't Use

Check This Out...

Register by Modem Many software companies now enable you to register your new programs via modem. Typically, after you install the program, a dialog box pops up on your screen, asking whether you want to register via modem. You select **Yes**, and then follow the onscreen instructions. The program takes care of the rest (dialing the phone, sending the information, and so on).

If you are running low on disk space, it's tempting to just delete folders for programs you no longer use. That gets rid of the program, right? Not entirely, especially if the program you're trying to get rid of is a Windows program. When you install a Windows program, it commonly installs files not only to the program's folder but also to the **\WINDOWS, WINDOWS\SYSTEM,** and other folders. To remove the program completely, you should use Windows' Add/Remove Programs utility:

1. Click the **Start** button, point to **Settings**, and click **Control Panel**.

2. Click the **Add/Remove Programs** icon. The Add/Remove Programs Properties dialog box appears.

3. Click the **Install/Uninstall** tab, if it isn't already selected. At the bottom of the screen is a list of programs you can have Windows uninstall.

4. Click the name of the program you want to remove.

5. Click the **Add/Remove** button.

6. One or more dialog boxes will lead you through the uninstall process, asking for your confirmation. Follow the onscreen instructions to complete the process.

If the name of the program you want to remove doesn't appear in the Add/Remove Programs list, you may be able to use the program's own setup utility to remove the program. Take one of the following steps:

➤ Use My Computer or Windows Explorer to display the contents of the folder for the program you want to remove. If you see a **Setup** or **Install** icon, double-click it, and follow the onscreen instructions to remove the program.

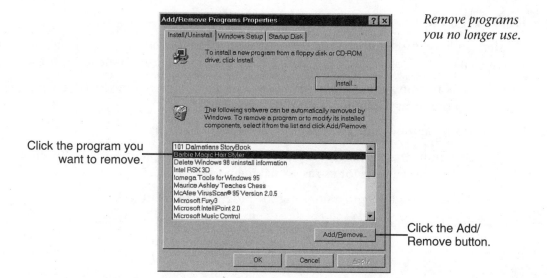

Remove programs you no longer use.

Click the program you want to remove.

Click the Add/Remove button.

➤ Click the **Start** button, point to **Programs**, and point to the program's menu name. Look on the submenu that appears for a **Setup**, **Install**, or **Uninstall** option. If the menu has such an option, select it and then follow the onscreen instructions to remove the program.

In many cases, the program's setup utility enables you to remove the entire program or only selected components. If you use the program but don't use its advanced features, you can save disk space by removing only the components you don't use.

Manually Delete Shortcut If the program you removed has a shortcut icon on the desktop, you might have to delete this manually. Right-click the icon, and choose **Delete**.

Uninstall Utilities

If you don't see a Setup or Install button, the best thing to do is to obtain a program that's designed especially to help you remove other programs from your hard drive. Remove-It and Clean Sweep are two of the more popular programs, although they both require a good amount of technical expertise to avoid deleting the wrong files. Don't play with these programs unless you know what you're doing.

85

Tech Check

After working through this chapter, you will no longer have to call your neighbor or in-law to help you install a new program. Just make sure you can do the following:

➤ Walk into any computer store, pull a program box off the shelf, and determine whether your computer can run the program.

➤ Figure out how much free space is left on your hard disk.

➤ Determine the amount of physical memory your computer has and the amount of disk space available for use as virtual memory.

➤ Install a Windows program using the program's setup utility.

➤ Remove a Windows program that you no longer use.

Chapter 7

Running and Juggling Programs

In This Chapter

➤ Five ways to run a Windows program

➤ Jumping from one program to another

➤ Scheduling programs to run automatically

➤ Running your old DOS programs

Although you might not consider Windows as user-friendly as Microsoft claims it is, it has significantly improved the way programs run. You can run programs from the Start menu or the Windows desktop, have Windows launch programs automatically on startup, flip from one program to another in the taskbar, and even automatically open a document in its program by double-clicking the document's icon.

However, in order to take advantage of these modern conveniences, you must first learn the basics of running programs and switching from one program to another. This chapter provides all the necessary basic instructions, plus a bushel of tips to make you feel like a pro.

Five Ways to Fire Up a Windows Program

The only hard part to running a Windows program is deciding *how* you want to run it. The standard way is to open the Start menu, point to Programs, and then click the program's name. In some cases, however, you have to follow a trail of three or four submenus to find the desired program.

Fortunately, Windows provides several alternative ways to run programs. You can launch programs from My Computer or Windows Explorer, create your own shortcuts on the Windows desktop, and even create your own toolbars to give your programs single-click access. The following sections explain your options.

1. Start It Up from the Start Menu

Check This Out...

Too Many Programs? If you have dozens of programs on your Programs menu, they may not all fit. In such a case, you will see an arrow at the bottom of the Programs menu. Rest the mouse pointer on the arrow to scroll additional program names into view.

Whenever you install a Windows program, the program's name is added to the Start, Programs menu. If the program consists of two or more programs, the setup utility may create a program group, which appears as a submenu on the Programs menu. To run the program, you take the following steps:

1. Click the **Start** button.

2. Point to **Programs**. The Programs submenu opens.

3. If the program's name is on the Programs menu, click it to run the program and skip the next step. Otherwise, point to the program's group name (marked with a folder icon). Another submenu appears.

4. Click the name of the program. Finally, the program runs.

Granted, the process is convoluted, and if your hand is shaky, you might have trouble navigating the submenus, but this procedure will get you there.

2. Launch Programs from My Computer

You can also launch programs from My Computer or Windows Explorer, although the procedure isn't any more efficient than using the Start menu. You simply change to the folder in which the program's files are stored (assuming you can find it) and then double-click the icon for running the program. You'll find most of your programs in a subfolder inside the Program Files folder.

The only trouble with this approach is that the folder containing the program's files is typically packed with files that don't run the program. Look for the prettiest icon in the bunch; it's usually the icon for the *executable file*, which is the file that launches the program. If you have Internet Explorer 4, the left pane displays the selected file's full name and indicates that it is an Application file.

Sometimes it's easier to just double-click the name of a document file you created using the program. When you install most programs, the program sets up a *file association* that links the program to the type of document you use the program to create. When you double-click a document file, Windows runs the associated program, which then opens the document.

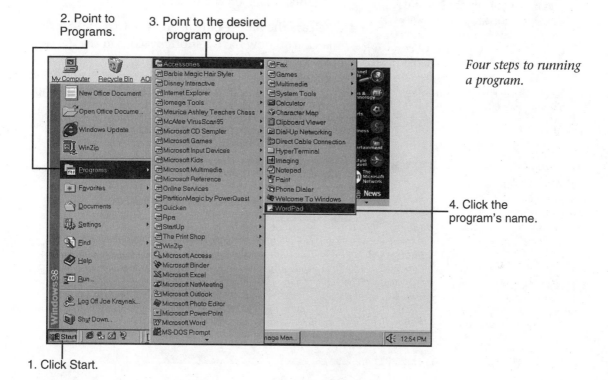

2. Point to Programs.

3. Point to the desired program group.

4. Click the program's name.

1. Click Start.

Four steps to running a program.

3. Make Your Own Program Shortcut

Had enough inefficiency? Here's what you do: Create a shortcut icon for every program you commonly use; place it on the Windows desktop. Then, rather than follow a trail of menus or folders to find the program, you double-click its shortcut icon. To make a shortcut icon for a program, take the following steps:

1. Run My Computer or Windows Explorer and resize the window so that you can see a blank spot on the Windows desktop.

Executables
The file that runs a program is called an *executable file*, and its name always ends in the .EXE, .COM, or .BAT extension. The trouble is that Windows may not display filename extensions. To display the extensions, open the **View** menu in My Computer and choose **Folder Options**. Click the **View** tab and remove the check mark from the **Hide File Extensions for Known File Types** box. Click **OK**.

2. Change to the folder containing the icon for the program you want to run. The Windows/Start Menu/Programs folder and its subfolders contain icons for all the programs on the Start, Programs menu. (Look for additional programs in the C:\Program Files folder.)

3. Hold down the **Ctrl** and **Shift** keys while dragging the icon from My Computer or Windows Explorer to a blank area on the desktop.

4. Release the mouse button and the **Ctrl** and **Shift** keys. You now have a shortcut icon on the desktop.

To quickly arrange icons on the desktop, right-click a blank area of the desktop, point to **Arrange Icons**, and click **Auto Arrange**. (If you turn off Auto Arrange, you can drag icons anywhere on the desktop.)

You can run programs from My Computer or Windows Explorer.

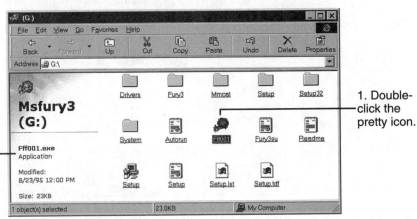

1. Double-click the pretty icon.

2. If you're running Internet Explorer 4, you can see the file type and extension here.

4. Assign a Shortcut Key Combination to Your Program

You can assign a key combination to program shortcut icons. Right-click the icon and choose **Properties**. Click the **Shortcut Key** text box and press the key that you want to use to run this program. You can use any key except Esc, Enter, Tab, Spacebar, Backspace, Print Screen, or any function key or key combination used by Windows.

If you press a function key (for example, F8), Windows inserts that key in the text box. (Don't use F1 because Windows uses that for Help.) If you press a number or character key, Windows automatically adds Ctrl+Alt+ to the key. For example, if you press 8, you will use Ctrl+Alt+8 to run the program. Click **OK**.

5. Do-It-Yourself Program Toolbar

If you have Windows with Internet Explorer 4 installed, the taskbar at the bottom of your screen contains a toolbar called the Quick Launch toolbar. It contains four icons for running Internet Explorer, Outlook Express, and Channels and for returning to the Windows desktop. To add your own toolbar to the taskbar, take the following steps:

1. Right-click a blank area of the desktop, point to **New**, and click **Folder**. A new folder appears on the desktop.

2. Type a name for the folder and press **Enter**.

3. **Ctrl+Shift+drag** any program icons that you want to appear on the toolbar over the new folder icon, and release the mouse button. This places a copy of each program icon in the folder.

4. Drag the folder icon over the taskbar and release the mouse button. Windows transforms the folder into a toolbar and places its icons on the taskbar.

To remove the toolbar, right-click a blank area of the taskbar, point to Toolbars, and click the toolbar's name. (You can also drag a program or submenu from the Start, Programs menu or any of its submenus to the desktop or to a toolbar displayed on the taskbar. To copy the items, hold down the Ctrl key.)

Start, Run You can also run a program by opening the Start menu, choosing Run, and then typing the location and name of the file that runs the program. However, this assumes that you know the location and name of the file you want to run. It's more trouble than it's worth.

Customizing Your Start Menu

Occasionally, you install a program, and it doesn't appear on the Start menu, or the program may appear on the third or fourth submenu down, making it difficult to access. Does that mean you have to live with it? Heck no, change it.

First, click the **Start** menu, point to **Settings**, and click **Taskbar**. This displays the Taskbar Properties dialog box. Click the **Start Menu Programs** tab. Now, do any of the following to customize your Start menu:

➤ To add a program to the Start menu or one of its submenus, click the **Add** button. This starts a *wizard* (a series of dialog boxes that leads you through the process). Follow the onscreen instructions to complete the operation.

➤ To remove a program from the Start menu, click the **Remove** button. This displays a list of all the Start menu items. To view the items on a submenu, click the plus sign next to the menu's name. Select the item you want to remove, and click the **Remove** button.

➤ To rearrange items on the **Start** menu, click the **Advanced** button. Again, you can click the plus sign next to a submenu name to view its contents. You can drag items up or down on the menu, drag programs to different submenus, and even delete items.

The contents of the selected
folder appear here.

*The Advanced option
lets you rearrange
items on the Start
menu.*

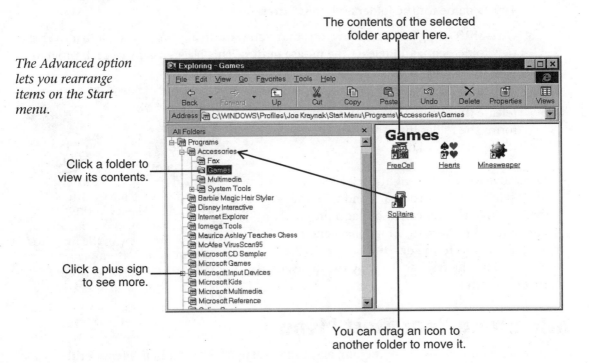

Click a folder to
view its contents.

Click a plus sign
to see more.

You can drag an icon to
another folder to move it.

Juggling Programs with the Taskbar

Multitasking (working with several programs at once) used to be a Zen lesson in resignation: If you clicked on the wrong spot, the window you were working in disappeared under an avalanche of other windows. If you were lucky, you might see an edge of the window that you could click to get it to jump in front of the other windows.

The latest versions of Windows have made it much easier to switch from one program to another. Windows displays a *taskbar* at the bottom of the screen, giving you a button for each program that's running. If you happen to lose a window at the bottom of a stack, just click its button in the taskbar to get it back.

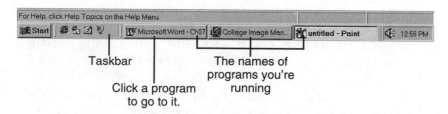

Use the taskbar to quickly switch to a program.

Taskbar

Click a program to go to it.

The names of programs you're running

Keep in mind that each program you have open (the program button appears on the taskbar) uses part of your computer's memory. As you use more memory, the program you're using runs slower. If you're not using a program, exit it. To exit a program, click the Close (X) button in the upper-right corner of the window, or open the program's File menu and choose Exit.

Program Juggling

There are other ways to switch from one program to another. Try this: Hold down the **Alt** key and press the **Tab** key. A box showing icons for all your running programs appears in the middle of your screen. As you continue to hold the **Alt** key and press the **Tab** key, each open program is selected in succession. When you release the Alt key, Windows switches to the selected program. You can also press **Ctrl+Esc** to open the Start menu.

Stupid Taskbar Tricks

Normally, the taskbar just lurks at the bottom of the screen until you need it. If you're bored, however, the taskbar offers some mild entertainment. Try the following:

➤ Drag the taskbar to the top of the screen or to the left or right side of the screen to move it. (Drag a blank, buttonless area of the taskbar.)

➤ Move the mouse pointer over one edge of the taskbar until the pointer turns into a double-headed arrow. Then, drag the edge up or down to resize the taskbar. You can make it very big, so it displays more rows of buttons and toolbars.

➤ Double-click on the time in the taskbar. This displays a dialog box that lets you set the time and date.

➤ Right-click on a blank area of the taskbar, and click **Properties**. A dialog box appears, allowing you to change the way the taskbar behaves.

➤ To resize toolbars in the taskbar, drag the horizontal line that appears on the left or right edge of the toolbar.

Taskbar Woes

If your taskbar disappears, you may have turned on the Auto Hide option in the Taskbar Properties dialog box. If Auto Hide is on, you can bring the taskbar into view by resting the mouse pointer at the edge of the screen where the bar typically hangs out (the bottom of the screen, unless you moved the taskbar). The taskbar pops into view. To turn off Auto Hide, right-click on a blank area of the taskbar, select **Properties**, click **Auto Hide** (to remove the check mark), and click **OK**.

The taskbar might also disappear if you shrink it. In this case, rest the mouse pointer at the edge of the screen where the taskbar usually appears; the mouse pointer will turn into a double-headed arrow. Hold down the mouse button, and drag away from the edge of the screen. This makes the taskbar bigger, so you can see it.

Running Programs Automatically

Internet Explorer 4 brings a new feature to Windows, called Task Scheduler, which allows you to set up programs to run and perform specific tasks automatically at a specified date and time. If you use Task Scheduler, it runs whenever you start Windows and remains in the background. When the scheduled time arrives, Task Scheduler launches the designated program, which then performs the specified task.

Like all programs that run in the background, Task Scheduler displays an icon in the system tray (on the right end of the taskbar) when it is running. You can double-click the Task Scheduler icon to view a list of scheduled tasks. You can then pause Task Scheduler to prevent it from automatically running programs (if you are currently working with another program).

Task Scheduler is particularly useful for automating system management tasks, such as backing up files on your hard disk, optimizing your hard disk, and checking disks for errors. (See Chapters 29 and 30 for details about maintenance tasks that you might want to automate.) To schedule a program, take the following steps (these steps may vary, depending on which version of Windows you are using):

1. Click the **Start** button, point to **Programs**, **Accessories**, **System Tools**, and click **Scheduled Tasks**. The Scheduled Tasks window appears.

2. Click **Add Scheduled Task**. The Add Scheduled Task Wizard appears.

3. Click the **Next** button. The Add Scheduled Task Wizard prompts you to select the program you want to set up from a list of installed programs.

4. Click the program that you want Task Scheduler to run automatically. Click **Next**.

5. Type the name of the program as you want it to appear in the task list (or accept the original program name).

6. Select the desired schedule for running the program: **Daily, Weekly, Monthly, One Time Only, When My Computer Starts**, or **When I Log On**. Click **Next**. The resulting options depend on what you selected in steps 5 and 6.

7. Enter the desired settings to specify the time and days you want the program to run. Click **Next**. The Completing the Add Scheduled Task Wizard dialog box appears.

8. Click the **Finish** button.

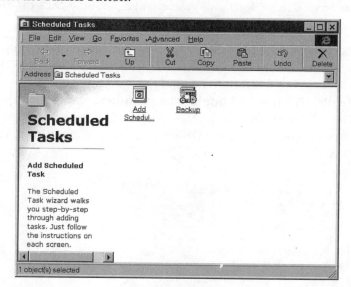

Task Scheduler can run a program automatically.

Running Stubborn DOS Games and Programs

Windows is designed to run DOS games better than they will run under DOS alone—in theory, anyway. To run the program, change to the drive and folder in which the program files are stored, and double-click the icon for running the program. (The files that execute DOS programs are typically displayed with an icon that looks like a tiny window.) You can add the DOS program to the Programs menu or create a shortcut to it, as explained earlier in this chapter.

In some cases, DOS programs, especially games, have trouble running from Windows. Windows may be consuming conventional memory that the

Additional Options

Successfully automating tasks requires some forethought. If you are automating backups so that they can proceed without your intervention, you must enter all your settings up front and enter options that allow the program to proceed without asking for your confirmation.

DOS program requires, or Windows and the DOS program may fight over control of the mouse, display, sound card, and other devices.

If you have trouble running a DOS program from Windows, create a shortcut icon for the DOS program. See "Do-It-Yourself Shortcut Icons" in Chapter 5 for instructions. Right-click the shortcut icon and choose **Properties**. Click the **Program** tab and click the **Advanced** button. Choose **MS-DOS Mode** and click **OK**. This gives the DOS program all available system resources. Click **OK** to save your changes. Double-click the shortcut icon to run the program.

If the program still doesn't run, right-click the shortcut icon and choose **Properties**. Click the **Programs** tab and click the **Advanced** button. Click **Specify a New MS-DOS Configuration**. Move the insertion point to the end of the **DEVICE=C:\WINDOWS\HIMEM.SYS** line and press **Enter** to create a blank line. Type **DEVICE=C:\WINDOWS\EMM386.EXE RAM**. This provides expanded memory for running programs that require it. Click the **OK** button. When you return to the Properties dialog box, click **OK** to save your changes.

You can coax Windows into running a stubborn DOS program.

Make sure MS-DOS mode is checked.

You can add startup commands here.

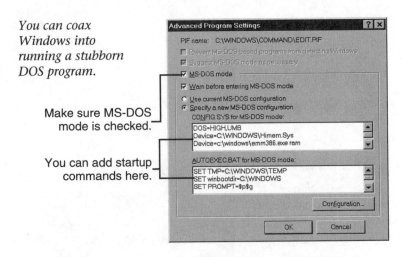

As a last resort, you can try running the program from the DOS prompt, using one of these methods:

➤ Click the **Start** button, point to **Programs**, and click **MS-DOS Prompt**. Type **cd\folder** (where *folder* is the name of the folder in which the program's files are stored) and press **Enter**. Type the command for running the program (refer to the program's documentation), and press **Enter**.

➤ Click the **Start** button, choose **Shut Down**, choose **Restart** in **MS-DOS Mode**, and click **OK**. Try to run the program from the DOS prompt. (See the program's documentation for details on how to run it.)

➤ If that doesn't work, restart Windows. As soon as your computer beeps, press and release the **F8** key. This displays the Microsoft Windows 98 Startup Menu. Choose **Command Prompt Only**. Run the program from the DOS prompt.

Tech Check

To do anything fun or productive in Windows, you need to know how to run programs and switch from one running program to another. Before you start working with your programs, make sure you can do the following:

➤ Run a program by choosing it from the Start, Programs menu.

➤ Find programs on your hard disk using My Computer.

➤ Make a shortcut icon for running a program and place it on the Windows desktop.

➤ Rearrange programs on the Start menu.

➤ Switch from one running program to another, using the taskbar.

➤ Set up a program to run automatically, using Task Scheduler.

➤ Get your favorite old DOS game or program to run from Windows.

Chapter 8

Barking Out Commands

In This Chapter

➤ Find out where a program hides its menus

➤ Bypass menus with toolbar buttons

➤ Bypass menus by pressing shortcut keys

➤ Display context menus with the right mouse button

Your computer is essentially an interactive television set. Press **F1**, and you get the Help channel. Press **Alt+F4**, and you exit your Windows program. You even get onscreen menus and buttons you can use to do everything from printing a file to zooming in on a page. The only thing you can't do is buzz in ahead of the other Jeopardy contestants. In this chapter, you'll learn how to take control of your television set (er...computer) with your keyboard and mouse.

As you work through this chapter, you'll notice that I tell you how to perform the same task three or four different ways. You might suspect that I'm trying to impress you or bore you. Nothing could be further from the truth. Windows provides several ways to perform the same task, so you can use the method that works best for you.

At first, you might want to use the menus, to see all the available options and commands. Then, when you're familiar with a program, you can bypass the menu system by clicking buttons. After you've mastered those time-savers, you may decide that you can become even more productive by using shortcut keys. This chapter leads you through this natural progression from menus to keyboard.

Ordering from a Menu

In the late '80s to early '90s, menus started popping up on all program screens. Some-times a big menu would appear front and center at startup. Other times, the menus would be hidden inside a menu bar near the top of the screen. Menus are great. They provide a comprehensive list of available commands and options and make entering commands easier than ordering a burger at McDonald's.

If Windows 95 is any indication, menus will soon be migrating south, to the bottom of the screen. No matter where they hide, the following steps will help you flush them out and make them do something useful:

Quick Windows Menu Selections To quickly select a menu option in Windows, move the mouse pointer over the desired menu name. Hold down the mouse button while drag-ging the mouse pointer over the desired option on the menu. When you release the mouse button, Windows executes the highlighted command.

➤ Click a menu name. If you can't find the menus, they're probably hidden in the menu bar. Look around the top of the window for a horizontal bar that has names in it such as File and Edit. To open one of these hidden menus, click its name. To select a menu item, click it, or use the arrow keys to highlight the item, and then press **Enter**.

➤ Press the **Esc** key. In some older DOS games and programs, pressing Esc displays a menu. Use the arrow keys to highlight the desired option, and then press **Enter**. This usually opens another menu and then another. Follow the menu trail until you get what you want.

➤ Hold down the **Alt** key. If you hold down the Alt key in some programs, the selec-tion letters in the menu names appear highlighted. To open the menu, hold down the Alt key while typing the highlighted letter.

➤ Press **F10**. In Windows programs (and some DOS programs), the F10 key activates the menu bar. Press the down-arrow key to open the highlighted menu. Use the left and right arrow keys to move from one menu to the next or previous menu.

➤ Cancel the menu. You can usually cancel a menu by clicking somewhere outside the menu or by pressing the **Esc** key.

Click a
menu
name.

Click the
desired
option.

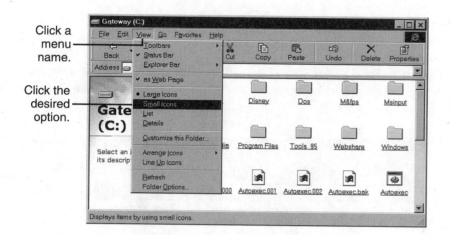

In Windows, and in most menu-driven programs, you can click a menu to open it.

As you flip through any menu system, you might start to notice that some of the menu options look a little strange. One option may appear pale. Others might be followed by series of dots. Still others might have arrows next to them. Their appearance tells all:

➤ Light gray options are unavailable for what you are currently doing. For example, if you want to copy a chunk of text and have not yet selected the text, the Copy command will not be available.

➤ An option with an arrow opens a submenu that requires you to select another option.

➤ An option with a check mark indicates that an option is currently active. To turn off the option, select it. This removes the check mark, although you won't know it because selecting the option also closes the menu.

➤ An option followed by a series of dots (...) opens a dialog box that requests additional information. For more about dialog boxes, keep reading.

Button Bars, Toolbars, and Other Shortcuts

In an effort to give you even less room to do your work, software developers have added toolbars to the screen. Each toolbar contains a set of buttons that you can click to bypass the menu system. The idea behind these time-savers is that it's faster to click a button than to pull down a menu and select a command, assuming, of course, that you know what each button does. After you become accustomed to using toolbars, you will quickly wean yourself from the menu system.

Programmers have figured out a way of telling you what these buttons do. In most new programs, if you move the mouse pointer over the button in question and let it rest there a couple of seconds, a box appears, displaying the button's name or function. These little labels are fondly known as *ToolTips* (or *ScreenTips*). To see how they work, rest the mouse pointer on the time displayed on the right end of the Windows taskbar and see what happens.

Toolbar buttons offer few clues as to what each button does.

Rest the mouse pointer on a button to display a ToolTip.

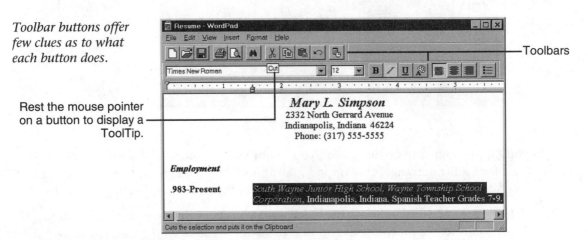

Toolbars

Quick Keyboard Commands

Techno Talk

Toolbars, Button Bars, and Other Names Each program has its own name for these button bands. The most popular names are *toolbar*, *button bar*, and *palette*.

If your boss still thinks WordPerfect 5.1 is the best word-processing program in the world, you may find yourself having to memorize a long list of keyboard commands: Shift+F7 to print, F3 for help, and so on. Most of these keystrokes are not intuitive; you have to memorize the keystroke-command combination. To help you get up to speed, you can purchase a keyboard template that contains a complete list of the commands and corresponding keystrokes. Although difficult to learn at first, these shortcut keys can save you loads of time.

Like the Great White Whale and the Siberian tiger, function key commands are disappearing fast. Most programs now use Ctrl+key combinations that allow you to bypass their pull-down menus. For example, you might press Ctrl+P to print, Ctrl+S to save a file, and Ctrl+C to copy selected text. These Ctrl+key combinations are a bit easier to memorize, and most Windows programs display shortcut keys next to their corresponding commands on the pull-down menus.

Right-Click Context Menus

I always thought that the second mouse button was there in case the left one grew tired or broke—like a reserve gas tank. You never use it, but you're glad it's there.

Recently, however, programs have been using the reserve button to do real work. You right-click some text, and a menu pops up that lets you copy, cut, or style the text. Right-click the window's title bar, and you get a menu that lets you print or save the file. Right-click the button bar, and you can turn it off (or turn on a different one).

Command-Driven Programs
Programs that depend on special keystroke commands are called *command-driven*, as opposed to *menu-driven*. However, menu-driven programs usually contain keyboard shortcuts that allow you to bypass the menu system.

These *context menus* give you a quick look at what's available. Each pop-up menu contains only those options that pertain to the object you clicked on, so you don't have to search the whole menu system to find your options.

Try it! In Windows 95 or 98, try the following right-mouse button moves to display context menus for various Windows objects:

➤ Right-click a blank area of the Windows desktop and choose **Properties** to display options for configuring your work surface.

➤ Right-click the **My Computer** icon and choose **Explore** to run Windows Explorer.

➤ Right-click the **Recycle Bin** icon and choose **Empty Recycle Bin** to remove deleted files from your hard disk.

➤ Right-click the **Start** button and choose **Explore** to display the items and folders on your Start menu.

➤ Right-click the speaker icon on the right end of the taskbar and choose **Open Volume Controls** to display the controls for adjusting the speaker volume on your computer.

What Do You Say to a Dialog Box?

If you choose a menu command that's followed by a series of dots (...), the program displays a dialog box that essentially says, "WHAT D'YA WANT?!" You click a few buttons, X a few check boxes, and then give your okay.

Use the right mouse button to display a context menu.

Right-click an object to display its context menu.

The context menu contains only those options that pertain to the selected object.

Tabs   Slider

A typical dialog box.

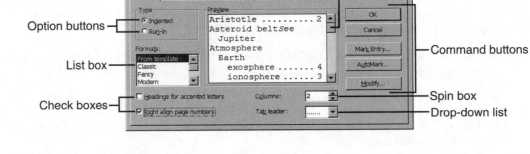

Option buttons

List box

Check boxes

Command buttons

Spin box

Drop-down list

The trouble is, you'll rarely meet a typical dialog box. As developers search for the perfect box, they continue to add items and alter the box design. However, in any dialog box, you can expect to find one or more of the following items:

Tabs   One of the newest dialog box innovations, the tab allows a dialog box to contain two or more pages of options. To switch to a set of options, click its tab.

Text boxes   A text box stands for *fill in the blank*; it allows you to type text, such as the name of a file. To replace an entry in a text box, double-click inside it and then type your entry. To edit an entry, click inside the text box, use the arrow keys to move the insertion point, and type your correction.

Option buttons   Option buttons (also known as **radio buttons**) allow you to select one option in a group. Click the desired option.

Check boxes   Check boxes allow you to turn an option on or off. Click inside a check box to turn it on if it's off, or off if it's on. You can select more than one check box in a group.

List box   A list box presents two or more options. Click the option you want. If the list is long, you'll see a scrollbar. Click the scrollbar arrows to move up or down in the list.

Drop-down list box   This list box has only one item in it. It hides the rest of the items. Click the arrow to the right of the box to display the rest of the list, and then click the item you want.

Get Help in a Dialog Box   In the upper-right corner of most dialog boxes is a button with a question mark on it. Click the button, and the question mark attaches itself to the mouse pointer. Click an option in the dialog box to display information about it. You can also right-click the option and choose **What's This?**

Spin box   A spin box is a text box with controls. You can usually type a setting in the text box or use the up or down arrows to change the setting.

Slider   A slider is a control that you drag up, down, or from side to side to increase or decrease a setting. Sliders are commonly used to adjust speaker volume, hardware performance, and similar settings.

Command buttons   Most dialog boxes have at least three buttons: OK to confirm your selections, Cancel to quit, and Help to get help.

To get around in a dialog box, you can click items with the mouse, use the **Tab** key to move from item to item (**Shift+Tab** to move back), or hold down the **Alt** key while typing the underlined letter in the option's name.

Automated Computing with Macros

Unlike humans, computers can perform the same mundane tasks over and over without getting bored or acquiring carpal tunnel syndrome. Humans, on the other hand, detest repetition. That's why we need progressively better commercials to keep us interested in the Super Bowl.

Macro   A macro records a series of keystrokes and/or menu selections and enables you to play them back with a single selection or keystroke.

Whenever you notice yourself performing the same computer task over and over, it's a sign that you need to delegate this task to your computer. You might need to create a *macro*.

Most programs have a macro feature that can record your actions or keystrokes for you. You enter the command to record a macro, and then you perform the task as you normally would. When you finish, enter the command to stop recording. The program then asks you to name the macro and assign it to a keystroke. To play back the macro, you select it from a macro list or press the unique keystroke you assigned to it. Many programs even let you create a button for the macro, assuming you're into buttons.

Of course, I can't tell you how to create macros here because the procedure differs from program to program. Use the index in your program's help system to find instructions for creating and playing macros. If your program has a Tools menu, you can usually find the macro commands on that menu.

Tech Check

Although each program sports its own command system and shortcut keys, you can usually navigate a program by using its menu system and dialog boxes. To master your programs, make sure you can do the following:

➤ Locate the menu bar and open a menu.

➤ From the mere appearance of a menu item, predict what will happen if you select it.

➤ Find shortcut key combinations for the commands you most frequently enter.

➤ Right-click at least five objects on the Windows desktop to view context menus.

➤ Locate the toolbar in your favorite program and display a ToolTip for each button in the bar.

➤ Explain macros to a kindergarten class.

Chapter 9

Making, Saving, and Naming Documents

In This Chapter

➤ Make a successful transition from typewriter to word processor

➤ Skip around inside a document

➤ Give your document files meaningful names

➤ Open your document files

➤ Find misplaced files in Windows

From the time you receive your first box of Crayolas until you draw up your last will and testament, you're driven to create. Maybe this drive comes from some primitive need to further the species. Perhaps the hostile natural environment forces you to invent. Maybe you're just trying to avoid boredom.

Computers further drive you to create. When you run a program, it presents you with a blank page, daring you to make something. In this chapter, you'll learn how to transform those blank pages into letters, ledgers, and other types of documents, save the documents you create, and open saved documents from your hard disk.

Type Away!

Most programs start you out with a blank "sheet of paper" or a work area. The screen is about one-third as long as a real sheet of paper, and it might be black instead of white, so you'll have to use your imagination. The program also displays a *cursor* or *insertion point*; anything you type will be inserted at this point. To try your hand at typing, start WordPad. Click the **Start** button, point to **Programs** and then **Accessories**, and click **WordPad**.

You start with a blank page.

The insertion point shows where the text will appear.

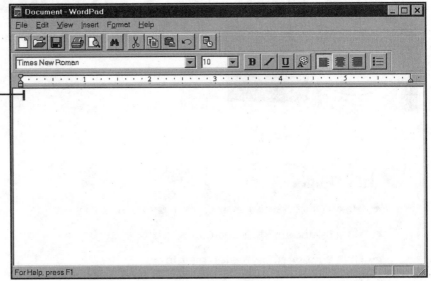

Prefab Documents

Some programs come with a bunch of *templates*, starter documents that are already laid out for you. For example, spreadsheet programs usually come with a budget spreadsheet, and word processing programs come with templates for business letters and newsletters. You can then customize the document for your own use. To view templates in most programs, open the **File** menu and choose **New**.

All Programs Differ

To type in a word processing program, you pretty much just do it. You type as you normally would, pressing the Enter key at the end of each paragraph. In other programs, typing is a little more complicated:

➤ In a spreadsheet, you tab to or click inside the *cell*, a rectangle formed by the intersection of a column and row. When you type, your entry appears on an input line near the top of the spreadsheet and may appear in the cell itself. Type your entry and press **Enter**.

➤ In a database program, you type each entry into a *field*—in a box or on a line. You typically press the **Tab** key to move from one field to the next, or click in the field with your mouse.

From Field to Record to Database A field is a fill-in-the-blank area on a database form. You type entries into the fields to create a *record*. Records make up the database. Think of a record as a single card in a Rolodex.

➤ In desktop publishing, graphics, and presentation programs, you have to draw a text box before you can type anything. To draw a text box, click the text box button and then use the mouse to drag a text box onto your work area. An insertion point appears in the text box, and you can start typing.

Rows   Input line   Columns

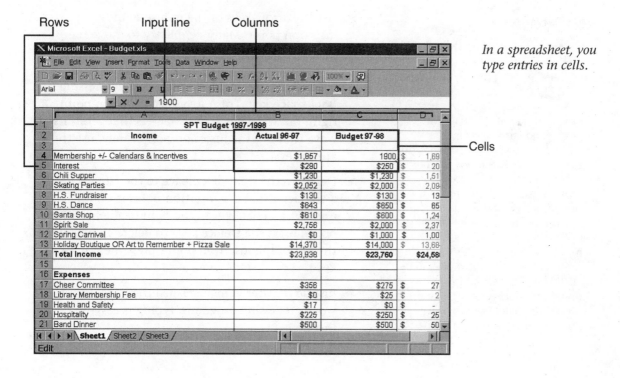

In a spreadsheet, you type entries in cells.

Cells

109

Easing the Transition

Moving from a typewriter to a keyboard can be a traumatic experience. I've known several people who developed nervous tics during the transition. To prevent you from going stark raving mad during your transitional phase, I'll give you some free advice:

➤ Press **Enter** only to end a paragraph. The program automatically wraps text from one line to the next as you type. Press **Enter** or **Return** only to end a paragraph or start a new line.

➤ Don't move down until there is something to move down to. If you press the down-arrow key on a blank screen, the insertion point usually will not move down. If you want to move the insertion point down on a blank screen, you have to press **Enter** to start a new paragraph.

➤ Text that floats off the top of the screen is *not* gone. If you type more than a screenful of text, any text that doesn't fit on the screen is scrolled off the top of the screen. You can see the text by pressing **Page Up** or using the up-arrow key to move the insertion point to the top of the document.

Check This Out...

Insert or Overstrike? Most of the time, you'll type in Insert mode; whatever you type is added at the insertion point, and surrounding text scoots over to make room. If you accidentally shift to Overstrike mode, whatever you type replaces existing text. In most programs, the status bar (at the bottom of the window) displays OVR when you are in Overstrike mode. Double-click OVR to switch back to Insert mode. If OVR is not displayed, try pressing the Insert key to change modes or check the program's help system for instructions.

➤ Use the arrow keys or the mouse to move the insertion point. Many people try to move the insertion point down by pressing the **Enter** key. This starts a new paragraph. Worse, some people try to move the insertion point left by pressing the **Backspace** key. This moves the insertion point all right, but it deletes any characters that get in its way. To move the insertion point safely, use the arrow keys.

➤ Delete to the right; backspace to the left. To delete a character that the insertion point is on (or under) or a character to the right of the insertion point, press the **Delete** key. To delete characters to the left of the insertion point, press the **Backspace** key.

➤ Just do it! After you've grasped the behavior of word processing programs, typing is easy— just do it.

Zooming In and Zooming Out

Nothing is more annoying than text that's too small to read or so large that it runs off the right edge of the screen. You could, of course, change the size of the text (as explained in Chapter 11, "Sprucing Up Your Documents with Formatting"), but that changes the size on the printed copy as well.

The solution is to change the display size. Most programs offer controls that enable you to zoom in on a document, so you can see what you're typing, or zoom out for a bird's-eye view. Check the menus and the button bar for zoom controls.

Skipping Around in a Document

Being in a document is like squeezing your way through a crowded city. You have all these characters onscreen, elbowing each other for a peek at the parade. You are the insertion point, attempting to weave your way through the crowds. To move the insertion point, you have several options:

Mouse pointer   To move the insertion point with the mouse pointer, simply move the pointer to where you want the insertion point, and then click the left mouse button.

Arrow keys   The arrow keys let you move the insertion point up, down, left, or right, one character at a time.

Ctrl+Arrow keys   To move faster (one word at a time), most programs let you use the Ctrl (Control) key along with the arrow keys. You hold down the Ctrl key while pressing the arrow key to leap from one word to the next.

Home and End keys   To move at warp speed, you can use the Home and End keys. The Home key usually moves the insertion point to the beginning of a line. End moves the insertion point to the end of a line.

Page Up and Page Down keys   Use the Page Up key to move up one screen at a time, or use Page Down to move down one screen at a time. Remember, a screen is shorter than an actual page.

Most programs also offer a scrollbar, as shown in the following figure, that lets you page up or down. However, scrolling doesn't move the insertion point. You must click on the spot where you want the insertion point moved.

Use the scrollbar to bring scrolled text into view.

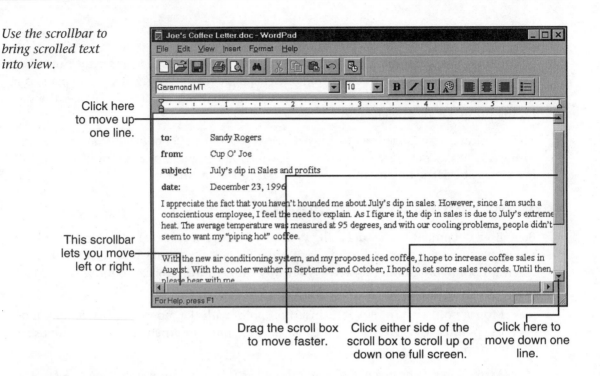

Click here to move up one line.

This scrollbar lets you move left or right.

Drag the scroll box to move faster.

Click either side of the scroll box to scroll up or down one full screen.

Click here to move down one line.

Saving Your Document for the First Time

What's a File? A file is a collection of information stored as a single unit on a disk. Each file has a name that identifies it.

As you smugly type away, your thoughts dancing across the screen, the computer stores your priceless creations in a very tentative area—RAM. If a squirrel fries himself on your power line, or someone trips the circuit breaker by running the toaster and microwave at the same time, your data is history. Why? Because RAM stores data electronically—no electricity, no data. That's why it's important to save your work to a disk, a permanent storage area.

The first time you save a file, your program asks for two things: the name you want to give the file, and the name of the drive and folder where you want the file stored. Here's the standard operating procedure for saving files in most Windows programs:

1. Click the **Save** button (usually marked with a picture of a floppy disk), or open the **File** menu, and select the **Save** command. A dialog box, usually called the **Save As** dialog box, appears and asks you to name the file.

2. Click inside the **File Name** text box, and type a name for the file. In Windows 95 or 98, the name can be up to 255 characters long, and you can use spaces. If you plan

on sharing the file with someone who is using DOS or an old version of Windows, the name can be only 8 characters long, no spaces. See "Filename Rules and Regulations" later in this chapter for details.

3. (Optional) Following the name you typed, type a period followed by a three-character *filename extension*. An extension indicates the file type. For example, you might type **.doc** (word processor DOCument file) or **.xls** (for an eXceL Spreadsheet).

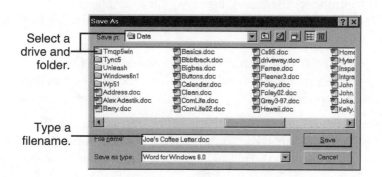

Omit the Extension If you don't supply an extension, most programs automatically add a period and the correct three-letter extension to the filename. For example, Word adds the extension .DOC, and Excel adds the extension .XLS. However, in some programs, such as WordPerfect, you still have to type the extension.

4. If you want to save the file, select the drive and folder (directory) where you want the file saved. If you don't specify a folder, the program picks a folder for you (see the following section, "Navigating a Directory Tree," for details).

5. Click the **OK** or **Save** button. The file is saved to the disk.

Select a drive and folder.

Type a filename.

The Save As dialog box asks you to name the file.

From now on, saving this file is easy; you don't have to name it or tell the program where to store it. The program saves your changes in the file you created and named. You should save your file every five to ten minutes to avoid losing any work. In most programs, you can quickly save a file by pressing **Ctrl+S** or by clicking the **Save** button in the program's toolbar.

When you save a file, most programs create a backup file (usually using the same name but adding the .bak extension). The new version of the file (the one with your changes) replaces the old version; the old version then becomes the BAK file. If you really mess up a file and save it, you can open the BAK file (typically stored in the same folder as the document you are editing) and use it to restore your file to its original condition (before you messed it up). (Some programs use other filename extensions for their backup files, such as BK!)

113

Navigating a Directory Tree

Whenever you choose to save a file for the first time or open a file you have saved, you have to deal with a dialog box that's not very friendly. The following list takes you on a tour of these dialog boxes and explains how to change to a drive or folder (directory) and pick a file:

➤ The Save In or Look In drop-down list in the upper-left corner of the dialog box lets you select a drive or folder. When you select a drive or folder from the list, the dialog box displays the contents of the active folder, which may contain subfolders.

➤ You can open a folder that is displayed in the main viewing area by double-clicking its icon.

➤ If you need to move up a level in the folder hierarchy, click the **Up One Level** button, which is just to the right of the Save In or Look In list.

➤ At the bottom of the dialog box is a **Save As Type** or **Files of Type** drop-down list, which enables you to pick a file format for saving the file or to specify the format of a file you want to open. In the Open dialog box, you can select a file type from this list to limit the number of filenames displayed; for example, if you pick something like Microsoft Word (*.DOC), the dialog box will display only those filenames that end in .DOC.

➤ If you are saving a file, the dialog box may have a **New Folder** button. You can click this button to create a new folder inside the current folder. You can then name the folder, double-click its icon, and save the file in this new folder.

➤ You might see additional buttons at the top of the dialog box, which enable you to control the way files are displayed. You might also see additional lists or text boxes, at the bottom of the dialog box, that help you search for misplaced files.

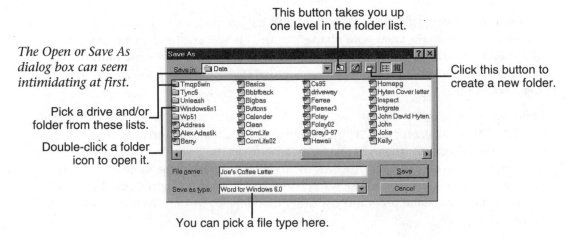

This button takes you up one level in the folder list.

The Open or Save As dialog box can seem intimidating at first.

Click this button to create a new folder.

Pick a drive and/or folder from these lists.

Double-click a folder icon to open it.

You can pick a file type here.

Filename Rules and Regulations

With the arrival of Windows 95, you can now give your files just about any name you can dream up: everything from LETTER.DOC to "Who came up with these numbers!" Windows 95 filenames can contain up to 255 characters, including spaces, but they can't include \, /, :, *, ?, ", <, >, or |. If you need to share a file with someone who is still running DOS or Windows 3.1, the rules are much stricter:

➤ A filename consists of a *base name* (up to eight characters) and an optional *extension* (up to three characters), for example, CHAPTER9.DOC.

➤ The base name and extension must be separated by a period.

➤ You can't use any of the following characters:

" . / \ [ ] : * < > | + ; , ? space

(You can use the period to separate the base name and extension, but nowhere else.)

➤ Although you can't use spaces, you can be tricky and use the underline character (_) to represent a space.

> **Is Report.doc a Good Name?** When naming files, keep the filename short but descriptive. If you name all your reports Report01.doc, Report02.doc, and so on, you'll quickly forget which document file contains the report you're looking for. A better name might be InvstrptQ498.doc. This indicates that the report deals with investments in the fourth quarter of '98. If you make the name too long (255 characters), the name will take up way too much space in My Computer and in the Open and Save dialog boxes.

What D'Ya Mean, Can't Save File?!

Occasionally, your program might refuse to save a file, rarely telling you what you're doing wrong. It could be something simple such as a mistyped filename, or maybe the disk is so full it can't store another file. If you receive a cryptic error message, use the following list to decipher it:

Invalid file name   Retype the filename following the filename rules given earlier.

Invalid drive or directory   You probably tried to save the file to a drive or directory (folder) that doesn't exist. Save the file to an existing folder, or create the folder before trying to save to it. If you are trying to save the file to a floppy disk, make sure there is a formatted disk in the drive.

Disk full   The file you're trying to save is too big for the free space that's available on the disk. Save the file to a different disk, or delete some files off the disk you're using.

Error writing to device You tried to save the file to a drive that doesn't exist or to a floppy drive that has no disk in it. Make sure you've typed the correct drive letter. If saving to a floppy disk, make sure there is a formatted disk in the drive and that the disk isn't *write-protected*.

Closing Up Shop

Check This Out...

How Does a Disk Become Write-Protected?
Look at the back of a 3 1/2" disk (the side opposite the label), and hold it so that the metal cover is at the bottom. If you can see through a hole in the upper-left corner of the disk, the disk is write-protected. Slide the tab down to cover the hole, and the disk is no longer write-protected. You can't save a file to a CD-ROM disc unless you have a special read/write CD-ROM drive, so you probably don't need to worry about protecting your CD-ROMs.

When you're done with a file, you should close it. This takes it out of your computer's memory (RAM), making that space available for other files and programs. Before closing a file, save it one last time; open the **File** menu and select **Save**. To close a file in most programs, you click the Close button (**X**) at the right side of the menu bar, or you open the **File** menu and select **Close**. Alternatively, you can double-click the **Control Menu** box (or logo) in the upper-left corner of the document's window.

Don't confuse the document window's Close button with the program window's Close button. Clicking the document window's Close button closes the file. The program window's Close button exits the program and closes any document windows that might be open.

Most programs have a safety net that prevents you from losing any changes you've made to a file. If you've made changes to a file and haven't saved your changes, and you choose to exit the program, it displays a prompt, asking whether you want to save the changes before exiting. After you've given your okay (or choose not to save your changes), the program closes itself down. The worst thing you can do to your data is to flip the power off before exiting your programs; doing this is a sure way to lose data.

Opening Saved Files

Saved files are essentially stapled to your disk drive. They stay there, waiting to be called into action. The quickest way to open a document is to double-click the document's icon in My Computer, Windows Explorer, or on the desktop. Windows launches the program used to create the document, and the program opens the document automatically.

If the program is already running, you can use the standard **File | Open** command to open a document. The specific procedure may differ, depending on the program.

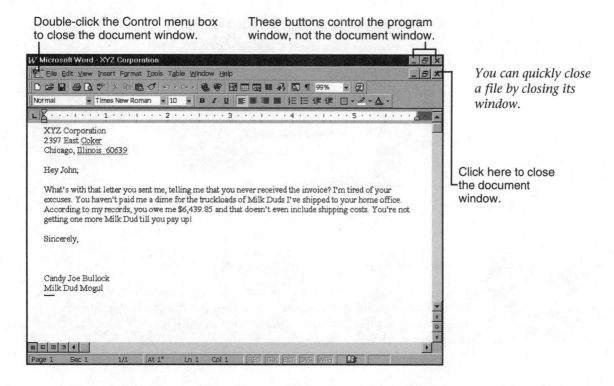

Double-click the Control menu box to close the document window.

These buttons control the program window, not the document window.

You can quickly close a file by closing its window.

Click here to close the document window.

However, the following steps provide a general guide for opening files in a Windows program:

1. Run the program you used to create the file.

2. If the file you want to open is on a floppy disk, insert the disk into the drive.

3. Open the **File** menu and select **Open**. A dialog box appears, asking you to specify the name and location of the file you want to open.

4. Open the **Look In** drop-down list and select the drive letter.

5. In the list of directories (or folders), double-click the desired folder.

6. To view the names of only those files that end with a specific extension, click the arrow to the right of the **Files of Type** list, and click the desired file type. The program displays a list of files.

Select the drive, folder, and name of the file you want to open.

The filename list

Pick a file type to narrow the filename list.

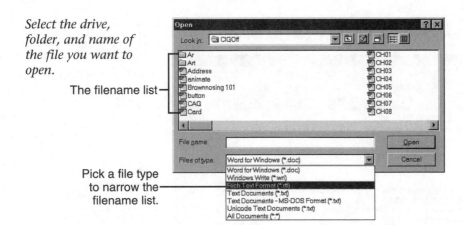

Opening Files from Other Programs

Most programs enable you to open files that were created using other programs. The program can convert the foreign file into a useable format. The Files of Type drop-down list typically displays the types of files that the current program can convert and use.

7. Click the desired file in the filename list.

8. Click the **Open** or **OK** button. The program opens the file and displays its contents onscreen.

Tracking Down Lost Files in Windows

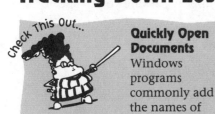

Quickly Open Documents Windows programs commonly add the names of the most recently opened files to the bottom of the program's File menu. To open one of these files, open the **File** menu and click the file's name.

When a program displays a dialog box asking where you want your file stored, it's tempting to just store it in the default folder. The trouble is that the default folder in one program may not be the same default folder in another program. You end up scattering your files like hayseed, making it difficult to find them later. Fortunately, Windows can help you track down misplaced files.

If you recently worked on the file, the first place to look is the **Documents** submenu (on the **Start** menu). This submenu lists the last 15 files you worked on. If you can't find the file there, try this:

118

1. Open the **Start** menu, point to **Find**, and click **Files or Folders**. The Find dialog box appears, asking what you're looking for.

2. Open the **Look In** drop-down list, and click the drive or folder you want to search.

3. In the **Named** text box, type the file's name (or a portion of it). If you don't know the name, you click in the **Containing Text** text box and specify some unique text that might be contained in the file.

4. Click the **Find Now** button. Windows searches your hard drive and displays a list of files and folders that match the name and/or text string you typed.

Type the file's name or a portion of it.

Select the drive or folder you want to search.

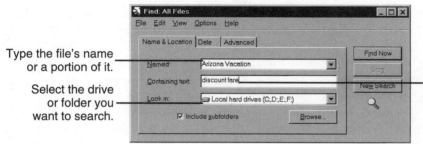

Windows can help you track down lost files.

If you can't recall the file's name, type a unique text string that appears inside the document.

After Windows has found the file you want to work with, you can open the file by double-clicking its name in the Search Results list. You also can drag the file from the list into the program window, or if you're working in older versions of Windows, you may need to make a mental note of the file's location and then use the program's **File | Open** command to open the file.

Using Your Program to Find Files Most Windows programs keep track of the last four or five files you've worked on in that program. Open the **File** menu, and look at the bottom of the menu for the names of recently opened files.

Tech Check

Now that you have saved your document and you know where it is stored, you can move on to fine-tune your document and make it look pretty. Before taking the next step, however, make sure you can do the following:

➤ Type a document in a word-processing program.

➤ Change from Insert to Overstrike mode in your word-processing program or in Windows WordPad.

➤ Save a document in a typical Windows program.

➤ Close your document without exiting the program in which it is displayed.

➤ Open a document file that you have saved.

➤ Find a misplaced file in Windows.

Chapter 10

Giving Your Documents the Editorial Eye

In This Chapter

➤ Delete a few characters here and there

➤ Chop and move chunks of text

➤ Undo mistakes with the click of a button

➤ Share data between two documents

➤ Check your spelling and grammar

The cool thing about computerized documents is that you can fling text on a page and go back later to perfect it. You can delete a few characters or an entire paragraph, move a section somewhere else, and quickly replace one word with another throughout the document. In addition, most programs include editing tools to help you correct spelling and grammatical errors and fix your typos. Perhaps best of all, programs enable you to undo your changes when you goof! In this chapter, you'll learn all this and more.

Making Minor Edits

You have probably figured out for yourself how to delete a character or word in a word processing program. You move the insertion point to the left of the character and then press the **Delete** key. You can also move the insertion point to the right of the character or word and press the **Backspace** key.

However, if you are working in a different program, such as a spreadsheet or desktop publishing program, you'll need to master a few additional techniques:

➤ In a spreadsheet program, you typically replace an entry in a cell by clicking the cell, typing the new entry, and then pressing **Enter**.

➤ To edit an entry in a spreadsheet cell rather than replace it, double-click the cell. The insertion point appears in the input box near the top of the window (or right inside the cell). Use the arrow keys to move the insertion point, and then use the **Backspace** or **Delete** key as you would in a word processor. Press **Enter**.

Automatic Rewrap As you type corrections, add or delete words, and insert phrases in your document, you'll notice that you don't have to adjust the surrounding text to accommodate the change. The word processing program does it automatically, rewrapping the words in a paragraph to compensate for whatever change you make.

➤ In a desktop publishing program, text typically appears inside a text box. Click inside the text box to activate it, and then edit the text just as you would in a word processor.

➤ In a database, you type each entry into a field. To replace an entry, double-click in the field and type the new entry. To edit the existing entry, click in the field, use the arrow keys to move the insertion point, and then use the **Delete** or **Backspace** key to delete individual characters.

➤ In some cases, you might want to replace a word or delete an entire sentence or paragraph. To do this, first select the text, as explained in the next section, "Cutting, Copying, and Pasting Stuff." Then, press the **Delete** key or just start typing. The selection is automatically deleted.

Cutting, Copying, and Pasting Stuff

Usually, revising a document isn't a simple matter of changing a word here or there or correcting typos. You might need to delete an entire sentence or even rearrange the paragraphs to present your ideas in a more logical flow. To help you do this, most word processing programs offer Cut, Copy, and Paste commands.

Before you can cut or copy text or change the text in any way (its type size, color, or position on the page), you must first *select* it. Although each word processing program has its own techniques for selecting text, the following are standard:

➤ Drag over text to select it.

➤ Double-click a word to select the entire word.

➤ Triple-click anywhere inside a paragraph to select the entire paragraph.

➤ Drag inside the selection area (the far left margin) to select lines of text. (When you move the mouse pointer to the selection area, the pointer typically changes direction, pointing to the right instead of the left.)

➤ Hold down the **Shift** key while pressing the arrow keys to *stretch* the highlighting over text.

➤ Open the **Edit** menu and click **Select All** (or press **Ctrl+A**) to select the entire document.

To try out some of these selection moves, open WordPad (**Start**, **Programs**, **Accessories**, **WordPad**). Open a document or type something and then start dragging, double-clicking, and triple-clicking to get a feel for selecting text. Try double-clicking in the selection area to see what happens.

After you have selected text, you can copy or cut the text. The Copy command leaves the selected text in your document and places a copy of it on the Windows Clipboard. The Cut command removes the text and places it on the Windows Clipboard. In either case, you can then use the Paste command to insert the text from the Windows Clipboard into the same document, a different document in the same program, or a document created in another Windows program. To cut, copy, and paste text, take the following steps:

1. Select the text.

2. Open the **Edit** menu and select **Cut** or **Copy**, or click the **Cut** or **Copy** button in the program's toolbar. (Press **Ctrl+X** to cut or **Ctrl+C** to copy.)

3. Move the insertion point to where you want the cut or copied text placed. This can be in the same document, a different document, or a document created in another program.

4. Open the **Edit** menu and select **Paste** or click the **Paste** button in the program's toolbar. (Press **Ctrl+V** to paste.)

Drag and Drop You don't need the clunky Cut and Paste commands to exchange text between documents. Display the source document in one window right next to the destination document. Select the text you want to copy in the source document, and then hold down the **Ctrl** key and drag it to the destination document.

You can move or copy
text from one place to
another.

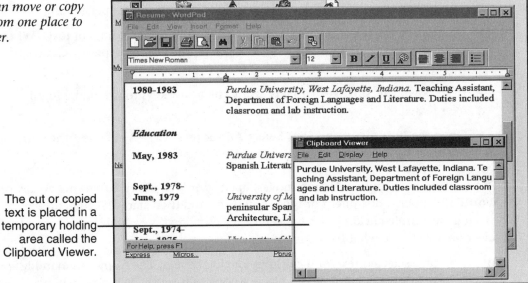

The cut or copied
text is placed in a
temporary holding
area called the
Clipboard Viewer.

Edit/Undo: The Editor's Safety Net

If you enjoy the slash-and-burn, never-look-back approach to editing your documents,
you might decide to live with whatever changes you enter. If you're a little more hesitant,
and you have that sinking feeling whenever you delete a sentence, you'll feel safe knowing that most programs have an Undo feature that enables you to take back any of the
most recent edits you've made.

To undo the most recent action, open the **Edit** menu and choose **Undo**, or click the
Undo button in the Standard toolbar (or press **Ctrl+Z** in most programs). You can continue to click the **Undo** button to undo additional actions.

The Undo button doubles as a drop-down list that enables you to undo an entire group of
actions or a specific action you performed some time ago. To view the list, click the arrow
to the right of the Undo button. Then click the action you want to undo, or drag over
two or more actions you want to undo. When you release the mouse button, Word
undoes what you did.

To recover from an accidental undo, use the Redo button (just to the right of Undo). It
works just like the Undo button: Click the **Redo** button to restore the most recently
undone action, or click the drop-down arrow to the right of the Redo button and select
one or more actions from the list.

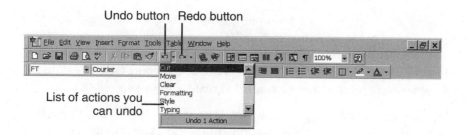

Undo button   Redo button

List of actions you can undo

If you act quickly after making a mistake, you can usually recover.

Dynamic Data Sharing with OLE

Although pasting the data inserts it in the document, the relationship between the two documents is usually static. For example, if you have a report in which you pasted a graph from your spreadsheet program, and you change the graph in your spreadsheet, the changes don't automatically appear in your report. In some cases, you might want the documents to share data dynamically so that changes you make in one document automatically appear in the other. You can share data dynamically in one of the following ways:

> **No Undo?!** Don't get too cocky with the Undo feature. After you save the file, your changes are usually final. If you reopen the document, you'll find that the Undo list is empty.

Link: Most documents support a data-sharing technology called OLE (pronounced "oh-lay" and short for object linking and embedding). If you're using programs that support OLE, you can share data by creating a *link*. With a link, the file in which you paste the data doesn't actually contain the linked data; the link is stored in a separate file. Whenever you edit the linked file, any changes you make to it appear in all other documents that are linked to the file. For example, say you insert a spreadsheet graph into a document you created in your word processing program as a link. Whenever you change the graph in your spreadsheet, those changes appear in the word processing document.

Embed: With OLE, you can also embed one file in another file. With embedding, the pasted data becomes a part of the file in which you pasted it. If you edit the file that contains the copied data, your changes will not appear in the document that contains the pasted data. However, the pasted data retains a connection with the program that you used to create it. If you double-click the embedded data, Windows automatically runs the associated program, and you can edit the data.

125

To embed data in a document from another document, simply use the Cut, Copy, and Paste commands, as explained in the previous section. If you copy and paste between two programs that support OLE (most Windows programs support OLE), the object is embedded in the destination document. If one of the programs doesn't support OLE, the data is pasted, but any link between it and the program used to create it is broken.

Creating a link is almost as easy as copying and pasting. First, you copy the data you want to paste as a link (using the program's **Edit, Copy** command). Then you change to the document in which you want to paste the data, open the **Edit** menu, and select **Paste Special** (or its equivalent command). This opens the Paste Special dialog box (shown in the next figure). Make sure **Paste Link** is selected, and then pick the format in which you want the link pasted (for example, Formatted Text or Picture). Click **OK**.

To create a link, you must specify how you want the data pasted.

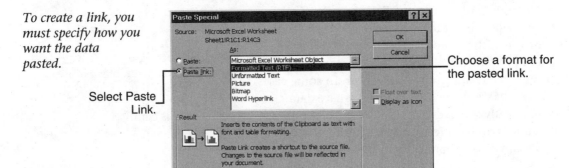

Choose a format for the pasted link.

Select Paste Link.

Finding and Replacing Text

Check This Out...

Be Careful When Moving Files Because a link points to another file in a folder on your hard drive or on the network, you must be careful when moving or deleting files. If you move or delete a file that is supplying data to another file, that other file won't be able to find the data it needs.

Most word processing programs have a tool, called *Search and Replace*, that can sift through your document, find a specific word or phrase, and replace it with a different word or phrase. If you typed **cog** and you meant to type **sprocket**, the Search and Replace can replace all the occurrences of *cog* with *sprocket* for you. Here's what you do:

1. Open the **Edit** menu and choose **Replace**.

2. Type the word or phrase you want to replace in the **Find What** text box and type the replacement word or phrase in the **Replace With** box.

3. To start the search and replace, click the **Find Next** button.

4. Word highlights the first occurrence of the text it finds and gives you the opportunity to replace the word or skip to the next occurrence. Click one of the following buttons to tell Word what you want to do:

Find Next: Skips this text and moves to the next occurrence.

Replace: Replaces this text and moves to the next occurrence.

Replace All: Replaces all occurrences of the specified text with the replacement text—and doesn't ask for your okay. Be careful with this one. If you choose to replace *play* with *performance*, the program will replace all occurrences of *play*, including its occurrences in other words, such as *players*, *playful*, and *playwright*.

Cancel: Aborts the operation.

Word highlights the text
it is about to replace.

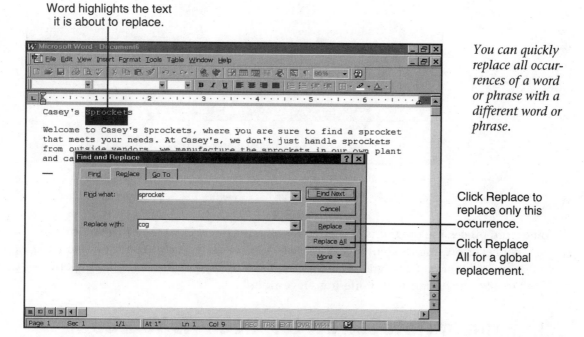

You can quickly replace all occurrences of a word or phrase with a different word or phrase.

Click Replace to replace only this occurrence.

Click Replace All for a global replacement.

Checking Your Spelling and Grammar

If spelling isn't your forté, your favorite word processing feature just might be the spell checker. Many word processing programs include a spell checker that can search your document for spelling errors, typos, repeated words (such as *the the*), and incorrect capitalization (*tHe*). A spell checker cannot, however, spot mistyped words; for example, it won't notice whether you type *two* instead of *too* or *its* instead of *it's*.

You'll find the spell checker on the Tools menu or in one of the program's toolbars. When you enter the command to spell check the document, the spell checker starts sniffing around in your document and then stops on the first questionable word it finds, as shown here. You can then skip the questionable word, replace it with a correction from the suggestion list, or type your own correction.

The spell checker stops on questionable spellings and offers suggestions.

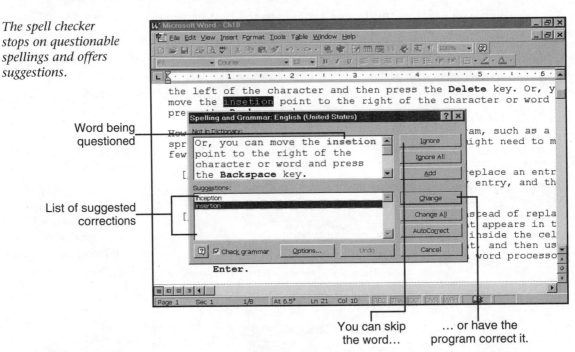

Word being questioned

List of suggested corrections

You can skip the word…

… or have the program correct it.

Some word processing programs also offer a tool that can check your document for grammatical errors, such as sentence fragments, subject-verb disagreement, passive voice, and run-on sentences. These grammar checkers work like spell checkers, stopping on questionable constructions and offering suggestions.

Redlining and AutoCorrect for Clean-As-You-Go Documents

The newest word processing programs automatically check your spelling on the go, giving you the feeling that your sixth grade English teacher is now living in your computer. For example, Microsoft Word displays a squiggly red line under any words you type that don't match a word in Word's dictionary. You can right-click the word in question and choose a correct spelling from the context menu. If you have the grammar checker on, green squiggly lines mark common grammar errors.

Word also features AutoCorrect, which automatically corrects commonly mistyped and misspelled words and uppercases the first letter of the first word of a sentence. For example, if you type *hte*, AutoCorrect automatically changes it to *the*. Sound great? Well, it is, assuming that when you type a string of characters, you agree with the correction. However, AutoCorrect also takes the initiative of replacing certain character strings with symbols, so if you meant to type *:)* and AutoCorrect inserts ☺, you're not going to be very happy.

If AutoCorrect is replacing your entry with a symbol you don't like, you can quickly press the **Backspace** key to retain your original entry. For a more permanent solution or to add words you commonly mistype, you can configure AutoCorrect. Choose **Tools, AutoCorrect**. You can then delete entries in the list of corrections or add your own entries. You can even use AutoCorrect to create your own electronic shorthand.

It Ain't Perfect Although you should never send a document without running a spell checker on it, don't think that the spell checker will catch everything. If you typed *to* when you meant to type *too*, the spell checker will not question you; *too* is spelled correctly. It's just the wrong word. The grammar checker might catch this, but you should proofread the document yourself.

Tech Check

In the next chapter, you'll start to format your document to make it look pretty. Before you start worrying about appearance, however, you should focus on content and make sure you can do the following:

➤ Use your Delete and Backspace keys to make minor edits.

➤ Select a word, sentence, or paragraph.

➤ Copy or cut selected text.

➤ Paste copied or cut text somewhere else in your document.

➤ Recover from accidental edits.

➤ Make your word processing program replace one word or phrase with another word or phrase throughout your document.

➤ Use a spell checker, if your word processing program has one.

Sprucing Up Your Documents with Formatting

Plain text just doesn't cut it anymore. People aren't satisfied with a typed page, no matter how ingenious its contents. If it doesn't look like the front page of *USA Today*, they probably won't even pick it up. You need to add some character, some attitude. You need to *format* your text.

Format

A document's *format* is the way the document looks on the page. When *formatting* a document, you change settings to improve the appearance of your document. Formatting includes changing the margins and line spacing, changing text size and style, adding lines and shading, and numbering the pages.

Messing with Margins

In most cases, margins are preset at about an inch, which is sufficient for business letters and other standard documents. However, if you're printing a poem or need to stretch a four-page report to five pages, you have to make some adjustments.

Margin settings often hide behind the **Page Setup** command, which is usually on the **File** menu. If you can't find the margin settings there, look for a similar command on the **Format** menu. When you find and select the command, you will see a dialog box that prompts you to enter new settings for the left, right, top, and bottom margins. Double-click in the text box of the setting you want to change, and enter your change.

The Page Setup dialog box contains the margin settings.

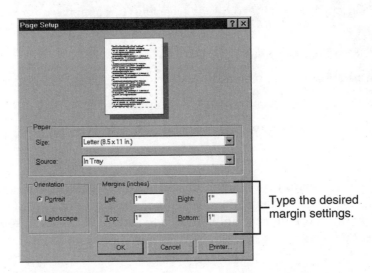

Type the desired margin settings.

Another way to set margins is to choose the **Print Preview** command, available in most programs (try the **File** menu or the Standard toolbar, usually the top toolbar). This displays an aerial view of the page. Drag the margin markers to where you want the new margins placed.

┌─Drag the margin marker.

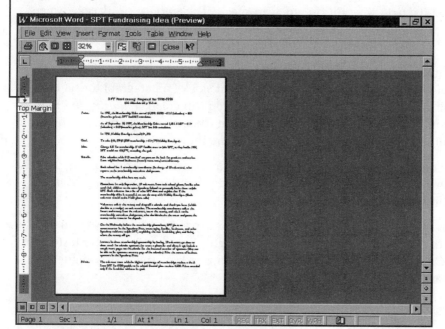

Use Print Preview to set your margins.

Primping Your Paragraphs

It's tempting to do most of your paragraph formatting with the two universal formatting keys: the Spacebar and the Enter key. Double-space? No problem, just hit **Enter** twice at the end of each line. Need to indent a paragraph? Just press the **Spacebar** five times. The trouble with this approach is that it's sloppy, it makes it difficult to adjust text later, and people will laugh at you.

Get Your Head Out of the Gutter! Some programs let you enter a setting for the *gutter margin*. The gutter margin adds space to the right side of the left page, and to the left side of the right page, so you can bind the pages in a book.

Word processors come with special paragraph-formatting commands. To format an existing paragraph, click inside the paragraph first; to format several paragraphs, select them (you need only select a portion of each paragraph you want to format). In most programs, you enter the **Format/Paragraph** command, and you see a dialog box that enables you to enter all your preferences:

Line spacing: You can single-space, double-space, or select a fraction, for example, 1.5 for a line and a half. In addition, you can specify the amount of space between paragraphs. For example, you can single-space the lines within a paragraph and double-space between paragraphs.

Indents: Normally, you indent the first line of each paragraph five spaces from the left margin. However, you can also indent the right side of a paragraph or set off a long quote by indenting both sides. In addition, you can create a *hanging indent* for bulleted or numbered lists. (With a hanging indent, the first line appears without an indent, but all subsequent lines in the paragraph are indented.)

Alignment: You can have text left-aligned (as normal), centered, right-aligned (pushed against the right margin), or fully justified (spread between margins like newspaper columns).

Tab Settings: Tab stops are typically set at every five spaces, so whenever you press the Tab key, the cursor moves five spaces to the right. You can change both the tab stop position and its type. The tab stop type determines how the text is aligned on the tab stop, as shown in the following figure.

Different tab stop types.

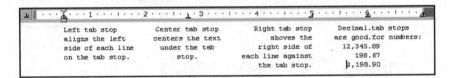

Giving Your Characters More Character

To emphasize key words and phrases, many word processing programs let you select from various fonts (also known as *typestyles*), sizes, and enhancements. In other words, you can make the letters look big and fancy like in a magazine.

So, what's a *font*? A font is a set of characters that have the same design, such as Courier or Garamond. The font size is measured in points. (For reference, there are 72 points in an inch.) An *enhancement* is any variation that changes the font appearance. Boldface, italics, underlining, and color are all enhancements; the character's design and size stay the same, but an aspect of the type is changed.

To change fonts or typestyles, you select the text you want to change and then open the **Format** menu and choose **Font** or **Character**. This opens a dialog box that enables you to select the font, size, and enhancements you want to use. If you enter settings before you start typing, whatever you type will appear as specified. (You can quickly change the font, size, or enhancements for selected words, phrases, or blocks of text by using buttons in the formatting toolbar. See "Quick Formatting with Rulers and Toolbars" later in this chapter.)

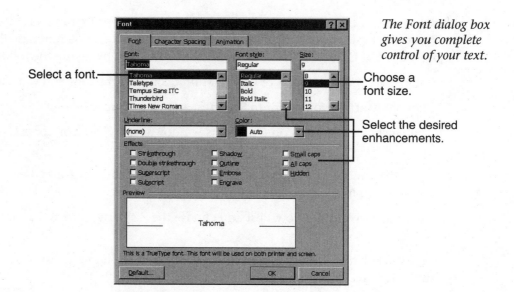

The Font dialog box gives you complete control of your text.

Select a font.

Choose a font size.

Select the desired enhancements.

Installing Additional Fonts

In the past, most fonts were installed on printers. When you installed a program, you also installed a printer driver for that program that included instructions telling the program how to use the printer's fonts. Although printers still come with installed fonts, most fonts you'll encounter are generated by Windows or your Windows programs. When you install Windows and when you install additional Windows programs, the installation utility typically places fonts on your computer. You will encounter three common font types:

➤ **Printer Fonts** Your printer has some basic fonts installed, which the printer can directly access for quick printing. Check your printer's manual to determine which fonts it came with. You can also determine which fonts are printer fonts by looking at the font's name in the Formatting toolbar's font list (you have to open the drop-down list). Windows marks printer fonts by displaying a printer icon next to the font's name.

➤ **Cartridge Fonts** Many printers have a slot in which you can plug a cartridge that contains additional printer memory or additional fonts. These fonts act as printer fonts. Windows displays a printer icon next to the names of these fonts.

➤ **Soft Fonts** Windows and most Windows programs come with special soft fonts called *TrueType* fonts. Unlike traditional fonts, which require a special font for each type size, TrueType fonts are *scalable,* giving you more flexibility to resize fonts. Windows displays *TT* next to the names of TrueType fonts. You might encounter additional fonts that aren't TrueType fonts and might not be scalable.

135

Although you can change the fonts on your printer, adding printer fonts is often expensive. You can add soft fonts much more easily and for less cost. You purchase these fonts on floppy disks or CD-ROMs. You can then install the fonts by taking the following steps:

1. If necessary, insert the disk or CD-ROM that contains the font you want to install.

2. Click the **Start** button, point to **Settings**, and click **Control Panel**.

3. Double-click the **Fonts** icon. The Fonts window displays an icon for each installed font.

4. Open the **File** menu and choose **Install New Font**. The **Add Fonts** dialog box prompts you to specify the location of the new font.

5. Open the **Drives** drop-down list and choose the disk drive where the fonts are stored.

6. Double-click the folder in which the font is stored. (You might have to double-click subfolders to access the fonts.)

7. The names of the available fonts appear under **List of Fonts**. Click the font you want to install. To select additional fonts, **Ctrl+click** their names. To install all the fonts in the list, click the **Select All** button.

8. Make sure **Copy Fonts to Fonts Folder** is checked. Click **OK**.

9. Windows copies the fonts to your hard disk and places them in the Windows\Fonts folders. Icons for the new fonts are added to the Fonts window.

You can install additional fonts from a disk or CD-ROM.

Select the fonts you want to install.

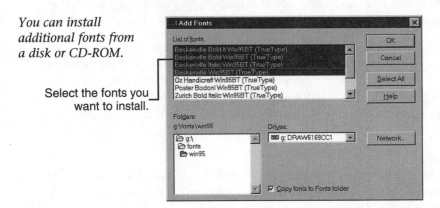

Low on Disk Space?

If you are running low on disk space, you should consider using Font Manager to remove fonts that you don't use. However, do not remove the font named *MS Sans Serif*. Windows uses this font, which is easy to read, to display text in its windows, menus, and dialog boxes. If you remove this font, Windows uses a different font, which might not display all onscreen text.

Cell Formatting in Tables and Spreadsheets

Spreadsheets and tables have additional formatting needs. Not only can you change the fonts and text color for your entries, but you can also add lines and shading to the cells and have values displayed as dollar amounts, percentages, or dates. You can usually access these options by choosing **Format**, **Cell** or **Format**, **Borders and Shading**. The following list provides a rundown of the most common table and spreadsheet formatting options:

Alignment: You usually want text left-aligned within a cell. Dollar amounts are usually aligned along the decimal points.

Lines and Shading: You can add lines around the cells and shade cells to help mark rows and columns.

Column Width and Row Height: If a column isn't wide enough for your entries, the spreadsheet might cut off the entry or display a value as a series of asterisks (*) or pound (#) symbols. When this happens, you have to widen the column. You can usually do this by dragging the right side of the column header (the box at the top of the column that contains the columns letter).

Value Formatting: When you type a number in a spreadsheet, it usually appears as a plain number (without a dollar sign or percent sign). To display these signs, select a value format.

Right-Click Formatting

Most new programs support the right mouse button. Drag over the text or cells you want to format, and then right-click the selected text. If you see a pop-up menu, you're in business. Select the desired format option and enter your preferences.

Quick Formatting with Rulers and Toolbars

To give you quick access to commonly used formatting tools, programs provide a formatting toolbar near the top of the screen. To apply a format, select the text you want the format to affect, and then click the format button or choose the desired setting from a list. Onscreen rulers help you quickly indent text and change margins and tab stop settings (see the following figure):

➤ To place a tab stop, click the button on the left end of the ruler to select the desired tab stop type (left, right, center, or decimal). Click in the lower half of the ruler where you want the tab stop positioned.

➤ To move a tab stop, drag it left or right. To delete it, drag it off the ruler.

➤ To indent the right side of a paragraph, drag the right indent marker to the left.

➤ To indent the left side of a paragraph, drag the left indent marker to the right. (The left indent marker is the rectangle below the upward pointing triangle.)

➤ To indent only the first line of a paragraph, drag the first line indent marker to the right. (This is the downward pointing triangle on the left.)

➤ To create a hanging indent, drag the hanging indent marker (or comparable control) to the right. (This is the upward pointing triangle on the left.)

Use the ruler to quickly indent paragraphs and set tabs.

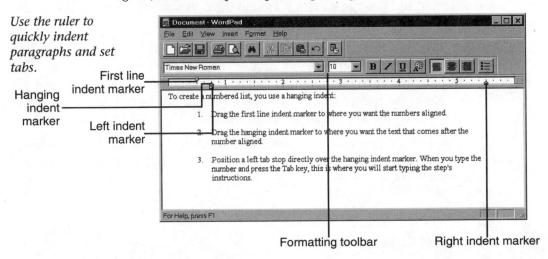

Topping It Off with Headers and Footers

Long documents often need some text that repeats at the top or bottom of every page. This text might include the document's title, a chapter name and number, the date, and the page number. You can add such text in the form of *headers* (printed at the top of every page) or *footers* (which appear at the bottom).

Don't count on finding the Header or Footer command on the Format menu or even on the Insert menu. Different programs have different hiding places for these commands. In Microsoft Word, the command is on the View menu.

When you enter the command, you'll see some sort of text box that enables you to type the text that you want to appear in the header or footer. In addition, you can enter special codes for inserting the date or page numbers, as shown in the following figure.

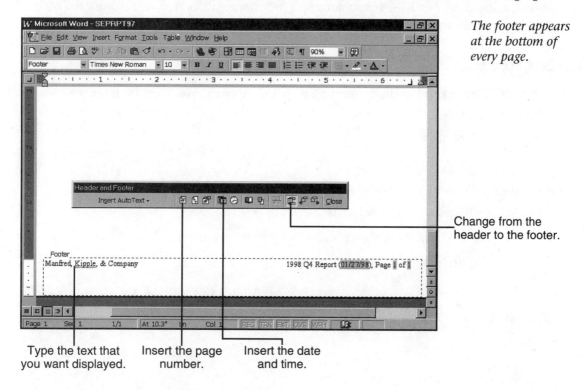

The footer appears at the bottom of every page.

Change from the header to the footer.

Type the text that you want displayed.

Insert the page number.

Insert the date and time.

Saving Time with Styles

Formatting is probably one of the most time-consuming and frustrating parts of making documents. You might spend hours tweaking your design before it looks just right. When you're done, you don't want to put on a repeat performance. Because of this, programs enable you to save your format settings and quickly apply them to other text in other documents. You do this with styles.

Say you are creating a book, and each chapter title is to be set in 24-point New Century Schoolbook font, italic, and centered. Rather than change the font, style, point size, and indentation each time you type a chapter title, you can create a style called *Chapter Title*.

This style would contain all the specified format settings. The next time you need to format a chapter title, you highlight the chapter title and choose the Chapter Title style.

The biggest advantage of using styles is that you can quickly change the formatting of all the text formatted with a particular style. Suppose (in the same example) that you decide the chapter title should be larger, say 36-point type. Because you formatted all the chapter titles with the Chapter Title style, you can edit the style's definition, changing the point size from 24 to 36. This changes all the chapter titles that were formatted with the Chapter Title style to 36-point type.

Tech Check

Although all programs handle formatting a little differently, you'll get by if you can do at least the following:

➤ Set the page margins.

➤ Center a paragraph.

➤ Change the font style and size for selected text.

➤ Create a bulleted or numbered list.

➤ Name all the buttons in your program's formatting toolbar.

➤ Install additional fonts.

Chapter 12

Picture This (Working with Graphics)

In This Chapter

➤ Add clip art to your letters, résumés, and spreadsheets

➤ Drag a picture to move or resize it

➤ Get text to wrap around a picture, just like in a magazine

➤ Play graphic artist with Windows Paint

➤ Make your text look more graphical

In this age of information overload, most of us would rather look at a picture than wade through a sea of words. We don't want to read a newspaper column to find out how many trillions of dollars we owe as a nation. We want a graph that shows how much we owed in 1995 and how much we'll owe in the year 2000, or maybe a map that shows how much of the nation could have built $100,000 homes given the amount of our debt. We want *USA Today*.

But what about your presentations and the documents you create? Are you as kind to your audience? Do you use pictures to present information more clearly and succinctly? Do you *show* as well as *tell*? After reading this chapter, you will know about several types of programs that will help you answer "Yes" to all these questions.

Clip Art for the Lazy and Untalented

Before we get into the nitty-gritty of graphics programs, I should let you know that you may not need a graphics program. If you want to add pictures to your newsletters and other documents, you can buy collections of computerized clip art, sketches that some person born with artistic talent created using a graphics program.

Here's the scenario: You're creating a newsletter and you want to spruce it up with some pictures. Nothing fancy, maybe a picture of a birthday cake for a company newsletter or a picture of a baseball player to mark upcoming games for the softball league. You create the newsletter and then enter a command telling the program to insert a piece of clip art. You select the piece you want, click the **OK** button, and voilà, instant illustration, no talent required!

Get It Where You Can: Sources of Clip Art

Some programs (such as desktop publishing, word processing, business presentation, and drawing programs) come with a collection of clip art on the disk. Some of this "free" clip art is very good—but some isn't fit for open house at the local kindergarten. The next figure shows a small portion of the clip art that comes with Microsoft Office. Just for reference, this is some of the good stuff.

Many programs come with a collection of clip art.

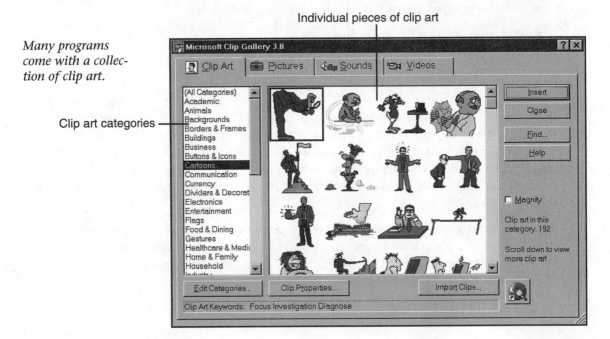

You can also purchase separate clip art libraries on disk, just as you would purchase a program. These libraries typically include hundreds or even thousands of clip art images that are broken down into several categories: borders and backgrounds, computers, communications, people and places, animals, productivity and performance, time and money, travel and entertainment, words and symbols—you name it.

You can find gobs of graphics on the Internet, too, especially on the World Wide Web, as you'll see in Part 4 of this book. You can use a Web search tool, as explained in Chapter 20, "Doing the Internet Shuffle," to find clip art libraries and samples. When you see an image you like, just right-click it and choose **Save Picture As**. (You shouldn't use a picture someone else created in your own publication without the creator's permission.) In addition, the Microsoft Office Clip Art library has a button you can click to copy additional clip art from Microsoft's Web site.

Check This Out...

Clip Art Shopping Savvy

Before you plop down 50 bucks for a clip art library, make sure your word processing or desktop publishing program can handle the graphic format of the clip art. For example, if you have a word processing program that can't use .PCX files (art created using a program called PC Paintbrush), don't buy a clip art library that consists of .PCX images. To determine which clip art formats your program supports, choose **Insert**, **Picture** (or its equivalent), and in the dialog box that appears, open the **Files of Type** drop-down list.

Pasting Clip Art on a Page

Now that you have a bushel full of clip art, how do you get it from the bushel into your documents? Well, that depends. Sometimes, you have to open the library, cut the picture you want, and paste it onto a page. Other times, you *import* or *insert* the image by specifying the name of the file in which the image is saved (it's sort of like opening a file). No matter how you do it, the program inserts the clip art in a box as shown here. You can then use your mouse to shove the image around, stretch it, or squeeze it.

You can paste a piece of clip art onto a page.

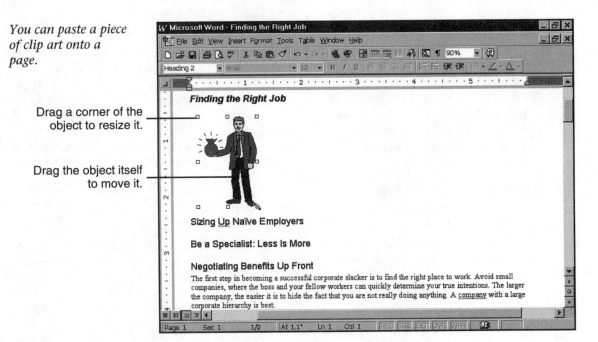

Drag a corner of the object to resize it.

Drag the object itself to move it.

Hey, the Picture Is Blocking My Text

When you lay a picture on top of text, the text typically moves to make room for the picture. In most programs, you can set *text wrap* options to control the way text behaves around a picture. To set the text wrap options, first select the picture, and then enter the command for formatting the picture (in Word, it's **Format**, **Picture**). The following list explains common text wrap options:

➤ **Square** places the picture on an imaginary rectangle and wraps the text around the rectangle. For example, if you have a circular picture, you can set text wrapping to Square to prevent the text from following the curves of the circle.

➤ **Tight** makes the text follow the contour of the picture.

➤ **None** places the picture right on top of the text. Choose this only if you have a see-through picture that you want to use as a watermark. Otherwise, it will hide your text.

➤ **Top and Bottom** places text above and below the picture, but does not wrap it around the sides.

➤ **Distance from Text** specifies how close the text can get to the image.

Making Slide Shows and Overhead Transparencies

Even if you are not in sales or marketing, you have probably seen a business presentation sometime in your life—probably on TV or in a movie. A sales or marketing representative stands up in front of the board of directors or some other group and shows a series of slides that pitch a new product or show how profitable the company is. How did that person create this presentation? Probably by using a presentation graphics program. Although we can't describe the ins and outs of using every major presentation program in this book, we can give you a pretty good idea of what they can do. Most presentation programs let you create the following:

➤ **Onscreen slide shows:** You can create a slide show that plays on a computer screen. If you have the right equipment, you can project the onscreen slide show onto a projector screen or wall, or play it on a TV. (This is the coolest way to go.)

➤ **35mm slide shows:** You can transform your presentation file into 35mm slides for viewing with a slide projector (great for getting uninvited guests to leave early). If you don't have the required equipment to do this, you can send your presentation to a company that converts presentations into slides.

➤ **Overhead transparencies:** Most printers will print your slide show on special transparency sheets instead of paper (or you can send them out to have them done). You can then display them with an overhead projector. (When printing transparencies, be sure to get transparency sheets that are specifically for printers; otherwise, you'll be sucking molten plastic out of your fancy laser printer.)

➤ **Audience handouts:** Many business people use presentation graphics programs to create audience handouts, which can be used alone or in conjunction with slide shows.

If you're creating an onscreen slide show, you may be able to add some special effects:

➤ **Sounds:** If your computer has a soundboard (such as SoundBlaster), you can plug in a microphone and record your voice, music, or other sounds that will play when you move from one slide to the next.

➤ **Transitions:** These are animated effects that control the movement from one slide to the next. For example, the current slide may open like vertical blinds, revealing the next slide.

➤ **Builds:** This animation effect adds items to the slide while the audience looks on. For example, instead of displaying an entire bulleted list at once, a build would add one bullet at a time while you're giving your presentation.

All presentation programs are not alike. For information on how to work with a specific program, check your software documentation or pick up a book that's devoted to your presentation program.

Paint Your Own Picture

Remember the old Lite Brite toy? It consisted of a box with a lightbulb in it, a peg board, and a bunch of colored, translucent pegs. You stuck the pegs in the board in various patterns to create pictures. The same principle applies to paint programs. You turn on a bunch of onscreen dots to create a picture.

Windows comes with a paint program, called Paint, which you can find on the **Start**, **Programs**, **Accessories** menu. Run Paint to display the following screen.

Paintbrush is a paint program that comes with Windows.

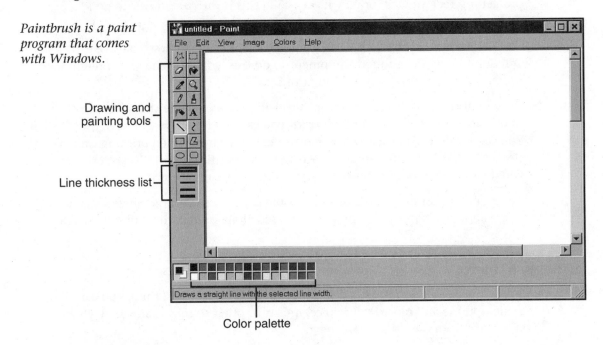

Drawing and painting tools

Line thickness list

Color palette

When you have the Paint screen up, play around with some of the line, shape, and paint tools. The procedure is pretty basic: You click a line, shape, or paint tool (such as the spray paint tool), choose a line thickness, and click a color. Then, you drag the mouse pointer over the page. To create a filled shape, click the desired color for the inside of the shape, right-click the color for the outside of the shape, and then drag your shape into existence.

Don't stop till you've tried out the paint can. Draw a closed shape on the screen (circle, square, whatever), and then click the paint can, click a color, and click anywhere inside the shape. I would tell you what to expect, but that would ruin the surprise.

You can do much more in Paintbrush, including adding text to your drawing, editing individual pixels (dots) on the screen, and using the color eraser to replace one color with another. Flip through the menus and play around with the Zoom tool and some of the other options.

Drawing Lines, Circles, and Other Shapes

You can purchase special draw programs such as CorelDRAW!, which allows you to create drawings by putting together a bunch of shapes. (The latest versions of word processors and desktop publishing programs include drawing tools that work much the same way.) For example, you might draw a cityscape by putting together a bunch of rectangles of various sizes and dimensions, or you might draw simple arrows, starbursts, or other objects right inside your documents. After working with Paint in the previous section, you might wonder how drawing tools differ from painting tools. Here are the main differences:

> ➤ In a drawing program, each shape is treated as a separate object. Think of each shape as being formed out of a pipe cleaner (you know, those fuzzy, flexible wire things). If you lay one shape on top of another, you can easily lift the shape off later, without disturbing the other objects.

> ➤ In a paint program, think of each shape as being formed out of marbles. If two shapes overlap, you can't just lift one shape without disturbing the marbles that make up the other shapes.

Techno Talk

Pixels Your computer screen is essentially a canvas made up of 150,000 to 700,000 tiny lights called *pixels*. Whenever you type a character in a word processing program, or draw a line with a paint or draw program, you activate a series of these pixels so that they form a recognizable shape onscreen.

Check This Out...

Object-Oriented Graphics Draw programs are often called *object-oriented* graphics programs, because they treat objects as individual units rather than as a collection of pixels.

You draw a shape the same way you paint a shape; click the shape you want to draw and then drag the mouse pointer to create the shape. You can then group shapes to move or resize them all at once, and you can shuffle the shapes to layer them on the page. If you have an advanced word processing or desktop publishing program, check its help system to see whether it has a collection of drawing tools.

In a draw program, you can layer several objects to create a complex drawing.

Moving and Resizing Your Graphics

After you've drawn an object or insert a piece of clip art or other picture in a document, handles appear around the object. You can then drag the object anywhere onscreen or change the object's shape, size, or orientation. To move an object, move the mouse pointer over the center of the object (not on any of the handles). Hold down the mouse button and drag the object to the desired location.

To change an object's size or dimensions, move the mouse pointer over one of the handles and hold down the mouse button (this is commonly called *grabbing* a handle). Drag the handle toward the center of the object to make it smaller; drag the handle away from the center to make it larger.

You can move or resize your graphics by dragging.

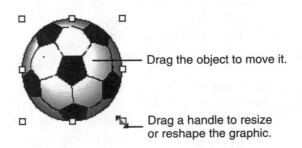

Drag the object to move it.

Drag a handle to resize or reshape the graphic.

The Painted Word: Text as Graphics

Although paint and draw programs are not designed to handle huge blocks of text, they do let you add labels and draw arrows to point out important areas of an illustration. Paint programs handle text as a series of pixels, making the text very difficult to edit. The process may require you to cut a portion of the text and paste in a revised portion. Aligning the revised text can be extremely difficult. Draw programs offer much more flexibility when dealing with text. The text is contained in a separate box, and you can edit the text just as if you were using a word processing program.

Many desktop publishing and word processing programs also offer features that allow you to insert text as graphic objects. For example, Microsoft Word's WordArt feature allows you to create text objects that look like graphical banners. You open the Insert menu, point to Picture, and click WordArt, and Word displays a selection of designs. After you choose the design you want and click OK, Word displays a dialog box that allows you to type your text.

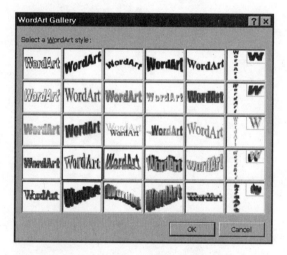

WordArt treats text as a graphic object.

A Word About Graphic File Formats

To insert a picture in a document, the picture must be saved in a graphic file format that your program supports. Most pictures are saved as .PCX, .BMP, .TIF, .JPG, or .GIF files, which most programs support. However, some specialized graphic programs save files in less common formats. If your program does not support the format in which the graphic file was saved, you cannot insert the graphic in your document. If you have the program used to create the graphic, open the graphic and try to save it in a file format that your word processing or desktop publishing program supports.

Tech Check

With an advanced graphics program and some artistic talent, you can create three-dimensional, life-like drawings that look like sleek color photos in a magazine ad. But for now, just make sure you can do the following:

➤ Insert clip art into a document you created in your word processing or desktop publishing program.

➤ Make text wrap around a picture you inserted.

➤ Paint a picture using Windows Paint.

➤ Draw basic shapes using a draw program or using drawing tools in your word processor.

➤ Move and resize a picture after inserting it.

Chapter 13

Okay, Now You Can Print It!

In This Chapter

➤ Install a printer in Windows

➤ Are you really ready to print?

➤ Check out your printing options

➤ Do other things while you print

When printing goes as planned, nothing is simpler. You open the **File** menu, select **Print**, click the **OK** button, and then make yourself a pastrami sandwich while the printer spits out your document. But rarely does a print job proceed without a glitch. You come back with your pastrami sandwich only to find a stack of paper covered with foreign symbols. Or you see an error message that says the printer's not ready. After hours of fiddling and mumbling, you find and correct the problem only to face a new problem: getting your printer back online. In this chapter, you'll learn all you need to know to print glitch-free and recover from the occasional print failure.

Setting Up Your Printer in Windows

You can't just plug your printer into the printer port on your system unit and expect it to work. No, that would be far too easy. You also need to install a *printer driver*—instructions that tell your programs how to use your printer. (If you have a printer that supports plug-and-play, Windows will lead you through the installation at startup.)

In Windows, you install one printer driver that tells Windows how to communicate with the printer. All your Windows programs communicate with the printer through Windows. When you set up a printer, Windows asks for the following information:

➤ **Printer make and model** Windows comes with printer drivers for most common printers. In addition, your printer may have come with a disk containing an updated printer driver.

➤ **Printer port** This is the connector at the back of the system unit into which you plug the printer. Most printers connect to the LPT1 port. If you're not sure, try LPT1.

Parallel and Serial Printers

All printers are commonly categorized as either *parallel* or *serial*. Parallel printers connect to one of the system unit's parallel printer ports—LPT1 or LPT2. A serial printer connects to the system unit's serial port: COM1, COM2, or COM3. Most people use parallel printers because they're faster; a parallel cable can transfer several instructions at once, whereas a serial cable transfers them one at a time. However, serial communications are more reliable over long distances, so if you need to place the printer far from your system unit (over 16 feet), a serial printer may be a better choice.

When you installed Windows, the installation program asked you to select your printer from a list. If you did that, Windows is already set up to use your printer. If you're not sure, double-click **My Computer**, and then double-click the **Printers** icon. If there's an icon for your printer, right-click it, and make sure there's a check mark next to **Set As Default**. If there is no icon for your printer, follow these steps to install a printer driver for your printer:

1. Click the **Start** button, point to **Settings**, and click **Printers**.

2. Double-click the **Add Printer** icon. The Add Printer Wizard appears.

3. Click the **Next** button. The next dialog box asks if you want to set up a network or local (desktop) printer.

4. Make sure **Local Printer** is selected, and click the **Next** button. A list of printer manufacturers and printer makes and models appears.

5. Do one of the following:

   ➤ If your printer came with a disk that has the printer driver for Windows, insert the disk, click the **Have Disk** button, and follow the onscreen instructions to select the printer driver. Click the **Next** button.

   ➤ If you don't have a disk for the printer, you must use a printer driver that comes with Windows. Click the manufacturer of your printer in the **Manufacturers** list, and then click the specific printer model in the **Printers** list. Click the **Next** button.

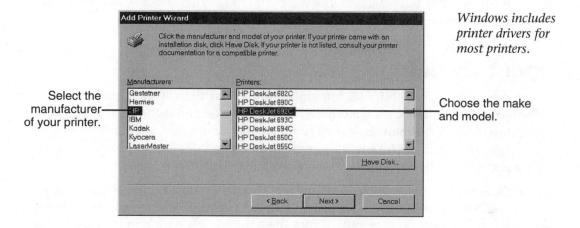

Windows includes printer drivers for most printers.

Select the manufacturer of your printer.

Choose the make and model.

6. Select the port into which you plugged your printer. This is usually LPT1. Click the **Next** button. You are now asked to type a name for the printer.

7. (Optional) Type a name for the printer. If you want to use this printer as the default printer, click **Yes**. Then click the **Next** button. Windows asks if you want to print a test page.

8. Make sure your printer is on and has paper, and then click **Yes** and click the **Finish** button. If you don't have a disk for the printer, a dialog box appears telling you to insert the Windows CD-ROM.

9. Insert the Windows CD into your computer's CD-ROM drive and click **OK**. Windows copies the specified printer driver and prints a test page to make sure it's working properly.

153

If your printer did not appear on the list of printers, and the printer did not come with its own Windows driver, you have several options:

➤ Select a printer that is like the one you have. For example, if an older model of your printer is listed, try selecting the older model.

➤ Select **Generic** in the Manufacturers list and click **Generic/Text Only** in the Printers list to print plain text. Do this only if you have a tight deadline and you need a printout of a document real quick. Setting up to use a text-only printer prevents you from printing any graphics or fancy fonts.

➤ Call the printer manufacturer and ask them to send you an updated Windows driver for your printer. (If you have an Internet connection, you can usually copy the required driver from the printer manufacturer's Internet site. See Chapter 33, "Help! Finding Technical Support," for details.)

Preprint Checklist

Most programs display a Print button in the toolbar that allows you to quickly send your document to the printer. It's tempting to click the button and see what happens. However, this usually just results in wasted paper or an error message. You can avoid nine out of ten printing problems by checking your document in Print Preview and making sure your printer is ready. The following checklist shows you what to look for:

➤ **Does the document look okay in Print Preview?** Most programs can display the document as it will appear in print. Open the **File** menu and choose **Print Preview** (or its equivalent command), or click the Print Preview button in the toolbar. Flip through the pages to see how they will appear in print, and look for the following:

Chopped text Many printers have a non-printing region near the margins. If you set your margins so that the text falls in these areas, the text will be chopped off (not printed).

Strange page breaks If you want a paragraph or picture to appear on one page, and it appears on the next or previous page, you may need to insert a page break manually.

Overall appearance Make sure your fonts look good next to one another, that text is aligned properly, and that no pictures are laying on top of text.

➤ **Does your printer have enough paper?** If your printer runs out of paper, it will usually prompt you to load paper and then continue printing. However, this pause in the printing operation can sometimes cause problems.

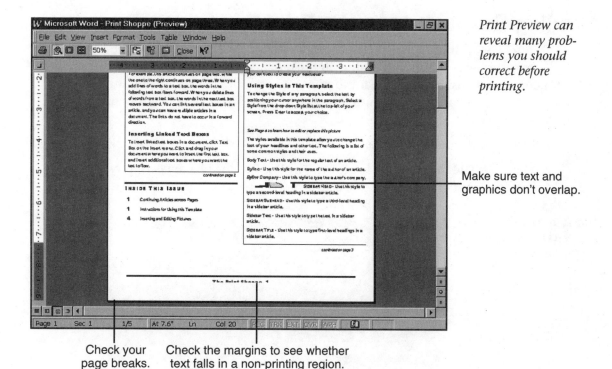

Print Preview can reveal many problems you should correct before printing.

Make sure text and graphics don't overlap.

Check your page breaks.   Check the margins to see whether text falls in a non-printing region.

➤ **Is the printer's On Line light lit?** When the On Line light is on, the printer has paper, is turned on, and is ready to print. If the printer is off line, Windows will display a message telling you so. You can usually put the printer back online by filling the printer with paper and then pressing the **On Line** button or its equivalent.

Check This Out...

No Blank Pages!

Did your printer spit out an extra blank page at the end of your document? If it did, you may have told it to! Sometimes people finish typing their documents by pressing the Enter key three or four times. That adds extra blank lines to your document and could add a whole extra blank page. If you see an extra page in Print Preview, delete everything *after* the last line of text in your document, and, in the future, try to resist those extra flourishes at the end of your documents. The End.

Sending Documents to the Printer

After your printer is installed and online, printing is a snap. Although the procedure for printing may vary depending on the program, the following steps work in most Windows programs. If you just want to print one copy of your document, using the default settings, click the **Print** button on the toolbar. If you need to customize a bit, follow these steps:

1. Open the document you want to print.

2. Open the **File** menu and select **Print**. The Print dialog box appears, prompting you to enter instructions. The figure below shows a typical Print dialog box.

The Print dialog box lets you enter specific instructions.

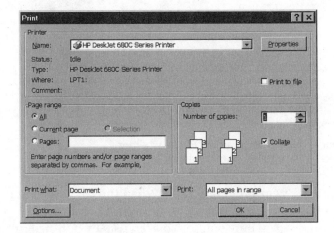

3. In the **Print Range** section, select one of the following options:

   All prints the entire document.

   Selection is available only if you highlighted text before choosing the Print command. Selection prints only the highlighted portion of the document.

   Pages prints only the specified pages. If you select this option, type entries in the From and To boxes to specify which pages you want to print. In some cases, you won't see a single text box into which you can type the range of pages you want to print; for example, 3–10 or 3,5,7.

4. Click the arrow to the right of the **Print Quality** option (or click the **Options** button), and select the desired quality. (If you have a color printer, you may have the option of printing in grayscale—black-and-white.)

5. To print more than one copy of the document, type the desired number of copies in the **Copies** text box.

6. Click **OK**. The program starts printing the document. This could take a while depending on the document's length and complexity; documents that have lots of pictures take a long time.

7. Go make yourself a pastrami and cheese sandwich.

Managing Background Printing

Windows has a funny way of printing. Instead of printing directly to the printer, Windows sends all the information needed to print the document(s) to your disk. The printing information is stored in something called a *print queue* (a waiting line in which documents stand to be printed). Windows then feeds (*spools*) the printing information from the print queue to the printer as needed. This prevents the printer's brain (memory) from suffering information overload. If you ever need to stop, cancel, or resume printing, you have to access the queue.

Whenever you print a document in Windows, a picture of a printer appears next to the time in the taskbar. Double-click the printer icon to view the print queue. You can then perform the following steps to stop or resume printing:

Printing Woes If your printer prints a font that looks nothing like the font that was displayed in Print Preview, you may have to revisit Chapter 11, "Sprucing Up Your Documents with Formatting," to learn about TrueType fonts. If you're having more serious problems with your printer than simple font miscues, see "My Printer Won't Print," in Chapter 32 to learn how to track down the cause of the problem and correct it.

➤ To pause all printing, open the **Printer** menu and select **Pause Printing**.

➤ To pause the printing of one or more documents, **Ctrl+click** each document in the queue, open the **Document** menu, and select **Pause Printing**.

➤ To resume printing, open the **Printer** or **Document** menu, and click **Pause Printing**.

➤ To cancel all print jobs, open the **Printer** menu and select **Purge Print Jobs**.

➤ To cancel individual print jobs, **Ctrl+click** each print job you want to cancel, and then open the **Document** menu and select **Cancel Printing**.

➤ To rearrange documents in the print queue, drag a document up or down.

If you choose to cancel printing, don't expect the printer to immediately cease and desist. Fancy printers have loads of memory and can store enough information to print several pages. You can turn off the printer, but then you'll end up with a Windows error message and you may have trouble getting the printer back online.

157

The Document menu controls printing
for selected documents.

*You can supervise
and control printing
using Print Manager.*

The Printer menu has
options for controlling
all printing.

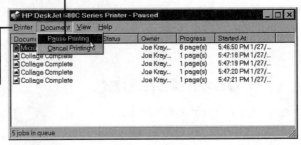

Tech Check

**Why Did It
Print Three
Copies?** If you
chose to print
only one copy
of a document,
and your printer spit out several
copies, this usually indicates that
you printed the document more
than once. When the printer
doesn't start printing right away,
many people lose patience and
keep clicking the Print button.
Each time you click the Print
button another copy of the
document is sent to the queue,
and your printer dutifully
prints it.

Your printer provides one of the few ways that your
computer can transform your documents into something useful, such as a letter or résumé, so mastering
printing basics is essential. Before you move on to the
next chapter, make sure you can do the following:

➤ Install your printer in Windows.

➤ Set your printer as the default printer.

➤ Preview your document before printing it.

➤ Check your printer to make sure it is ready to
print.

➤ Print a document created in any Windows
program.

➤ Cancel and resume printing.

Chapter 14

Surviving Without Documentation

In This Chapter

➤ Find and navigate the help system in most Windows programs

➤ Search for specific help in a Windows programs

➤ Get immediate help for the task you're trying to perform

➤ Get late-breaking information about your programs

Worst-case scenario—you get a program, and there's no documentation. None of your friends knows how to use the program, and the local bookstore doesn't have a book on the topic. What do you do? The following sections provide some tactics for dealing with such situations. Although they won't work for all programs, they will work for most.

Fake It with Online Help

Not so long ago, you used to get a book with your new program—real documentation that told you how to enter commands and do something useful. Nowadays, you're lucky to get a pamphlet with installation instructions. In most cases, you get a CD, that's it... consider yourself lucky if you get a case for it!

More and more software companies are cutting expenses by reducing or eliminating printed documentation. As a replacement, they provide the instructions via the program's help system or on special files that you'd never think of looking at. In most cases, you just open the **Help** menu, click **Contents and Index**, and then follow a trail of topics till you find the answer. In this chapter, you'll learn how to use standard help systems and take a peek at less obvious help files.

Help menu

Most programs have a Help menu.

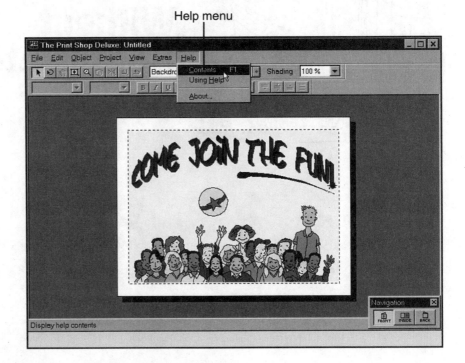

Skipping Around with Hypertext Links

No matter how you get into a program's help system, you need some way to navigate the system once you're there. Most help systems contain *hypertext links* that let you jump from one topic to another. The hypertext link is a highlighted word or phrase that, once selected, displays a definition of or additional information concerning that word or phrase. You usually have to click or double-click the hypertext link to display the additional information. Or you can tab to the link and press **Enter**.

Most help systems that allow you to jump from one topic to another also provide a way for jumping back. Look for the **Back** and **History** options. The Back option usually takes you back one topic at a time. The History option provides a list of topics you have looked at and allows you to select a topic from the list. These buttons vary from one help system to another, so be flexible.

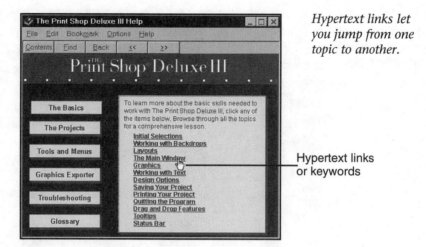

Hypertext links let
you jump from one
topic to another.

Hypertext links
or keywords

Working with the Online Librarian

Advanced help systems usually provide a way for you to search for information on a specific topic or task. For example, you might want to search for information about setting margins or printing. Here's what you do:

1. Open the **Help** menu and select **Search**, or enter the **Search** command in the help system. (The Help window may have a Find button or tab, or some other way of searching.)

2. Start typing the name of the term or topic. As you type, a list of available topics that match what you type scrolls into view.

3. When you see the desired topic, double-click it, or highlight it and press **Enter**. A list of subtopics appears.

4. Double-click the desired subtopic. A Help window appears, showing information that pertains to the selected subtopic.

What? No Help Menu?!

If you can't find a Help menu, don't give up. Some programs like to hide their help systems behind a keystroke. Try the following to call up the help system:

➤ **Press the F1 key.** The F1 key is the 911 of the computer industry. Most programs use this key to call up the help system.

➤ **Press the F3 key.** Some older programs prefer to use the F3 key for dialing help.

The Help window enables you to search for information on a particular topic.

Type here.

Double-click here...

...then double-click here.

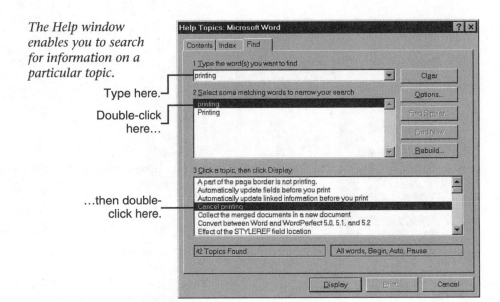

Context-Sensitive Help One of the best ways to use a help system is to start performing the task, and then press F1 when you get stuck. In most programs, this displays a context-sensitive help screen that provides the specific information you need to continue.

➤ **Look for a Help button.** Some programs display a Help button in a button bar or in dialog boxes (it usually has a question mark on it). Click the **Help** button.

If these techniques don't work, use My Computer or Windows Explorer to display the contents of the folder in which the program's files are stored. Look for a Help icon, typically displayed as a book with a question mark on it. Double-click the Help icon. Windows opens the program's Help menu.

Find Help Files

The names of help files for Windows programs all end in .HLP. If you can't find the help file or you're just curious, click the **Start** button, point to **Find**, and click **Files and Folders**. In the **Named** text box, type ***.hlp**. Choose the disk you want to search from the **Look In** drop-down list and click the **Find Now** button.

A Built-In Tutor? You've Struck Gold

Some programs come with a tutorial that leads you through the process of using the program's major features. If you ran the Welcome to Windows tutorial, as explained in Chapter 4, "Windows Survival Guide," you have already encountered an online tutor.

In most Windows programs, you can get to the tutorial through the Help menu. In some programs, however, you may have to run a separate program. In such cases, use My Computer or Windows Explorer to display the contents of the folder in which the program is stored and look for a file with a name like TUTOR.EXE, TUTOR.COM, LEARN.EXE, or LEARN.COM. If you find such a file, double-click its name.

> **Cutesy Help Systems** In an attempt to make your computer seem more personal, some programs, including Microsoft programs, offer animated characters that pop up on your screen whenever *they* think you need help. For example, if you start typing a letter in Microsoft Word, a cartoon character called Clip-It pops up and asks if you need help. Just click the links as you would in a standard help system, or click the Close button to tell him to go away.

Getting Help in a Dialog Box

Some dialog boxes contain over a hundred options spread out over a dozen or so tabs. Although the options are labeled, the labels may not tell you much. If you encounter a cryptic option in a dialog box, try the following to obtain additional information:

> ➤ **Press F1.** If you're lucky, a context-sensitive help window appears, displaying information about the dialog box and the options it contains.

> ➤ **Click the question mark button.** If there's a question mark button in the upper-right corner of the dialog box, click the button and then click the option about which you want more information. This typically displays a brief description of the option.

> ➤ **Right-click the option.** In many dialog boxes, right-clicking an option displays a menu containing a single option: What's This? Click **What's This?** to display a description of the option.

Finding Answers in README.TXT

Most programs come with a help menu of some type, which is the most logical place to look for help. However, if you can't even get the program running (or running right), you won't be able to get into the help system. When that happens, the first thing you should do is look for a README file.

Context-sensitive help is available for most dialog box options.

Right-click the option and choose What's This?

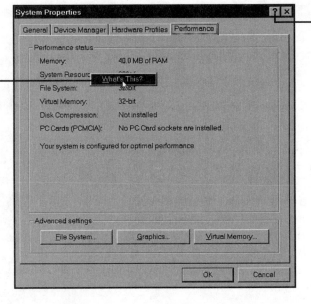

Click this button and then click the desired option.

A README file usually contains information about installing and running the program, details about how the program works, information about new features, and descriptions of known bugs.

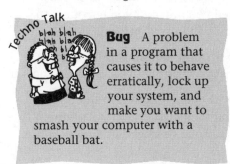

Bug A problem in a program that causes it to behave erratically, lock up your system, and make you want to smash your computer with a baseball bat.

To view a README file, use My Computer or Windows Explorer to display the contents of the folder in which the program's files are stored or the contents of the program's installation disk or CD-ROM. Look for a file called README.TXT or README.DOC. If you have My Computer set up to hide filename extensions, you won't see the .TXT or .DOC. Instead, Windows indicates the file type graphically. A text (.TXT) file icon looks like a small spiral notebook, and a document (.DOC) file icon appears with your word processor's logo on it (W, if you have Word). Double-click the file to open it in Notepad, WordPad, or in your word processor. The following figure shows the contents of a typical README.TXT file.

In rare cases, the README file may be in the form of a program. If you find a file called README.BAT, README.COM, README.EXE or a similar name with the extension .BAT, .COM, or .EXE, you can run the README file as you can run any program file; just double-click its name.

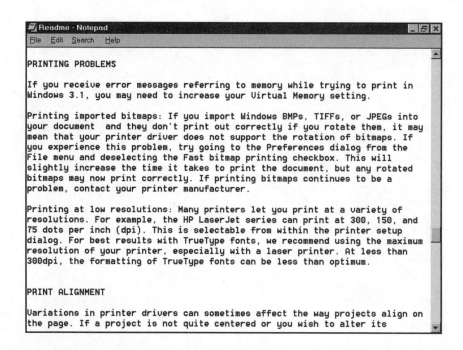

A typical README.TXT file displayed in Notepad.

Tech Check

As you become accustomed to using a computer, you'll be more and more tempted to try using each program without looking at the documentation. Before you rely entirely on online documentation, make sure you can do the following:

➤ Get help in most Windows programs via the **Help** menu.

➤ Use the Index or Search features to find specific help.

➤ Get context-sensitive help with the F1 key.

➤ Display descriptions for options in a dialog box.

➤ Find and open at least one README.TXT file on your hard disk or on a program disk or CD.

Part 3
Get Organized! (Managing Disks, Folders, and Files)

You're a slave to your computer. You install programs where it tells you to install them. You save your document files to the default drive and folder. And even when you stop using a program, you leave its files on your hard drive, afraid that any deletion will bring your system to a grinding halt.

In this part, you'll learn how to take control of your disks, folders, and files. You'll learn how to format floppy disks, create your own folders, rearrange files, and even remove some of the vagrant files that are cluttering your hard disk. And if you work on a network, you'll learn how to navigate its drives and resources.

Chapter 15

Doing the Floppy (Formatting and Copying Disks)

In addition to acting as second-rate Frisbees and first-rate drink coasters, floppy disks store files and enable you to transfer files from one computer to another. Before you can use them in this capacity, however, you need to know how to format (prepare them to store data) and copy disks.

Making a Floppy Disk Useful

You get a brand new box of disks. Can you use them to store information? Maybe. If the disks came *preformatted*, you can use them right out of the box. If they are not formatted, you have to format them, with the help of Windows.

Before you dive into this formatting thing, you should know that not all floppy disks are the same. Standard 3.5-inch disks come in two different capacities—720KB (kilobytes) and 1.44MB (megabytes). Unless your computer is from the Stone Age, you have a

Add FAT to your Disk Formatting divides a disk into small storage areas and creates a *file allocation table* (FAT) on the disk. When you save a file to disk, the parts of the file are saved in one or more of these storage areas. The FAT functions as a classroom seating chart, indicating for your computer the location of information on all its storage areas.

1.44MB drive, which can format and use 720KB or 1.44MB disks. When formatting a disk, make sure you format to the disk's capacity, not the drive's capacity; otherwise, you might lose data that you try to store on the disk. (The disk's capacity should be marked on the disks or on the box that the disks came in. HD indicates high-density or 1.44MB, DD indicates double-density or 720KB.)

You can format disks using either My Computer or Windows Explorer. I prefer using My Computer because it's right there on my desktop. Just insert the unformatted disk and double-click its icon in My Computer or Windows Explorer. Windows displays a series of dialog boxes to lead you through the rest of the process.

Enter your formatting preferences.

Specify the disk capacity.

Select Quick to reformat a disk, or Full to format a new disk.

You can name the disk (its name or label appears in My Computer).

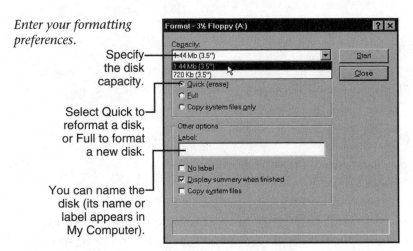

Reusing Disks Without Losing Data

After you've formatted a floppy disk, you shouldn't format it again. If you want to reuse the disk, make sure you no longer need the files it contains and delete them (see Chapter 16, "Copying, Moving, and Nuking Folders and Files").

If you have problems with a disk, you might fix it by reformatting the disk. To reformat a disk, insert it in the floppy disk drive, right-click the drive icon in My Computer, and follow the onscreen instructions. Keep in mind, however, that formatting destroys any data on the disk, so if the disk contains files you need, copy those files to another floppy disk or your hard disk before reformatting.

Disk Errors

Several factors might cause disk errors. The read/write head inside the disk drive might go out of alignment over years of use, storage areas on the disk might start to go bad, or the data on the disk may have become corrupted by dirt or a magnetic field. If you get disk errors with several floppy disks, have the disk drive cleaned, repaired, or replaced. If you're having trouble with a single disk, run ScanDisk on the disk, as explained in "Refreshing and Repairing Disks with ScanDisk" in Chapter 28. If ScanDisk makes the disk readable, copy files from the disk to a different disk or to your hard disk, and throw away the damaged disk.

Copying Disks for Friends and Colleagues

Although illegal, the main reason people copy floppy disks is to pirate software. For ten bucks, you can make Christmas presents for the entire family! I'm not going to lecture you on the evils of this practice. You know it's wrong, and if you thought there was any way you might get caught, you'd probably stop. The only reason you *should* copy floppy disks is so that you can put the original program disks in a safe place and use the copies for installing and using the program. Having done my duty for the software industry, let us proceed.

Get Some Blank Disks

To copy disks, first obtain a set of blank disks that are the same *size* and *density* as the program disks you want to copy. You cannot copy low-density disks to high-density disks or vice versa. And you can't copy a 5 1/4" disk to a 3 1/2" disk either. Don't worry about formatting the disks; your computer can format the disks during the copy operation. The copying goes faster, however, if the disks are formatted.

While you're at it, write-protect the *original* disks (the ones you want to copy, not the blank disks). This prevents you from accidentally copying a blank disk over an original disk and ruining it.

Copying Disks in Windows

You can copy disks using either My Computer or Windows Explorer. In My Computer, take the following steps:

1. Insert the original disk you want to copy into one of the floppy disk drives.

2. Double-click **My Computer**.

3. Right-click the icon for the floppy disk drive and choose **Copy Disk**. A dialog box appears, asking from and to which drives you want to copy.

4. Click the same drive letter in the **Copy from** and **Copy to** lists.

Windows asks which drives you want to use.

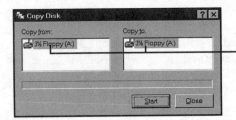

If you have only one floppy disk drive, you must use the same drive for the source and destination disks.

Dual Drive Copy If you have two floppy disk drives of the same size and capacity, insert the original disk in drive A and the blank disk in drive B. In the **Copy from** list, click drive A, and in the **Copy to** list, click drive B.

5. Click the **Start** button.

6. Wait until a message appears telling you to insert the destination disk.

7. Remove the original disk and insert the destination disk.

8. Click **OK**, and then wait until the copying is complete.

Copying Programs from Your Hard Drive

New computers always come with a bunch of software on the hard disk. The manufacturer may also include CDs or diskettes containing the same software, just in case anything happens to the programs on your hard disk.

Can you copy a program from the hard drive to a set of floppy disks? Usually not. When you install most Windows programs, the installation utility typically places files in the Windows folder, the Windows/System folder, and any other folders you'd never think of looking in. Unless you're a super sleuth, you never find all the files that make up a program. Another problem is that most programs can't fit on a single floppy disk.

If you want to lift a program off of your hard disk, the best option is to back up your entire system when you first get your computer. See Chapter 31, "Backing Up for the Inevitable Crash," for details.

Tech Check

Few people use floppy disks anymore. They buy everything on CD-ROM, store all their data on the hard disk, and exchange files via email. When you can't avoid working with a floppy disk, just make sure you can do the following:

➤ Format a floppy disk.

➤ Reuse a disk without reformatting it.

➤ Copy a disk.

Copying, Moving, and Nuking Folders and Files

In This Chapter

➤ List the similarities between a landfill and a hard disk

➤ Jump from folder to folder in Windows

➤ Move files into a different folder

➤ Wipe out selected folders and files with a single command

➤ Name a folder after your favorite actor

Right now, you might be thinking of your hard disk as an information age landfill. Each time you install a program, you can almost hear the dump truck beeping as it backs up to your disk, your hard disk groaning under the added burden. You start to wonder where future generations are going to dump their files.

Without folders (also called directories), this image might be accurate but folders help organize the files into logical groups, making them much easier to find and manage—assuming that you know what you're doing. In this chapter, you learn how to take control of the files and folders on your hard disk to clean them up and make them more organized.

Climbing the Directory Tree

Before you lay your fingers on any folders or files, you should understand the basic structure of a *directory tree*. Shake that landfill analogy out of your mind, and start thinking of your disk as a big, sterile filing cabinet, stuffed with manila folders. Each folder represents a directory that stores files and/or additional folders.

The structure of a typical hard disk is shown here. The monkey at the top of the tree, c:\, is the *root directory*; other directories branch off from the root. In the figure, the HOME folder branches off from the root directory (C:\) and includes four *subfolders*—MEGHAN, RYAN, MEDICAL, and TAXSTUFF. Each of these subfolders contains files. (Don't ask me why the root is at the *top* of the tree; that's just the way it is.)

A typical directory tree.

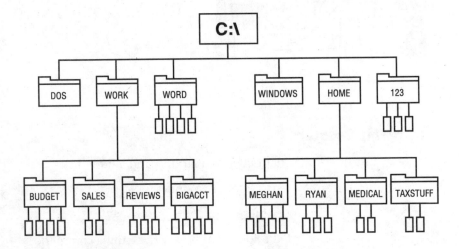

Selecting Folders and Files

What's a Path? A path is a map to the desired drive and folder. For example, in the figure, the path to the MEGHAN folder is C:\HOME\MEGHAN. Backslashes (\) are used to separate the folder names. When opening a file, you can type a path to its folder, rather than double-clicking a series of folders and subfolders.

If you're copying, deleting, or moving a single file or folder, selecting it is about as easy as picking a losing lottery number. You simply click the file or folder (in Windows Explorer, or My Computer). You would think that if you clicked on another file or folder, you'd select that one, too, but it doesn't work that way. Selecting another file deselects the first one. This can be maddening to anyone who doesn't know the tricks for selecting multiple files or folders:

➤ To select neighboring (contiguous) files and folders, click the first file or folder and then hold down the **Shift** key while clicking the last one in the group.

➤ To select nonneighboring (noncontiguous) items, hold down the **Ctrl** key while clicking the name of each item.

➤ To deselect an item, hold down the **Ctrl** key while clicking its name.

➤ You can also select a group of items by dragging a box around them. When you release the mouse button, all the items in the box are highlighted.

Now, if you have Web Style or View as Web Page turned on in My Computer, forget all this clicking nonsense. Clicking opens a file or folder. Simply point to (rest the mouse pointer on) a file or folder to select it. Ctrl+point to select additional items, and Shift+point to select a group of neighboring items.

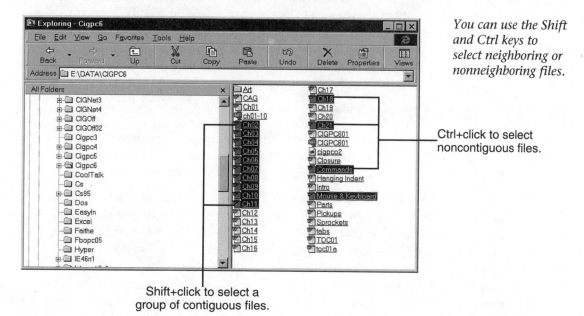

You can use the Shift and Ctrl keys to select neighboring or nonneighboring files.

Ctrl+click to select noncontiguous files.

Shift+click to select a group of contiguous files.

If you're selecting groups of files, it often helps to change the way the files are sorted or arranged. Open the **View** menu and choose to sort files by name, by type (using their file name extensions), by size, or by date. For example, you can sort files by type to list all the document files that end in .DOC. You can also arrange the icons by opening the **View** menu and selecting one of the following options:

➤ **Large Icons** Good if you want to select only a few files or folders.

➤ **Small Icons** Displays tiny icons. Folders appear at the top, and files at the bottom. In this display, you can drag a box around items down and to the right.

➤ **List**   Displays tiny icons (just like Small Icons view), but folders (directories) are listed on the left, and files are listed on the right.

➤ **Details**   Displays additional information such as the date and time at which files were created. (This view makes it tough to manage large numbers of files.)

Check This Out...

Small Icons Versus List

In Small Icons view, if you click an item in one column, and then **Shift+click** an item in another column, you select a rectangular block of items, just as if you had dragged a box around them. In List view, items snake up and down a page like newspaper columns. If you click an item in one column and then **Shift+click** an item in another column, you select all the items between the two items you selected.

Making Your Own Folders

You rarely have to create your own folders. When you install a program, it usually makes the folders it needs or uses existing folders. You need to make folders, however, for your own data files so that they don't get mixed up with all your program files.

When creating folders, try to follow one rule: *keep the folder structure shallow*. If you bury a file eight subfolders deep, you're going to have to do a lot of digging to get it out. On my drive, I have one folder for everything everyone in the family creates. It's called DATA. Under it, I have a subfolder for each book I write, a subfolder for my personal files, a subfolder for tax records, and a subfolder for the files that my kids and wife create. Most of the files are buried only two levels deep. This structure also makes it easy to back up only the data files we have created. I simply tell my backup program to back up the DATA folder and all its subfolders. In Windows, you can create folders all over the place: in My Computer, Windows Explorer, or even on the Windows desktop. Give it a shot; try creating a new folder on drive C. You can always delete the folder later if you don't need it. Take the following steps:

1. Double-click the **My Computer** icon.

2. Double-click the icon for drive C. A window opens showing all the folders currently on drive C.

3. Right-click a blank area inside the window to display a shortcut menu.

4. Rest the mouse pointer on **New**, and then click **Folder**. Windows creates a folder on drive C called **New Folder**.

5. Type a name for the folder (255 characters or fewer). As you start typing, the New Folder name is deleted and is replaced by what you type. You cannot use any of the following characters: \ / : * ? " < > |

6. Press **Enter**.

Right-click a blank area.

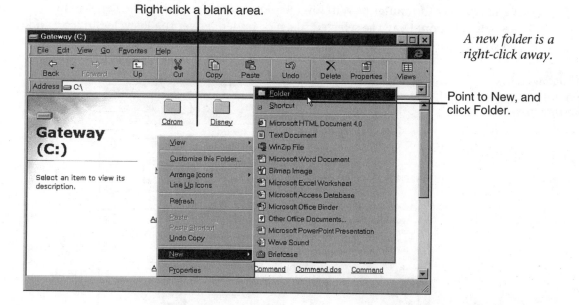

A new folder is a right-click away.

Point to New, and click Folder.

Long names (255 characters for folders and files) are great for programs that support them, but some older programs and DOS cannot display long names. In such cases, the program displays a portion of the name, such as letter~1.doc. This does not affect the contents of the file, and you can still open it.

You can also create folders inside folders (subfolders). To do that, first double-click the folder in which you want the new folder placed. This displays the contents of the folder. Then follow the same steps given above to create a new folder.

> **Desktop Folders** If the Windows desktop becomes too crowded with shortcuts and other icons, you can create folders to help organize the desktop. Right-click a blank area of the desktop, point to **New** and click **Folder**.

Nuking Folders and Files

With Windows 95, you have all sorts of ways to delete folders and files. Take any of the following steps:

➤ Select the file(s) or folder(s) you want to delete and click the **Delete** button (the button with the big X on it) on the toolbar.

➤ Select the file(s) or folder(s) you want to delete and press the Delete key.

➤ Right-click a selected file or folder and click **Delete**.

➤ Resize the My Computer or Windows Explorer window so that you can see the Recycle Bin icon. Drag the selected file(s) or folder(s) over the Recycle Bin icon and release the mouse button.

Windows offers several ways to destroy files.

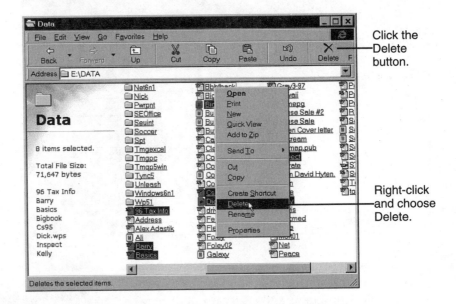

Click the Delete button.

Right-click and choose Delete.

Undo It! My Computer and Windows Explorer both sport a toolbar that contains an Undo button. If you delete a file or folder by mistake, you can quickly get it back by clicking the **Undo** button or pressing **Ctrl+Z**.

When you choose to delete one or more files or folders, Windows displays a dialog box or two asking you to confirm the deletion. Respond accordingly, and the selected items go away. If you accidentally delete a file or folder, you can drag it out of the Recycle Bin, as explained in Chapter 4, "Windows Survival Guide."

Renaming Folders and Files

Managing your folders and files is an exercise in on-the-job training. As you create and use folders, you find yourself slapping any old name on them. Later, you find that the name doesn't really indicate the folder's contents, the name is too long, or you are just plain sick of seeing it snake across your screen. Fortunately, renaming a folder or file is easy:

Chapter 16

➤ If you click files and folders to select them, click the icon for the file or folder you want to rename. Then, click the name of the file or folder and type the new name.

➤ If you point to files and folders to select them, right-click the file or folder you want to rename and choose **Rename**. Type the new name and press Enter or click a blank area in the window.

When you choose to rename a file or folder,
Windows highlights the current name.

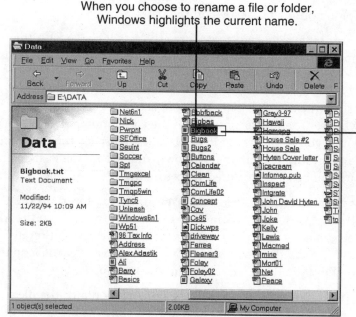

You can easily rename files and folders.

Type a new name
and press Enter.

Moving and Copying Folders and Files

You can quickly move files and folders to reorganize your hard disk. To move an item, simply drag it over the folder or disk icon to which you want to move it. When moving or copying files and folders, keep the following in mind:

➤ To copy or move multiple files or folders, first select the items, as explained earlier in this chapter. When you copy or move one of the selected items, all the other items follow it.

➤ If you drag a folder or file to a *different* disk (or a folder on a different disk), Windows

Don't Rename Program Folders or Files Windows uses the names of program folders to find the program files it needs to run the programs. If you rename a program folder or file, Windows usually throws a fit and won't run the program for you.

assumes that you want to *copy* the item to that disk. If you want to *move* the item, hold down the **Shift** key while dragging.

➤ If you drag a folder or file to a different folder on the *same* disk, Windows assumes that you want to *move* the item into the destination folder. If you want to *copy* the item, hold down the **Ctrl** key while dragging.

➤ To move a file or folder to the Windows desktop, drag it from My Computer or Windows Explorer onto a blank area on the desktop.

➤ If you're not sure what you want to do, drag the folder or file with the right mouse button. When you release the button, a context menu appears, presenting options for moving or copying the item.

Sometimes, the easiest way to move a file or folder is to cut and paste it. Right-click the icon for the item you want to move, and choose the **Cut** command. Now, change to the disk or folder in which you want the cut item placed. Right-click the disk or folder icon (or right-click a blank area in its contents window), and choose the **Paste** command. The following are a couple of other convoluted ways to move files and folders:

➤ Run Windows Explorer (**Start, Programs, Windows Explorer**). In the **Contents** list (on the right), display the file or folder that you want to move. In the **All Folders** list (on the left), make sure you can see the icon for the destination disk or folder, but don't select it. Drag the item that you want to move over the icon for the destination disk or folder and release the mouse button.

➤ Use My Computer to display two windows: one that contains the file or folder that you want to move, and another that displays the contents of the destination disk or folder. Drag the item that you want to move over a blank area inside the destination window and release the mouse button.

Tech Check

Consider this chapter basic training for Chapter 28, in which you use your folder and file management skills to optimize your hard disk. Until then, make sure you can do the following:

➤ Draw a rough sketch of a directory tree, starting at drive C.

➤ Select neighboring files or folders in a list.

➤ Select nonneighboring files or folders.

➤ Make your own folder.

➤ Delete selected files and folders and undelete them.

➤ Drag and drop a file or folder to another folder or disk.

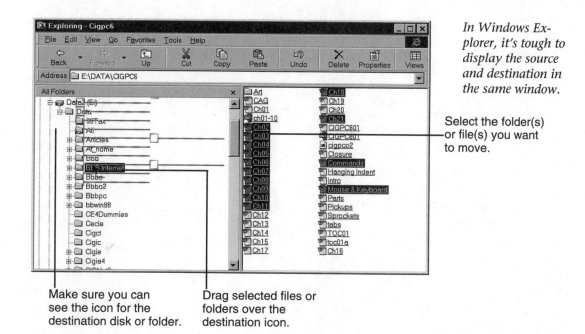

In Windows Explorer, it's tough to display the source and destination in the same window.

Select the folder(s) or file(s) you want to move.

Make sure you can see the icon for the destination disk or folder.

Drag selected files or folders over the destination icon.

Chapter 17

Networking (for Those Corporate Types)

In This Chapter

➤ Learn enough about networking to fake your way through your next job interview

➤ Log on to a network, so you can use stuff that's not on your computer

➤ Check out what's available on your network

➤ Make a folder on the network look like a folder on your computer

➤ Print a document from your computer to a printer that's not even connected to your computer

You have mastered the basics of using your computer. You can run programs; make documents; print, copy, and move files; and even dazzle colleagues with the Windows tricks you've learned. But now your boss has informed you that your company is going to install a network. Perhaps you've heard about networks, and maybe you even have a general understanding of the concept behind them, but you've never actually worked on a network, and you don't know what to expect. In this chapter, you learn how to use several Windows features designed especially for networks so that you can get up to speed in a hurry.

What Is a Network, Anyway?

Back in the old days when computers used to cost a lot of money, many companies used networks to save money. The company would install a big, powerful, expensive computer called a *server* as the central computer and then give each worker a *workstation*, consisting basically of a keyboard, monitor, and a cable connecting the workstation to the *server*.

When the cost of desktop computers started to drop, companies started to move away from networks, providing workers with their own powerful desktop computers. However, by doing this, companies lost a valuable aspect of the network: the fact that its workers could communicate and share files more easily on a network. As companies started realizing that they had lost something, software developers were coming up with new programs that took advantage of network computing, providing tools for sending and receiving email, collaboratively creating and editing documents, and sharing expensive hardware. As a result, networks have been growing in popularity.

The two basic types of networks are *client-server* and *peer-to-peer*. The following sections describe the two types of networks.

Client-Server Networks

On a client-server network, all computers (the clients) are wired to a central computer (the network server). Whenever you need to access a network resource, you connect to the server, which then processes your commands and requests, links you to the other computers, and provides access to shared equipment and other resources. Although somewhat expensive and difficult to set up, a client-server network offers two big advantages: it is easy to maintain through the network server, and it ensures reliable data transfers.

Network Administrators

Client-server networks typically have a *network administrator* who is in charge of assigning access privileges to each computer on the network. For example, some users may only be able to open data files on the server and may not be able to run certain programs. The administrator assigns each user a name and password. You must then log on to the network.

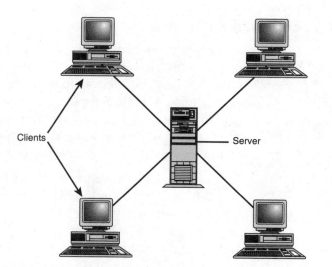

On a client-server network, clients are connected to a central server.

Clients

Server

Peer-to-Peer Networks

On a peer-to-peer network, computers are linked directly to each other, without the use of a central computer. Each computer has a network card that is connected via a network cable to another computer or to a central *hub* (a connection box). Many small businesses use this peer-to-peer configuration because it doesn't require an expensive network server and because it is relatively easy to set up. A peer-to-peer network does, however, have a few drawbacks: it is more difficult to manage, more susceptible to packet collisions (which occur when two computers request the same data at the same time), and is not very secure because no central computer is in charge of validating user identities.

On a peer-to-peer network, each computer acts both as a client and a server.

Do I Need a Network?

What About Intranets?
An intranet is simply a network that is set up to look and act like the Internet, which you learn more about in Part 4, "Going Global with Modems, Online Services, and the Internet."

When you think of networks, you usually think of large corporations. However, networks are starting to pop up in churches, small businesses, home offices, and anywhere else that two or more computers live. Why? Because people find that when they have two or more computers, they need an easy way to exchange data between those two computers and share expensive hardware.

For example, say you work out of your home and you have two kids, each of whom has his or her own computer. Without a network, you need three of everything: three modems, three color printers, and so on. With a network, you can buy a top of the line printer and the best modem on the market, connect the devices to any one of the computers on the network, and you can all share those devices. In addition, you can quickly send each other messages and use a central calendar to keep everyone up to date. Of course, you have to shell out some money for the network cards and cables to connect the computers, but you still save money in the long run.

The easiest way to install a simple peer-to-peer network is to purchase a networking kit from your local computer store. A typical kit includes two network cards, cables, and instructions. Windows includes the required network support, so you don't need special network server software required by a client-server configuration. The procedure for setting up a network, however, is beyond the scope of this book. The instructions accompanying your network kit should walk you through the procedure in detail.

Quickly Connect Two Computers

If you need to connect only two computers (say your desktop and laptop computers), don't waste your time and money installing network cards. You can connect the two computers with a parallel printer cable or a special serial cable. (See "Linking Your Notebook and Desktop Computers," in Chapter 29, for details. You can link two desktop computers using the same techniques described in that chapter.)

Logging On and Logging Off

To connect your computer to the network, you must log on with your username and password. This identifies you on the network, and Windows establishes the connection between your computer and the other computers on the network so that you can access shared files and resources. If the network has one, the administrator assigns the username and password. If you are on a small network, you and the other people on the network can discuss the usernames and passwords you want to use. The procedure for logging on is easy:

1. When you start your computer, Windows displays the Enter Network Password dialog box with your name in the **User Name** text box.

2. Type your password and click **OK**.

If you are working on a client-server network, you should be aware that when you are using a program or file on the server, you can lose your work if the server is shut down for any reason. Often, the network administrator shuts down the server for maintenance. The administrator should notify all users in advance so that they can save their work and exit any programs before the shutdown. If the server crashes, however, you are automatically disconnected from the network and any changes you have made to a network file are lost.

On a peer-to-peer network, you can also lose your connection with another computer on the network if that computer happens to lock up or its user decides to shut it down without asking for your okay.

Checking Out the Network Neighborhood

When you connect to the network, you can access any shared disks, folders, and printers on other computers that are connected to the network, assuming you have the right password (if a password is required). Locating shared resources, however, can be difficult, especially on a large network. Fortunately, Windows has tools to help you track down network resources and manage them. The most basic tool is the Network Neighborhood. When you click the Network Neighborhood icon on the Windows desktop, a window displays icons for all the computers that are on the network. You can then browse the shared resources on that computer, just as if they were on your computer. The following figure shows drive C on a network computer, not on your computer.

> **Find a Computer on the Network** If your network is large, you can use the **Start**, **Find**, **Computer** command to search for a specific computer on the network, assuming that you know its name.

A disk on the network computer appears as
a folder on your computer.

*The Network
Neighborhood
displays icons for
network resources.*

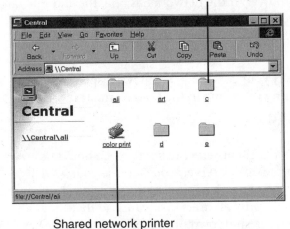

Shared network printer

Mapping a Network Drive to Your Computer

If you frequently access a particular disk or folder on the network, you can *map* the disk
or folder to a drive on your computer. Your computer then displays the disk or folder as a
folder in My Computer and in the Save As or Open dialog box in any Windows program
you use. This enables you to access the disk or folder just as easily as if it were on your
computer. To map a disk or folder to your computer, take the following steps:

1. In the Network Neighborhood, right-click the network disk or folder that you want
   to map to your computer and choose **Map Network Drive**. The Map Network Drive
   dialog box appears.

2. Open the **Drive** drop-down list and choose a drive letter to assign to the network
   disk or folder.

*You can map a
network disk or folder
to your computer.*

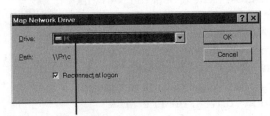

Choose the desired drive letter.

3. To have Windows automatically log on to this disk or folder on startup, click
   Reconnect at Logon and then click **OK**.

4. Switch back to the opening My Computer window. A new icon appears for the mapped disk or folder.

Using a Network Printer

To use a network printer, you must add the printer to your Printers folder. Before you can add a network printer, however, you must set printer sharing options on the computer that is connected to the printer (as explained in the next section, "Sharing Resources on Your Computer"). You can then run the Add Printer Wizard and select the network printer from a list of available printers. Take the following steps:

1. Click the **Start** button, point to **Settings**, and click **Printers**. The contents of the Printers folder appears.

2. Click **Add Printer**. The Add Printer Wizard appears.

3. Click **Next**. The wizard asks if you want to install a local or network printer.

4. Click **Network Printer** and click **Next**. The wizard prompts you to specify the path to the printer.

5. Click the **Browse** button. The Browse for Printer dialog box displays a list of all computers on the network.

6. Click the plus sign next to the computer that is connected to the printer. The printer's icon appears.

7. Click the printer's icon and click **OK**. You are returned to the wizard where the path to the network printer is displayed.

8. Click **Next**. The wizard displays the name of the printer as it appears on the network computer. You can change the name, if desired.

9. To use this printer as the default printer for all your Windows applications, click **Yes** and then click **Next**. The wizard now asks if you want to print a test page.

10. Click **Yes** or **No** and click **Finish**. If you choose to print a test page, the wizard sends the page to the network printer. Windows copies the necessary printer files from the network computer to your computer and returns you to the Printers folder. An icon for the network printer appears.

After the network printer is set up, you can use it to print documents just as if the printer were connected to your computer. If you did not set up the network printer as your default printer, however, you must select the printer when you choose to print your document.

Sharing Resources on Your Computer

Before you can access disks, folders, files, and printers on your network, the person whose resources you want to use must give you access to his or her computer. For example, a person may want everyone on the network to have access to a customer database but probably would not want to allow everyone on the network to modify that database.

The user or network administrator can assign various levels of access to specific users or resources to prevent unauthorized use of a particular resource on the server. In addition, before anyone else can access files or folders on your computer, you must enter settings that give that person access to your computer. To enable other users to access folders or files on your computer in Windows 95 or later versions, take the following steps:

1. Run My Computer or Windows Explorer.

2. Right-click the icon for the disk or folder that you want to share and choose **Sharing**. The Properties dialog box for the selected disk or folder appears with the Sharing tab in front.

3. Click **Shared As**.

You can mark disks or folders as shared.

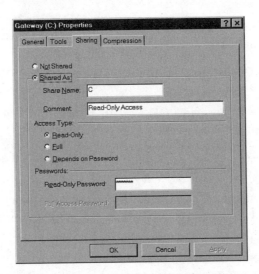

4. The **Share Name** text box automatically displays the drive's letter or the folder's name as it will appear to users who access your computer. You can type a different entry in this text box, if desired.

5. (Optional) Type any additional information in the **Comment** text box.

6. Under **Access Type**, choose the desired share option: **Read-Only** (to enable people to look at files on the disk or folder but not change them), **Full** (to authorize people to open and save files to the disk or folder), or **Depends on Password** (to use a different password for read-only or full access).

7. Under **Passwords**, type the password that people must enter in order to access the drive or folder. (If you chose Depends on Password in the previous step, enter a different password for read-only and full access.) Click **OK**.

8. If you entered a password, Windows prompts you to confirm it. Type the password again and click **OK**.

9. You are returned to My Computer or Windows Explorer, and a hand appears below the icon for the shared disk or folder.

No Password Required To provide access to a disk or folder without prompting the person for a password, leave the Password text boxes blank. This saves time on a small network on which you fully trust the other users.

Share No More To terminate sharing, right-click the icon for the disk, folder, or printer and choose **Sharing**. Select **Not Shared** and click **OK**.

You can also enable other users to share your printer. Open the **Start** menu, point to **Settings**, and click **Printers**. Right-click your printer icon and choose **Sharing**. Enter the requested information and click **OK**.

Tech Check

Although you may not feel confident enough to set up your own network, you should now feel competent enough to navigate a network. Before you boast about your network mastery, make sure you can do the following:

➤ Tell the difference between a client-server and peer-to-peer network.

➤ Figure out whether you need to network your computers.

➤ Log on to a network.

➤ Check out what's available on your network using the Network Neighborhood.

➤ Map a network disk to your computer.

➤ Use a network printer.

Part 4
Going Global with Modems, Online Services, and the Internet

How would you like to play a computer game against a friend in another town? Get the latest news, weather, and sports without taking your fingers off the keyboard? Connect to an online encyclopedia, complete with sounds and pictures? Order items from a computerized catalog? Send a postage-free letter and have it arrive at its destination in a matter of seconds? Mingle with others in online chat rooms? Or even transfer files from your computer to a colleague's computer anywhere in the world?

In this part, you'll learn how to do all this and more. You'll learn how to buy and install a modem that can keep up with traffic on the Internet, connect to America Online (the most popular online service in the world), and tour the Internet. With this section, a modem, and the right software, you'll be primed to master the information age.

Chapter 18

First You Need a Modem

In This Chapter

➤ Name the three things your computer needs in order to communicate with another computer over the phone lines

➤ Read a modem ad and understand what it says

➤ Figure out which type of software you need to do what you want to do

➤ Hook up an internal or external modem and get it to work

Okay, I admit it; the part opener was a tease. I wanted to tell you all the neat things you could do with a modem, so you would start thinking that you simply can't live without one. I conveniently left out all the complicated information about shopping for a modem, hooking it up, and figuring out what software you need. Now that I've sucked you in, I'll hit you with the hard stuff.

Shopping for a Modem

Before you start shopping for a modem, you need a brief lesson in "modemese," the language of modem ads. Do you think I'm exaggerating? Then read the following ad I lifted from my favorite computer catalogue:

Internal Connecta 33.6 Modem

This internal modem is fast, providing up to 33.6Kbps V.34 industry standard speeds. What's more, it's fully upgradable to x2 technology to deliver the Internet to you at speeds up to 56Kbps! Your ticket to the fast lane is a simple software upgrade away. The firmware for this Cardinal Connecta Fax Modem is in FlashROM. When you're ready to move up to x2 speeds, simply access the upgrade from the Cardinal Web site.

If you're in shock, try to calm down. You'll be able to translate this gobbledygook by the time you finish this section. Take it slow, and read on.

Inside or Out? Internal and External Modems

Modems come in two types—*internal* and *external*. An internal modem is a board that plugs into an expansion slot inside your computer. Yeah, you have to flip the hood on your system unit, and plug the thing in. It's not all that difficult to do, but if you've never done it, skip to Chapter 27, "Upgrading Your Computer to Make It the Best It Can Be," to learn how to install an expansion board.

An external modem plugs into a serial port (a receptacle) on the back of your computer. (Most modems do not come with the required serial cable; you must purchase it separately.) To use an external modem, you must have an extra serial port. Look at the back of your system unit to see whether it has an extra outlet called COM.

PCMCIA A PCMCIA (also known as *PC card*) modem is the size of a credit card, and it slides into a PCMCIA slot on a portable computer. If you have a laptop or notebook computer, get a PCMCIA modem. (See "Adding and Removing PCMCIA Cards," in Chapter 29, for details on installing PCMCIA cards.)

Which is better? Internal modems are less expensive (they have no case or indicator lights), take up less desk space, and require only one connection (the phone line). If you have an open expansion slot inside your computer (or a slot that's occupied by a modem from the Stone Age), get an internal modem. External modems have a couple of advantages—they are easy to install, and most come with indicator lights that show you what the modem is doing. (The lights can help you troubleshoot common problems, if you know what to look for. Your modem's documentation identifies each light and its purpose.)

Go Hayes-Compatible

The Hayes modem, made by a company called Hayes Technologies, has set the standard in the modem market. Hayes modems use a set of commands that enable you to tell the modem what you want it to do and how you want it to operate. (For example, to dial the phone number 555-1234, you would enter the Hayes command ATDT followed by the phone number.) This set of commands is called the *Hayes command set*. When a modem is advertised as being Hayes-compatible, it means that it understands Hayes commands. Fortunately, most communications programs enter the required Hayes commands behind the scenes, so you don't have to mess with them. You just type the phone number, and the program takes care of the rest.

Get a Speedy Modem

Modems transfer data at different speeds, commonly measured in *bits per second (bps)*. The higher the number, the faster the modem can transfer data. Common rates include 28,800bps, 33,600bps, and 56,800bps. Because these modem speed numbers are becoming so long, manufacturers have started to abbreviate them. You commonly see speeds listed as 33.6Kbps (for 33,600bps). When they start dropping the bps, and list something like 56K, you know it's really fast. Also look for fast words, such as "blistering" and "searing." Although you pay more for a higher transfer rate, you save time and decrease your phone bill by purchasing a faster modem.

Some ads claim that the modem is *downward-compatible* (or *backward-compatible*). This means that if you connect the 56Kbps modem with a slower modem (say 28.8Kbps), the two modems can still communicate. Most modems are downward-compatible even if the ad doesn't say so.

The bottom line is that if you're buying a new modem, you should look for a 56Kbps modem. But before you run out and buy one, you should know a few things:

➤ **56K Limits**   56K pushes the limits of phone line communications. The phone company limits connection speeds to 53K, although there is some talk of raising the speed limit. You rarely see data transfers at 56Kps. Expect a maximum speed of about 40-45Kbps, and that's only when your modem is receiving data. A 56K modem still sends data at 28.8-33.6Kbps due to limitations on the phone lines in your house. Also, make sure your online service supports 56K modem connections.

➤ **x2 and 56KFlex**   These are competing 56K standards. x2 was developed by U.S. Robotics, and 56KFlex was developed by Rockwell. Before buying a 56K modem, find out which standard your online service supports.

➤ **ITU**   Short for International Telecommunication Union, ITU is the international standard for 56K modems. If given the option of buying an x2, 56KFlex, or ITU, get the ITU. Because many modem manufacturers were making 56K modems following either the x2 or Flex standard before the ITU standard was finalized, you can upgrade most x2 and 56KFlex modems to the ITU standard by running special software. Just make sure the modem is software upgradable.

56K Modem Magic

The upper speed limit of modem communications stands at about 33.6Kbps, due to the nature of phone lines, which are designed to carry voice communications via *analog* signals. The new 56K modems speed up modem communications by using an encoding technology that enables data to be transmitted via *digital* signals. Although the encoding technology works over digital lines (typically connecting your online service provider to the phone system), these signals hit a bottleneck at the line that comes into your home (a copper cable designed to carry analog signals). A 56K modem may slightly increase the speed at which you receive signals (assuming your online service supports the encoding technology), but outgoing communications still crawl through the lines at 33.6Kbps or slower.

V.34bis, V.42bis, and Throughput

Nothing perks up a modem ad like a list of standards—V.34bis, V.42bis, MNP 2–4. You don't know what these standards represent, but you just have to have them. To understand the standards, keep in mind that they fall in three categories:

➤ **Modulation**   A way of sending signals, a little like AM and FM. You commonly see standards, such as V.32 in modem ads. V.32 is the modulation standard used for most 33.6Kbps modems.

➤ **Error correction**   A feature that automatically checks data to ensure that it has been sent and received properly. Error correction standards include MNP 1, 2, 3, and 4; LAPM; and V.42.

➤ **Data compression**   Enables modems to decompress data. The only trick is that the sending and receiving modems must be using the same data compression standard. Common data compression standards include MNP 5, MNP7, and V.42bis.

Don't worry too much about these standards. Speed is what is most important, and conforming to these standards (especially the modulation and data compression standards) is what gives the modem its speed.

What About the New ISDN and Cable Modems?

The trouble with most modems is that they have to use phone lines, which were designed for voice communications, not data communications. (You know how little useful data is transferred during a typical voice conversation.) Voice is carried over the phone lines by analog (wave) signals, which aren't the most efficient carriers of digital information.

33.6Kbps modems push the limits of standard phone lines. Even if you have a 33.6Kbps modem, you usually find that your connection is slightly slower because of line noise or because your online service's modems do not support higher speeds. If you want to go beyond this speed, you need an ISDN (Integrated Services Digital Network) modem, a cable modem, or a PC satellite dish.

ISDN modems use special phone lines to transfer data at up to 128Kbps (128,000bps). That's over four times faster than a 28,800bps modem. In addition, an ISDN phone line is like having two phone lines. You can carry on a voice conversation on one line and connect to the Internet on the other line (although the connection is half the speed— 64Kbps). If you're considering an ISDN modem, check out the following:

➤ Call your phone company first. Ask if they offer ISDN service and find out how much it costs for connecting and monthly fees. This information alone is usually enough to convince you that you don't need ISDN service.

➤ Before you buy an external ISDN modem, make sure that you have a super-fast serial port connection or that the modem connects to a parallel port (and that you have an open parallel port). Otherwise, the modem transfers data over the phone lines faster than it can transfer data to and from your computer.

➤ Make sure the modem can handle analog data transfers at 28,800bps. You may still have to establish analog connections with some services.

The newest modems on the market are cable modems, which make a computer cable-ready. They act like the cable connection on your TV set, and like the cable connection on your TV set, they require you to call the cable company and have a person come out to install the cable service. Because these coaxial cables can carry so much information (30MB per second!), they are ideal for video connections, the Internet, and *WebTV*. (WebTV typically consists of a control box that connects your TV to an Internet cable and your phone line. You use a remote control to navigate the Web and watch it all happen on your television screen.) The trouble is that TV cables are made to bring information into your house, not out of it (you still need a phone line to carry your outgoing signals). Cable companies, however, are working hard to update their lines for two-way communications.

Breaking the Speed Barrier with a PC Satellite Dish

Should I Worry About Sending Speed? When you're cruising the Internet or an online service, the speed at which your modem sends information is not very important. Typically, your modem sends small packets of data to request something. It's the speed at which your modem receives data that is most important. If, however, you plan on doing video-conferencing over a modem, your modem is required to send huge chunks of data, and you should consider going with an ISDN modem.

Before cable TV, television signals were transmitted through the airwaves. What a crazy idea! Well, we're back to transmitting television signals through the airwaves via satellite, and it has revolutionized television. The same revolution is currently under way on the Internet via satellite PC. Promising 400Kbps data transfers, satellite PC triples the speed at which an ISDN modem can yank data into your computer. So, what are the drawbacks? The following is a list of them.

➤ **It's expensive** $300 for the dish, plus installation ($100 or more), plus a one-time activation fee ($50 or more), plus a monthly service charge (about $40). Some services charge per kilobyte you download, so it can get even more expensive. Read the subscription plans thoroughly before you sign on the dotted line.

➤ **It's tough to install**   Get a techie friend who's not afraid of heights to do it for you.

➤ **You need to install another expansion board in your system unit**   Assuming you have any expansion slots left, this isn't too hard. (See Chapter 27, "Upgrading Your Computer to Make It the Best It Can Be.")

➤ **You still need a modem**   The satellite dish can shovel data into your computer, but it can't carry signals out. For outgoing signals, you still need a modem connected to your phone line.

If you have the money and you spend a lot of time on the Web, you love the noticeable increase in speed and never want to go back to a slow modem connection again.

Flash ROM Is Good

Modem manufacturers are constantly developing new technology to increase data transfer rates, and many of these technologies are available before anyone thinks about creating a standard. For example, 56K x2 and Flex modems hit the market long before the 56K ITU standard was finalized. The instructions that tell the modem how to transfer data are stored in the modem's ROM (read-only memory). A flash ROM enables you to update the instructions to take advantage of the new technology. You obtain the ROM update from the modem manufacturer (either on disk or over the phone lines) and install it in your modem. Without flash ROM, you would have to buy a whole new modem or replace the ROM chip.

To Fax or Not To Fax?

Some modems, called *fax modems*, come equipped with the added capability to send faxes or send and receive faxes. Like fully equipped fax machines, a fax/modem enables you to dial a number and transmit pages of text, graphics, and charts to a conventional fax machine or to another computer that has a fax/modem. You can also use the fax modem to receive incoming calls.

Shop carefully. Some fax/modems are capable only of sending faxes, not receiving them. If you want to receive faxes, make sure the fax/modem can handle incoming faxes. Also, make sure your modem supports Class 1 and 2, Group III fax machines. Nearly 90 percent of faxes in use today are of the Group III variety.

> **Fax, Copy, Scan, and Print** A fax modem enables you to send faxes only from your computer. If you need to fax printed or signed documents, the fax modem won't do you much good. You can, however, purchase printers that act as standard fax machines. They may also copy paper documents and scan text and graphics.

Voice and Video Support

If you plan to have your computer answer the phone and take messages, make sure the modem offers voice support. Without voice support, your modem can answer the phone, but it can only emit annoying screeching noises (which, on the other hand, is useful for making telemarketers back off).

Some modems are also designed to handle video calls, something like on *The Jetsons*. If, however, modems are too slow to handle simple file transfers, you can imagine how slow they are to transfer live video images. Also, you and your friend would each need a camera connected to your computer while you're talking.

Avoiding Headaches with Plug-and-Play

Windows supports plug-and-play technology, which enables you to plug a device into your computer without having to worry about the device conflicting with other devices on your computer. You just connect the device. When you turn on your computer, and Windows starts, Windows detects the device and installs the necessary driver for the device or prompts you to install the driver from the disk that came with the device. If you get a modem that does not support plug-and-play and if it conflicts with another device, such as your mouse, you're going to face some complex troubleshooting steps to remedy the situation.

Do You Need Another Phone Jack for the Modem?

If you already have a phone jack near the computer, but your phone is plugged into it, you don't need to install an additional jack. Most modems come with two phone jacks—one that connects the modem to the incoming phone line and another one into which you can plug your phone. When you are not using the modem, you use the phone as you normally would. If your modem doesn't have two phone jacks, you can purchase a split phone connector from an electronics store. The split phone connector enables you to plug both your phone and your modem into the same jack.

If your computer is far from an existing phone jack, get a long phone cable or have an additional phone jack installed. If you're good with a screwdriver and pliers (and maybe a drill, hammer, or other instrument of destruction), you can probably do it yourself in less than an hour. It took me four hours, but I had to remove a few ceiling tiles in the basement.

Installing Your Modem

Modem installation varies depending on whether you are installing an internal or external modem. With an internal modem, you must get under the hood of your PC, plug the modem into an open expansion slot, and plug the modem into the phone jack. (If you're a rank beginner, see Chapter 27 for a few pointers on installing expansion cards.)

Just about anyone can install an external modem. All you have to do is turn off the computer and make three connections:

➤ **Modem to serial port** Connect the modem to the serial port (usually marked COM) on your computer using a serial cable.

➤ **Modem to power source** Plug the modem's power cord into a receptacle on your wall or into your power strip or surge protector.

➤ **Modem to phone line** Connect the modem to the phone jack. This is just like plugging a phone into a phone jack. (You might also want to connect your phone to the modem, as shown here.)

Whenever you install a new device, you must also install a driver that tells Windows how to use the device. If your modem is plug-and-play compatible, the Windows Add New Hardware Wizard runs when you start your computer and leads you through the necessary steps. If your modem is not plug-and-play compatible and the Add New Hardware Wizard does not start, open the Windows Control Panel (click **Start**, point to **Settings**, and click **Control Panel**) and double-click the Add New Hardware icon.

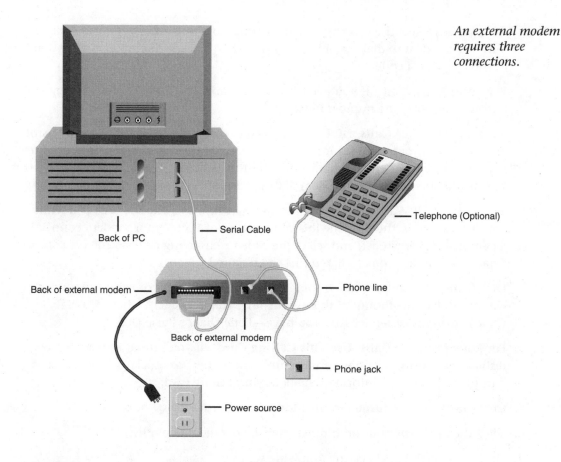

An external modem requires three connections.

Back of PC

Serial Cable

Telephone (Optional)

Back of external modem

Phone line

Back of external modem

Phone jack

Power source

Checking Your Modem Settings

After installing your modem, you should check your modem settings in Windows to make sure your modem is ready to dial. Take the following steps:

1. Click the **Start** button, point to **Settings**, and click **Control Panel**.

2. Double-click the **Modems** icon.

3. In the Modems Properties dialog box, click the **Dialing Properties** button.

4. Enter the following information:

   I Am Dialing From This is initially set at Default Location. If you take your computer on the road, you can click the **New** button and create a new dialing from location so that you can enter different dialing properties for dialing from other places.

205

Area Code   Select the country you are dialing from and enter your area code. This tells your modem to dial the area code only when you are dialing a number that is outside your area code.

For Local Calls, Dial   If you need to dial a number (such as 9) before dialing an outside line, enter the number here.

For Long Distance Calls, Dial   If you need to dial a special number for accessing an outside line for long distance calls, enter the number here. If you only need to dial the standard 1 before dialing a number that is outside your area code, leave this box blank; otherwise, your modem dials 1 twice.

To Disable Call Waiting   If you have call waiting and someone calls you while your modem is on the line, the incoming call disconnects your modem connection. Open the drop-down list, and select the code for disabling call waiting (usually *70). Check your phone book to determine the required code.

Dial Using   If you have touch-tone service, you hear tones of various frequencies when you dial the phone. With pulse-dialing, you hear clicks when you dial. Choose the type of service that you have—Tone Dial or Pulse Dial.

For Long Distance Calls, Use This Calling Card   If you intend to place long-distance calls using a calling card number, check this box, click the Calling Card button, and enter the information about your calling card.

5. Click **OK**. You are returned to the Modems Properties dialog box.

6. Click the **Properties** button (immediately below the modem list).

7. On the General tab, check the following settings:

Port   This setting tells Windows where to look for your modem. Leave this setting alone for now. If you get a message saying that Windows cannot find your modem or if your modem fails to dial, try changing the port setting.

Speaker Volume   If this option is available for your modem, you can drag the slider to increase or decrease your modem's speaker volume. (Modems make a lot of noise when they dial.) If this option is unavailable (grayed), proceed to steps 8 and 9.

Maximum Speed   Choose the highest speed on the list. In some cases, this can actually increase the speed at which your modem connects. If you have trouble connecting later, try choosing a lower setting.

8. Click the **Connection** tab and check the following settings:

   Data bits   Indicates the number of bits in each transmitted character. The common setting is Eight.

   Parity   Tests the integrity of the data sent and received. The common setting is None or No Parity.

   Stop bits   Indicates the number of bits used to signal the end of a character. The common setting is One bit.

9. Click the **Advanced** button.

10. If you could not set the speaker volume in step 7, type one of the following codes in the Extra Settings text box to set the volume (these codes work for most Hayes compatible modems):

    ATM0 to turn the speaker off

    ATM1 to turn the speaker down

    ATM2 to set the speaker volume at medium

    ATM3 to turn the speaker up

    Click **OK**, click **OK**, and click **Close** to save your settings and close all the modem dialog boxes.

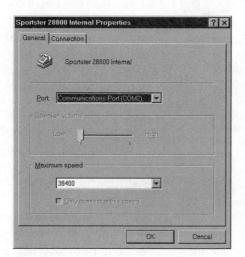

Check your communications settings.

Now, What Do You Want to Do with Your Modem?

Before you begin using your modem, you might need some additional software. To determine what software you need, ask yourself what you want to do with the modem. The following list describes some of the common uses for a modem and the type of program required for each use.

Online information services   If you want to connect to an online service (such as Prodigy or America Online), you have to start an account and obtain a special program from the service. (Skip to the next chapter for details.)

Surf the Internet   This is sort of like connecting to an online service (in fact, you can connect to the Internet through an online service). You can also connect by using a local *Internet service provider*. The service provider usually equips you with the software that you need and any other instructions that you need to get started. (See Chapter 20, "Doing the Internet Shuffle.")

Games in two-player mode   If you have a game that enables you to play games in two-player mode by using a modem, the program probably contains all the tools you need to play the game over the phone lines. Refer to the user manual that came with the game.

Place a Phone Call   To make sure that your computer acknowledges having a modem, use your modem to make your next phone call (assuming you have a phone connected to your modem). Click **Start, Programs, Accessories, Phone Dialer**. Type the phone number you want to dial, and click **Dial**. When someone answers, pick up the receiver on your phone and start talking.

Remote computing   Say you have a computer at work and one at home. You can call your computer at work to get any files you may have forgotten to bring home, or you can dial into your company's network. (See "Calling Your Desktop Computer or Network Via Modem" in Chapter 29 for details.) You can also obtain a special program, such as *PC Anywhere*, that enables you to use a remote computer just as if you were sitting at its keyboard.

"Free" long-distance calls   You can't avoid long-distance charges to your pal across the country simply by placing the call with your modem. You and your pal both need an Internet connection and special software. (See Chapter 24, "Reaching Out with Chat and Internet Phone," for details.)

All these tasks require different steps for dialing out and establishing a connection. Check the documentation that came with the telecommunications program or skip to the chapter referenced in the previous list to determine the steps that you need to take.

What Went Wrong?

Rarely do modem communications proceed error free the first time. Any minor problem or wrong setting can cause a major disruption in the communications between your computer and the remote computer. If you run into a glitch that prevents your modem from dialing, connecting, or communicating with a remote system, see "My Modem Doesn't Work," in Chapter 31 for possible fixes.

Tech Check

The most difficult aspects of telecommunications are in picking out a good modem and setting it up. Before you move on to the next chapter, where you actually use your computer to connect to an online service, make sure you can do the following:

➤ Decipher a modem ad.

➤ Tell the difference between a 56K x2, 56KFlex, and 56K ITU modem.

➤ Decide whether you need an ISDN modem or PC Satellite dish.

➤ Make a checklist of everything you want in a modem.

➤ Install a modem.

➤ Check your modem settings in Windows.

➤ Figure out what you want to do with your modem.

Chapter 19

"You've got mail!"

Going Online with America Online (and Other Online Services)

In This Chapter

➤ Connect to one of the big four online services

➤ Pick a local access number (to avoid long-distance charges)

➤ Send and receive mail electronically

➤ Chat live with friends and strangers

➤ Access the Internet

One of the first things most people do with a modem is to connect to one of the big four online services—America Online, Microsoft Network, Prodigy, or CompuServe. When you subscribe to the service (usually for about 10 to 20 bucks a month), you get a program that enables you to connect locally to the service (assuming you live near a major town), and you get access to what the service offers. This includes electronic mail, chat rooms (where you can hang out with other members), news, research tools, magazines, university courses, the Internet, and much, much more.

How Much Does This Cost?

What's the price you pay for all this? When you're shopping for an online service, compare subscription rates and consider the focus of each service. The following is a rundown of the four biggies (keep in mind, the prices quoted here are current as of this writing but are subject to change; check with the service for price specifics):

America Online   Charges a flat rate ($19.95) for unlimited use, or $4.95 for three hours per month (plus $2.50 for each additional hour). America Online is the most popular online service on the planet. It offers simple navigational tools, great services, and a friendly, hip social scene. Call 1-800-827-6364 for a startup kit (complete with a free trial offer).

CompuServe   Charges $9.95 for five hours per month, plus $2.95 for each additional hour, or $24.95 for unlimited use. Special services cost extra. CompuServe has traditionally been more technical and business oriented. Call 1-800-524-3388, extension 664 for a startup kit (complete with a free trial offer).

Microsoft Network   Has two main plans (and several special plans). The Standard plan charges $6.95, which includes five hours of usage per month. Each additional hour is $2.50. The Unlimited plan charges $19.95 per month. If you have Windows 95, you can double-click the **Microsoft Network** icon on the Windows desktop and sign up right now (you get one month free to try it out).

Check This Out...

Canceling Your Membership
Online services typically waive the first month's usage fee. If you choose to no longer use the service, be sure you cancel your membership before the next month's billing period begins. Check out the service's online help system.

Prodigy Internet   Gives you unlimited access for $19.95 per month. Prodigy is a family-oriented online service. Call 1-800-PRODIGY for a startup kit. Prodigy Internet provides a connection to the Internet and enables you to navigate the Internet with Internet Explorer (see Chapter 21, "Whipping Around the World Wide Web," for details.) Prodigy seems to be phasing out Prodigy Classic, its old online service.

Although all these online companies offer different services and sport their own unique look, they are all becoming more like online service providers for the Internet. Every online service listed here can connect you to the Internet, and all of them offer the programs you need to surf the Web, exchange email messages, and perform other Internet-related tasks, as explained in later chapters.

This chapter focuses on America Online, because it is such a popular online service, and because it serves as a good representation of what's available on a commercial online service. I'm not promoting one service over another, and, no, I'm not an employee (or relative of an employee) of America Online.

When you first connect to any of the online services, keep tabs on your phone bill. If you use a modem to call long distance, your friendly neighborhood phone company charges you long-distance rates, so keep this in mind when you chat on the modem. Most online services, however, provide you with a local number for connecting to the service. You can then communicate with other people in different states by way of the local connection, thus avoiding long-distance charges.

No Local Number?

If you live in a small town or in an area code that the online service doesn't serve, you could be in for a larger bill than expected. You either have to pay long-distance charges to connect to the nearest town or fork over additional money to get a special 800 number to dial. So much for the joys of living in the country!

Starting Your Online Account

Before you run to the phone and dial those numbers I listed in the previous section, check your Windows desktop for an icon named MSN or Online Services. The MSN icon is for The Microsoft Network. The Online Services icon contains additional icons for America Online, CompuServe, Prodigy, and AT&T WorldNet. Click one of these icons and follow the onscreen instructions to install the online service's program from the Windows CD, connect to the service, and sign up.

The installation program uses the modem to dial a toll-free number that lists local numbers. By selecting a local number, you avoid long-distance charges. After you select a local number (and usually an alternate number, in case the first number is busy), the installation program disconnects from the toll-free connection and then reconnects you locally. Most services then ask you to supply the following information:

➤ Your modem's COM port. To determine the COM port, double-click the Modems icon in the Control Panel, click your modem's name, and click Properties.

➤ Your modem's maximum speed. (Most services support up to 56K connections.)

➤ Any special dialing instructions, such as a number you must dial to connect to an outside line.

➤ Your name, address, and telephone number.

➤ A credit card number and expiration date. (Even if the service offers a free trial membership, you have to enter a credit card number.)

➤ The name (screen name) and password you want to use to log on to the service. (Write down the name and password that you use, in case you forget it. Without this information, you are not able to connect.)

Screen Name/Email Address

Your screen name acts as your email address, which people using the same service can use to send you messages. People using other online services can send you messages by tacking on the service's *domain name* to the email address. (A domain name is the address of the service, sort of like your city, state, and ZIP code.) For example, if your screen name is blondiex123 and you use America Online, the sender enters blondiex123@aol.com as your email address.

➤ An acceptance of the terms of service (TOS) or rules you must follow to continue to use the service. If you break the rules, the service may terminate your account. Read this so that you know what you're getting into.

Enter the requested information.

Before you can use an online service, you must register.

Connecting to an Online Service

After you have a local number to dial, you can log on to the service at any time and start using it. Select the online service from the Start, Programs menu or double-click its icon on the Windows desktop. Enter your screen name (user name) and password, and then click the **Dial** or **Connect** button.

The service dials the local access number, connects you, and displays an opening screen that enables you to start using the service. With CompuServe, you may need to select a feature (for example, News or Mail) before you sign on. CompuServe then dials the local access number, connects to the service, and takes you immediately to that feature.

To log on to America Online, select your username, type your password, and click Sign On.

America Online Nickel Tour

Although each online service offers different tools for moving around in the service, the tools are very similar. Most services display buttons and menus that enable you to use popular features, such as mail, news, and games. In addition, you can use *keywords* to quickly access a feature. To orient you to the world of online services, let's take a tour of America Online.

When you first connect to America Online, the service typically throws a bunch of ads at you. Just keep clicking **No Thanks**, **Cancel**, or whatever other buttons are displayed to make the messages go away. You finally come to a Welcome window (shown in the following figure), that contains buttons or icons for the Mail Center (where you can check your email), the Internet, the People Connection (for chatting online), Channels (for popular content categories), What's New (new features of the service), and additional buttons for news headlines.

Click the **Channels** button. The Channels window appears. It acts like a kiosk, displaying buttons for various content categories, including News, Sports, Entertainment, and Games. You simply click a button for the area that you want to explore. As you click buttons and other text and graphics, you may notice that whenever you position the mouse pointer over an object that can take you somewhere else, the mouse pointer appears as a hand. This indicates that the object under your mouse pointer is a *hyperlink* (an object that points to another resource). Keep clicking to follow the trail of links to the desired destination.

News headlines and other stuff

The Welcome Screen enables you to jump quickly to various features of the service.

Check out popular content categories.

Check and send email.

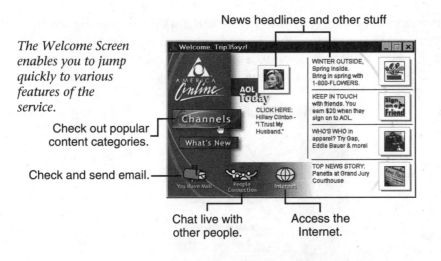

Chat live with other people.

Access the Internet.

The Channels window acts as an online kiosk.

Click a button for the area you want to explore.

When the mouse pointer is over a hyperlink, the pointer appears as a hand.

In addition to enabling you to meander to your destination, America Online provides a keyword feature that enables you to take a direct flight to your destination. You click the **Keyword** button in the toolbar or press **Ctrl+K**, type the name of your destination (for example, Newsweek), and click **Go**. If you don't know the keyword for what you want, click the **Find** button in the toolbar, and then click the type of resource you want to find—areas of interest, members, programs, or online events. Type one or two words (or a person's name) to describe what you're looking for, click the **Find** button, and flip through a list to find a link that points to the desired person or resource.

In addition to the Keyword and Find buttons, America Online's toolbar contains the following buttons for quickly navigating the service:

 Read New Mail Opens a window that displays a list of descriptions for messages that you have received. Double-click the description to read the contents of the message.

Compose Mail   Displays a window for addressing and typing a message you want to send to someone else. See the next section, "Keeping in Touch with Email," for details.

 Channels   Displays the Channels window, which you saw earlier in this section.

 What's Hot   Calls up a list of hot new features of the service.

 People Connection   Displays a window with links for hooking up with other people who use America Online. For example, you can click the Chat link to display chat rooms where you can chat with other members by typing messages back and forth. (See "Conversing in Chat Rooms," later in this chapter for details.)

 File Search   Enables you to search for games, pictures, programs, and other files.

 Stocks & Portfolios   Connects you to a personal finance center, where you can obtain information about investing in stocks and mutual funds.

 Today's News   Displays the current ABC headlines along with links to departments, such as Business, Sports, Politics, and Weather.

 World Wide Web   Connects you to the Internet. (See "Wandering Off to the Internet," later in this chapter.)

 Marketplace   Takes you to an online mall, where you can shop for computer accessories, electronic gadgets, clothes, plane tickets, cars, and much more. Have your credit card handy.

 My AOL   Displays a window with configuration options for America Online. After you've played on the service for awhile, you should check out these options. They can save you time and make your encounters with America Online more productive and enjoyable.

 Online Clock   Shows you how much time you have wasted... er... spent online so that you can decide whether you need to sign off and eat something.

How Much Time Do I Have Left?

The online clock won't indicate how much time you have left on your free introductory offer. To find out, check your billing summary. Press **Ctrl+K**, type **billing**, and press **Enter**. Click the **Current Bill Summary** link.

Print   Prints the contents of the current window.

 Personal Filing Cabinet   Displays a list of the folders that America Online uses for storing files and messages that you have downloaded and saved.

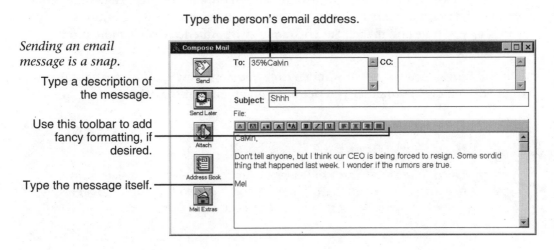 **Favorite Places**   Displays a list of places you have marked as your favorite places. As you wander the service, you may notice a heart icon in the upper right corner of most windows. To add a place to the Favorite Places folder, click the heart icon and click **Yes** to confirm.

 Member Services   This is your online help. Here you find links to billing information, account options, and common help topics.

Keeping in Touch with Email

How would you like to send a letter and have it reach its destination in less than a minute? With electronic mail (*email* for short), you can enjoy warp speed delivery at a fraction of the cost.

To send an email letter, you first enter the **Compose Mail** command (or its equivalent). This opens a dialog box that enables you to compose and address your correspondence. Type the email address of the person to whom you want to send the message (this is usually the person's screen name, if she is a member of the same service). Click inside the **Description** area, and type a brief description of your message. Finally, type your message (or paste it) in the **Message** area, and then click the **Send** button. In a matter of seconds, the message appears in your friend's mailbox. When your friend connects to the service, your message appears in her mailbox.

Sending an email message is a snap.

Type the person's email address.

Type a description of the message.

Use this toolbar to add fancy formatting, if desired.

Type the message itself.

Everyone on your online service (including you) has an electronic mailbox. Whenever you sign on, the program indicates in some way if you have mail waiting. To get your mail, you enter the **Get Mail** command or click the **Mail** button. This displays a list of waiting messages. Double-click the message that you want to read. The message appears inside a dialog box, which usually contains a **Reply** button, enabling you to respond immediately to the message.

A list of messages you received

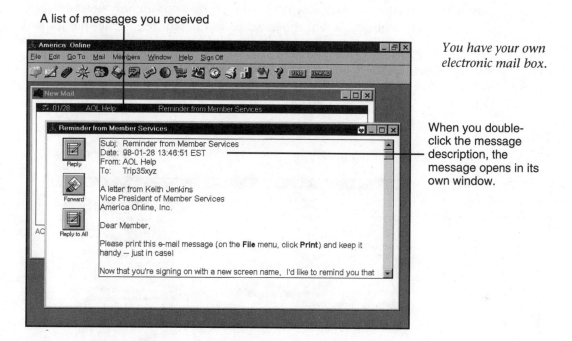

You have your own electronic mail box.

When you double-click the message description, the message opens in its own window.

Conversing in Chat Rooms

If you don't like waiting for mail, you can converse with your friends and colleagues in one of the many chat rooms the online service provides. You pick a room in which 20 or so people are hanging out and then start typing. Your messages appear on the screens of the other people in the room, and their messages appear on your screen. If you prefer to talk in private with one or more users, you can create your own private room and invite other users to join you.

To go to an America Online chat room, click the **People Connection** button and click the **Chat Now** link. This takes you to a lobby, where you can immediately start chatting. Chat windows consist of the following three areas:

Chat Window Displays the ongoing conversation. As you and others type and send messages, all the messages appear in this window. If the chat room has a talkative crowd, the messages scroll pretty quickly, so you need to stay on your toes.

List of Chatters Displays the screen names of everyone in the chat room. Double-click a member's name to display a dialog box with options for checking the person's profile (information the person entered about herself) or for sending the person an IM (instant message). An instant message pops up only on the screen of the person to whom you sent the message, so nobody else in the chat room can see it.

Message Area Below the chat window is a text box into which you type your messages. Click the text box, type your message, and click the **Send** button or press **Enter**. Your message pops up in your chat window and in the chat window of each person in the room.

Follow the discussion and check out the other chatters.

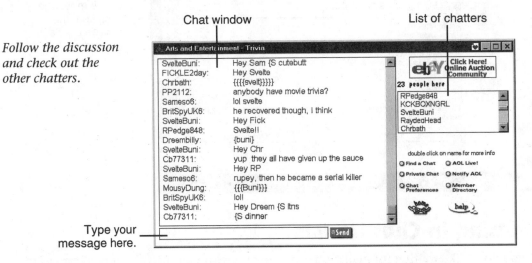

Watch Your Back

Although most chatters are harmless, you might bump into some less desirable types. Be careful about giving out sensitive information online, including your password, your last name, address, phone number, or anything else someone could use to track you down or use your account.

220

Although it's okay to hang out in a lobby, most people in lobbies are in transit to other rooms that interest them. To view a list of different chat rooms, click the **Find a Chat** link. This displays a window with two lists. In the list on the left, double-click the general chat area that interests you, such as Arts and Entertainment or Romance. The list on the right displays specific chat rooms in the selected category. Double-click the name of the room that you want to enter. (If the room has 23 members, it's full, and you have trouble gaining entrance.)

Sharing Common Interests

Online services started as computerized community centers where people could share their ideas, problems, and solutions. This tradition is still alive in online *forums* and *boards*. You can find a forum or board for almost any special interest category—from gardening and parenting to computers and automobiles. If you have a question, you simply post a message on the board. In a day or so, other members post answers in an attempt to help you out. You can get free legal advice, information on how to grow prize-winning roses, and help finding long-lost relatives. Forums and boards are also a great place to talk about your favorite books, movies, and TV shows, although not all users will agree with your tastes.

On some online services, the forums are scattered throughout the service. For instance, on America Online, you can find places to read and post messages in Member Services, Gardening, and HouseNet. Just press **Ctrl+K**, type a couple words describing your interest, and click the **Go** button. You receive a list of places to go, which may include links that take you to a message center on that topic.

Wandering Off to the Internet

You learn all about the Internet in the next few chapters. Before you leave, however, you should know that most online services offer full access to the Internet. On America Online, for example, you can quickly access the Internet by clicking the **Internet** button in the Channels window. This displays a window with links for the Web, newsgroups, and other Internet features. Click **Go to the Web** to start America Online's Web browser and open America Online's starting Web page. (America Online uses a modified version of Microsoft's Internet Explorer as its Web browser.)

To navigate the Web, click links, just as you do for navigating America Online. The only difference is that the links may look a little different from what you are accustomed to on America Online. Because you are wandering off the service to other services and sites, you don't get the consistent look and feel of America Online. To search for other sites and pages on the Web, click the **Search** button in the browser toolbar. A search form appears. Enter one or two words to describe what you're looking for and click the **Search** button. (For more information about navigating the Web, see Chapter 21.)

The America Online Web browser

America Online has the tools that you need to wander the Web.

You can type a page address to open a specific page.

Click links to go to other pages.

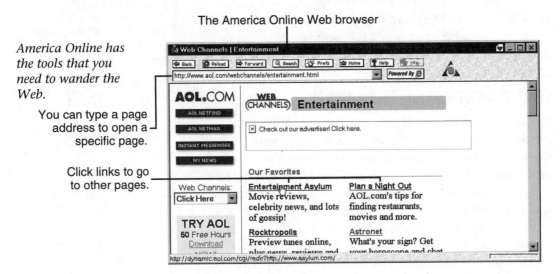

When you are done, simply click the Close (X) button in the browser window. This returns you to the America Online service. To sign off, you can click the Close button in the upper-right corner of the America Online window or open the **Sign Off** menu and click **Sign Off**.

Tech Check

Okay, you've read enough. Now, get hold of a couple free online trial-membership kits, and get connected. As you're cruising your online service, make sure you can do the following:

➤ Name the four most popular online services.

➤ Take advantage of an online service free trial offer using an icon on the Windows desktop.

➤ Connect to your online service.

➤ Navigate America Online.

➤ Send an email message to someone, assuming you know the person's email address.

➤ Find chat rooms.

➤ Open a Web page and skip to other Web pages.

Doing the Internet Shuffle

Unless you've set up permanent residence in the New York tunnel, you've probably heard the terms *Internet* and *Information Superhighway*. The Internet is a massive computer network connecting thousands of computers all over the world, including computers at universities, libraries, businesses, government agencies, and research facilities.

By connecting to the Internet, you can tap many of the resources stored on these computers. You can copy (*download*) files from them, use their programs, send and receive electronic mail (*email*), chat with other people by typing messages back and forth, get information about millions of topics, shop electronic malls, and even search for a job or a compatible mate. (Of course, if this compatible mate searches for a mate using a computer, you might both need counseling before you can even meet.)

What You Need to Get Started

Just because the Internet offers some pretty cool stuff does not mean that you're going to have to retool your computer. In fact, you probably already have everything you need to connect to the Internet now.

28.8Kbps (or faster) Modem   Web pages contain graphics, video clips, and other media objects that take a long time to travel over phone lines. You should have a modem that can receive data at least at a rate of 28.8Kbps. If you only want email, you can get by with a slower modem. (See Chapter 18, "First You Need a Modem," for details.)

SVGA Monitor   The same graphics and video clips that take so long to download look fuzzy on anything less than an SVGA monitor. (See Chapter 26, "Savvy Consumer Guide to Buying a Computer.")

Speaker and Sound Card   If you want to listen to recordings or music clips on the Internet, you had better have a sound card and speakers. (See Chapter 26.)

Internet Service Provider   The Internet service provider connects you to the Internet. Your modem dials the service provider's computer, which then establishes the required connection. If you have a commercial online service, such as America Online, you can use the service as your Internet service provider as well. (If you don't have an account with a commercial online service, you learn how to find an Internet service provider in the next section.)

TCP/IP Program   This program dials into your Internet service provider's computer using your modem and establishes the basic connection. You can then run specialized programs, such as a Web browser, email program, and news reader to access specific Internet features. Fortunately, the TCP/IP program that you need comes with Windows. (You learn how to set it up later in this chapter, using the Internet Connection Wizard.)

Credit card   Perhaps the most important item, the credit card, enables you to start an account with an online service provider.

Finding an Entrance Ramp

Before you can navigate the Internet, you have to find an entrance ramp—a way onto the Internet. You have several options:

Online service connection   The easiest way to connect to the Internet is to use an online service. All the major online services (Prodigy, America Online, CompuServe, and The Microsoft Network) offer Internet access. You can, however, usually get a better monthly service rate and better Internet service from a local Internet service provider.

Permanent connection   If your company or university has a network that is part of the Internet, and your computer is connected to the network, you have access to the Internet through the network. This is the least expensive (and fastest) way to go. Ask your network administrator if you're connected. If his eyes light up and he starts raving about a T1 line, you're connected.

Internet service provider (ISP)   One of the least expensive ways to connect to the Internet is through a local service provider. Most local Internet service providers charge a monthly fee of $15 to $20 for unlimited connect time (or for a huge chunk of time, say 200 hours). You use your modem to connect to the service provider's computer, which is wired to the Internet.

Although an Internet service provider is the least expensive way to go, it's a little more complicated than simply signing on to an online service. Most service providers, however, provide the instructions that you need to get up and running in a hurry. If you don't know of any service providers in your area, ask at a computer store or users group in your area, or check in the phone book.

To set up your account, you need information and settings that indicate to your computer how to connect to the service provider's computer. Obtain the following information:

> **Finding an Internet Service Provider Online**   If your search for a service provider comes up short, use the Internet Connection Wizard (as explained later in this chapter) to set up your account. The Internet Connection Wizard can display a list of popular service providers in your calling area, and you can start your account simply by providing some billing information.

Username   This is the name that identifies you to the ISP's computer. It is typically an abbreviation of your first and last name. For example, Bill Fink might use bfink as his username. You can choose any name you like, as long as it is not already being used by another user.

Password   The ISP may enable you to select your own password or may assign you a password. Be sure to write down the password in case you forget it. Without the right password, you are not able to connect to the service provider's computer.

Connection Type   Most ISPs offer PPP (Point-to-Point Protocol), but you might encounter a service provider who uses the older SLIP (Serial Line Internet Protocol). Point-to-Point Protocol is easier to set up and provides faster data transfer, so if given a choice, choose PPP.

Domain Name Server   The domain name server is a computer that's set up to locate computers on the Internet. Each computer on the Internet has a unique number that identifies it, such as **197.72.34.74**. Each computer also has a domain name, such as **www.whitehouse.com**, which makes it easier for people to remember the computer's address. When you enter a domain name, the domain name server looks up the computer's number and locates it.

Domain Name   This is the domain name of your service provider's computer—for example, internet.com. You use the domain name in conjunction with your username as your email address—for example, **bfink@internet.com**.

News Server   The news server enables you to connect to any of thousands of newsgroups on the Internet to read and post messages. Newsgroups are electronic bulletin boards for special interest groups. The news server name typically starts with news and is followed by the service provider's domain name—for example, news.internet.com.

Mail Server   The mail server is in charge of electronic mail. You need to specify two mail servers—POP (Post Office Protocol) for incoming mail, and SMTP (Simplified Mail Transfer Protocol) for mail that you send. The POP server's name typically starts with pop and is followed by the service provider's domain name—for example, **pop.internet.com**. The SMTP server's name typically starts with smtp or mail and is followed by the service provider's domain name—for example, **smtp.internet.com** (See Chapter 22, "Email: Postage Free, Same-Day Delivery," for details.)

Email Address   If you plan to receive email messages, you need an email address. Your address typically begins with your username followed by an at sign (@) and the domain name of your service provider—for example, **bfink@internet.com**.

Signing on with the Internet Connection Wizard

After you have all the information you need, you can run the Internet Connection Wizard and enter the connection settings. The wizard displays a series of screens prompting you to enter each piece of information. The wizard then creates a Dial-Up Networking icon that you can click to establish your connection.

Although I would really like to give you step-by-step instructions for using the Internet Connection Wizard, the steps vary depending on which Internet Connection Wizard you are using. The wizard that's included with Internet Explorer 3 is vastly different from the one included with Internet Explorer 4; however, I can tell you how to start the wizard and what to watch out for. Keep the following in mind:

➤ To start the Internet Connection Wizard, click **The Internet** or **Internet Explorer** icon on your Windows desktop. You use this same icon to run Internet Explorer, but the first time you click it, it runs the Internet Connection Wizard.

➤ If the previous step didn't work, the Connection Wizard may be hiding on your system. Check the **Start**, **Programs**, **Accessories**, **Internet Tools** menu for an option named **Get on the Internet**, or check the **Start**, **Programs**, **Internet Explorer** menu for an option called **Connection Wizard**.

Install Dial-Up Networking To connect to the Internet, a Windows component called Dial-Up Networking must be installed. If it is not available, see "Installing and Uninstalling Windows Components" in Chapter 5 to install Dial-Up Networking. You find it listed in the Communications category.

➤ After the wizard starts, follow the onscreen instructions to set up your Internet account. The second screen (Setup Options) is the most important screen. If you already have an ISP, choose **Manual** or **I Want to Set Up a New Connection....** If you need to find an ISP, click **Automatic** or **I Want to Choose an Internet Service Provider and Set up a New Account**.

➤ If you need to find an ISP, the wizard asks for your area code and the first three digits of your phone number; it then downloads a list of ISPs available in your area, as shown in the following figure. You need to register with the service and provide a credit card number. The wizard downloads the required connection settings for you, so you won't have to enter them manually.

➤ If you already set up an account with a service provider in your area, you have to manually enter the connection settings. This is no biggie; the wizard steps you through it. When asked whether you want to view the Advanced settings, however, click **Yes** so that you can check the settings.

➤ If asked to specify a logon procedure, leave **I Don't Need to Type Anything When Logging On** selected, even though your ISP requires you to enter a name and password. This option is for services that require you to manually log on using a terminal window or logon script. Most ISPs do not require this.

➤ Most ISPs automatically assign an IP (Internet Protocol) address to you when you log on, so don't choose to use a specific IP address unless your ISP gave you one.

➤ Most ISPs provide a specific DNS Server address. Choose **Always Use the Following** and enter the DNS address in the **DNS Server** text box. If your ISP offers a secondary DNS, enter it so that you can still navigate if the first DNS is busy.

➤ Don't worry about setting up your email and news server accounts at this point. You can set these up later.

The Internet Connection Wizard can help you locate an ISP in your area.

Select an Internet service provider.

> **Microsoft**
>
> Welcome to the **Microsoft Internet Referral Service**. From the list below, choose the service provider whose offer best fits your Internet needs.
> If you need help figuring out what to do next, click here.
>
> ### Premier Internet Service Providers
>
> | | More Info | Sign Me Up |
> |---|---|---|
> | **Sprint Internet Passport** Sprint Internet Passport Only ISP with the Get-Connected Guarantee-if we can't connect you, we'll credit you a week. Sprint's fiber optic network delivers fast, reliable connections. Rated #1 in page download speed (Inverse). First month FREE, then $19.95 | | |
> | **SPRYNET** 1996 PC Magazine Editor's Choice Award for Best National ISP! $19.95/month unlimited pricing plan, 5MB free home page hosting, 24-hour online support, more local access points than any other ISP, easy-to-use e-mail, online resources, and one month FREE. | | |
> | **Concentric Network** Easy, reliable, ultra-fast, unlimited active Internet access in over 3,000 areas-$19.95/mo, Basic-$7.95/mo; No set-up fees. Great deals, Customizable Start/Home Pages, Email, news, games, chat, 24-hr customer support & more! Click here for 1st month FREE! | | |
> | **IDT Corporation** 2 FREE MONTHS: Featured in PC magazine, Wall Street Journal, NY Times etc. Rated #1 for network reliability by Smart Money magazine. $19.95 includes 1000's of newsgroups, 33.6 kbps 24/7 live tech support: Sign up and get 1st & 13th MONTHS FREE !! | | |
> | **MCI Internet** The easiest way to access the Internet! Quick and easy access to all the news, information and ideas you need 24 hours a day. Explore the Internet with unlimited access for only $19.95 a month. Sign up now and get the first month FREE! | | |
> | **AT&T WorldNet Service** World Class Award (PC World July 1997), First Place Ranking (Smart Money May 1997), MVP Award (PC Computing Nov. 1996), $19.95 a month unlimited usage, 1st. Month | | |

After running the Internet Connection Wizard, run My Computer and double-click the **Dial-Up Networking** icon. The Dial-Up Networking folder contains icons for any ISPs that you have set up. Drag the icon for your ISP to a blank area of the Windows desktop.

Connecting for the First Time

After you have an icon, you can double-click it to connect to the Internet. When you double-click the icon, a dialog box appears as shown in the following figure, prompting you to type your username and password (supplied by your service provider).

Type your username and password. If desired, check the **Save Password** check box. This saves your username and password, so you won't have to type it again the next time you logon. If you share your computer with someone else, and you do not want that person using your Internet connection, leave the check box blank. Click the **Connect** button.

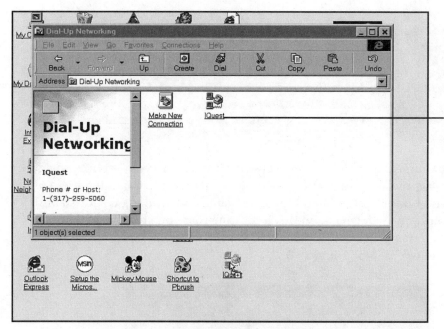

The Dial-Up Networking icon you just created is your passport to the Internet.

Drag the Dial-Up Networking icon that you created to a blank area of the Windows desktop.

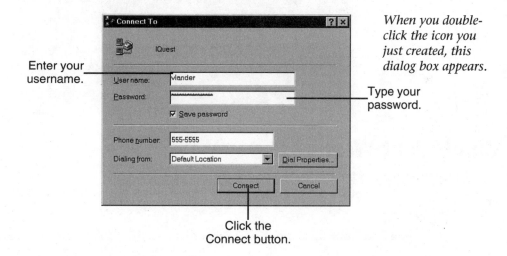

When you double-click the icon you just created, this dialog box appears.

Enter your username.

Type your password.

Click the Connect button.

231

No Save Password Option?

If you don't have the Save Password option, Client for Microsoft Networks is not installed. In the Control Panel, double-click the **Network** icon, click the **Add** button, and double-click **Client**. Click **Microsoft** and then double-click **Client for Microsoft Networks**. Make sure that **Client for Microsoft Networks** is selected as the **Primary Network Logon** and click **OK**.

After you click the Connect button, Dial-Up Networking dials into your service provider's computer and displays messages indicating the progress—Dialing..., Checking username and password..., and Connecting.... Assuming that Dial-Up Networking could establish a connection, the following dialog box appears, indicating that you are now connected. You can now run Internet programs (explained in later chapters) to navigate the World Wide Web, send and receive email, and so on.

Congratulations! You're wired.

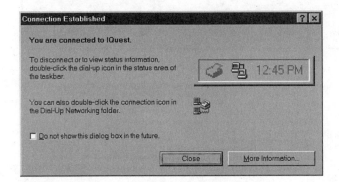

What Went Wrong?

If your connection proceeds smoothly the first time, lucky you. Most first attempts fail for some reason or another (these are computers, after all). If the connection fails, check the following:

➤ Did you type your username and password correctly? (If you mistyped this information or if your service provider entered it incorrectly on the system, Dial-Up Networking typically displays a message indicating that the system did not accept your password.) Retype your username and password and try connecting again. (Passwords are typically case sensitive, so type the password *exactly* as your service provider specifies.)

➤ Was the line busy? Again, Dial-Up Networking typically displays a message indicating that the line was busy. If several people are connected to the service, you may have to wait until someone signs off. Keep trying to connect.

➤ Did your modem even dial? Go to the Windows Control Panel and check your modem setup. Make sure that you've selected the correct modem and COM port. (If you muted your modem in Chapter 18, turn the speaker back on so that you can determine whether the modem is even dialing.)

➤ Do you have reliable phone lines? Unplug your modem from the phone jack and plug a phone into the jack. Do you get a dial tone? Does the line sound fuzzy? If you don't hear a dial tone, the jack is not working. If the line is fuzzy when you make a voice call, it has line noise, which may be enough to disconnect you.

➤ Check your Dial-Up Adapter settings. Display the Windows Control Panel, and double-click the **Network** icon. Click **Dial-Up Adapter**, and click the **Properties** button. Click the **Bindings** tab and make sure there is a check mark next to TCP/IP-->Dial-Up Adapter. (If NetBEUI or IPX/SPX are listed, make sure they are NOT checked.)

➤ Make sure you have selected the correct server type. In the Control Panel, double-click the **Dial-Up Networking** icon. Right-click the icon for connecting to your ISP, and choose **Properties**. Click the **Server Type** tab. Open the **Type of Dial-Up Server** drop-down list and choose the correct server type (specified by your service provider)—PPP or SLIP.

Make sure that you have selected the correct server type.

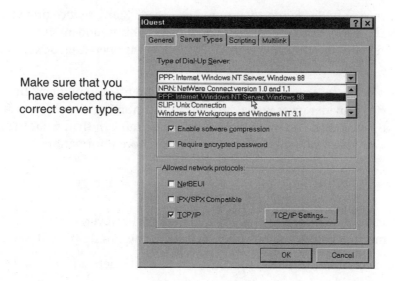

Check the settings for your Dial-Up connection.

Speeding Up Your Internet Connection

Modem Troubleshooting
If your modem does not respond, see "My Modem Doesn't Work," in Chapter 31, for additional troubleshooting tips.

When Dial-Up Networking establishes a connection, it displays the speed at which data is being transferred. Expect the speed to be slightly less than your actual modem speed. For example, if you have a 28.8Kbps modem, expect an actual speed of 24 to 26Kbps. If you're using a 56K modem, expect speeds in the range of 40 to 45Kbps. These speed dips may be the result of line noise or problems with your service provider.

If Dial-Up Networking shows that the speed is half of what your modem is capable of, then you should be concerned. For example, if your 28.8Kbps modem is chugging along at 14,400bps, you should check the following:

➤ The trouble could be line noise. If you typically connect at a higher speed, you may have a bad connection. Try disconnecting and reconnecting. If the connection is always slow, check the phone lines in your house and call your local phone company to report line noise.

➤ Check your modem setup. In the Control Panel, double-click the **Modems** icon. Click the name of your modem and click the **Properties** button. Under Maximum Speed, open the drop-down list and choose a speed that is higher than your modem's speed. Try the highest setting. Disconnect and reconnect to see if your connection speed has increased.

➤ Does your service provider support your modem speed? Many service providers support only up to 33.6Kbps modems. If you have a 56Kbps modem, it transfers data only at the rate that the service provider's modem is operating. 56Kbps modems can *send* data at speeds only up to 33.6Kbps.

➤ Does your service provider know that you're using a high-speed modem? In many cases, the service provider gives you a different phone number to use to connect at a specific speed. You may be set up to dial into a slower modem than what the service provider has available. Call your service provider for more information.

Tech Check

After you're connected, You don't need to remember much; however, if you're planning on going into the Internet consulting business, make sure you can do the following:

➤ Write a list of everything you need to connect to the Internet.

➤ Find a local Internet service provider.

➤ Gather all the information required to connect to an ISP.

➤ Run the Internet Connection Wizard and use it to enter the required connection settings.

➤ Use the Internet Connection Wizard to find a new ISP when your free trial period expires.

➤ Connect to the Internet.

➤ List five common causes of failed or slow connections.

Whipping Around the World Wide Web

The single most exciting part of the Internet is the World Wide Web (or Web for short). With an Internet connection and a Web browser, you have access to billions of electronic pages stored on computers all over the world. Whatever your interest—music, movies, finances, science, literature, travel, astrology, body piercing—you find hundreds of pages to explore.

What Exactly Is the Web?

The Web is a collection of *documents* stored on computers all over the world. Each computer that has Web documents is called a *Web server;* it serves up the documents to you and other users on request. (The other computer, the *client,* which is your computer, acts as a customer, demanding specific information.) What makes these documents unique is that each contains a *link* to other documents on the same Web server or on a different Web server (down the block or overseas). You can hop around from document to document, from Web server to Web server, from continent to continent, by clicking these links.

By document, I don't mean some dusty old text document like you'd find in the university library. These documents contain pictures, sounds, video clips, animations, and even interactive programs. When you click one of these multimedia links, your modem pulls the file into your computer, where the Web browser or another program plays the file. All you have to do is tilt your chair back, nibble on popcorn, and watch the show.

First, You Need a Web Browser

To do the Web, you need a special program called a *Web browser*, which works through your service provider to pull documents up on your screen. You can choose from any of several Web browsers, including the two most popular browsers—Netscape Navigator and Internet Explorer. In addition to opening Web pages, these browsers contain advanced tools for navigating the Web, finding pages that interest you, and marking the pages you like.

Check This Out...

Get Internet Explorer 4
This book covers Internet Explorer 4. If you have an older version, connect to the Internet Explorer home page at **www.microsoft.com/ie** and get the latest version. (See "Copying (Downloading) Files from the Internet," later in this chapter.) You download a small file and run it when you're connected to the Internet. The file leads you through the process of installing Internet Explorer.

Windows comes with Internet Explorer, which should already be installed on your computer. Internet Explorer also has several additional Internet programs, including Outlook Express (for email and newsgroups), NetMeeting (for Internet phone calls), and FrontPage Express (for creating Web pages).

If a friend or colleague recommended that you use Netscape Navigator instead, you can use Internet Explorer to download Netscape Navigator from Netscape's Web site. You can download Navigator (the Web browser) or Netscape Communicator—a suite of Internet programs that includes Messenger (for email), Collabra (for newsgroups), Composer (for creating Web pages), and Conference (for Internet phone calls). To connect to Netscape's Web site, run Internet Explorer, type **www.netscape.com** in the **Address** text box (below the toolbar), and press **Enter**. Follow the trail of links to download Navigator or Communicator. (For details on downloading files, see "Copying (Downloading) Files from the Internet," later in this chapter.) After the program is on your computer, you can double-click its icon to run the installation utility.

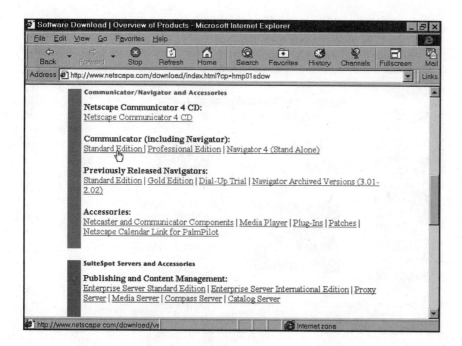

You can use Internet Explorer to get Netscape Navigator.

Navigating the Web with Internet Explorer

To run the Internet Explorer Web browser, click the icon named **The Internet** or **Internet Explorer** on the Windows desktop or choose Internet Explorer from the Start, Programs, Internet Explorer menu. If your computer is not connected to your service provider, the Connect To dialog box appears. Type your username and password, as explained in the previous chapter, and click the **Connect** button. After Dial-Up Networking establishes your Internet connection, Internet Explorer loads the Microsoft home page, as shown here.

You can start to wander the Web simply by clicking links (highlighted text or pictures). Click the **Back** button to flip to a previous page, or click **Forward** to skip ahead to a page that you've visited but backed up from.

Which One's Better?
Depends who you ask. For rank beginners, I recommend Internet Explorer. It's free, comes with Windows (at least so far), and has some cool features that integrate your desktop with the Web. Navigator has been said to be faster and more reliable, but performance and reliability vary depending on the pages you open.

Internet Explorer makes it easy to navigate the Web.

Click the Back button to display the previous page.

Click a link to flip to a page.

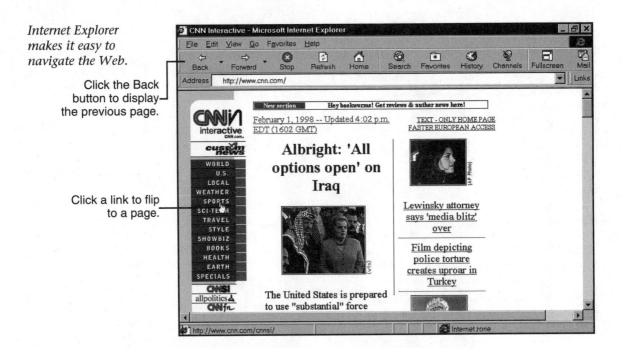

Cruising the Web with Netscape Navigator

Before big, bad Microsoft got serious about the Internet, Netscape Navigator was, by far, the most popular Web browser around and is still considered by many to be the best. It's fast, handles most of the media you encounter on the Web, and it's not a Microsoft product. Otherwise, it's pretty similar to Internet Explorer.

After you install Navigator (or Communicator), you should have an icon on your Windows desktop named **Netscape Navigator** or **Netscape Communicator**. Double-click the icon. Again, if your computer is not connected to the Internet, the Connect To dialog box appears. Type your username and password, as explained in the previous chapter, and click the **Connect** button. The Netscape Navigator window appears and opens Netscape's home page.

The procedure for wandering the Web with Navigator is fairly standard; you click links to jump from one page to the next. Links typically appear as blue, underlined text or as buttons or icons. After you move from one page to another, you can click the **Back** button to return to previous pages, or click the **Forward** button to move ahead to pages you've visited but backed up from. To view a list of pages you have visited, click the **Back** or **Forward** button, and hold down the mouse button. You can then click the name of the page that you want to revisit.

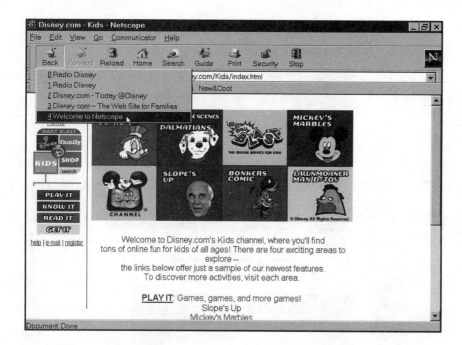

In Netscape Navigator, the Back and Forward buttons double as drop-down lists.

Hitting Specific Sites with Addresses

You've seen them on TV, in magazines, maybe even in your daily newspaper: bits of odd looking text, such as **www.whitehouse.gov** or **www.nfl.com**. What are these things? They're addresses of specific Web pages. These addresses are called *URLs* (Uniform Resource Locators). You enter the address in your Web browser, usually in a text box called Go to or Address, near the top of the window, and your Web browser pulls up the page.

URLs Dissected

To give you some idea of how these addresses work, let's dissect one. First, all Web page addresses start with **http://**. Newsgroup sites start with **news://**. FTP sites (where you can get files) start with **ftp://**. You get the idea. *HTTP* (short for Hypertext Transfer Protocol) is the coding system used to format Web pages. The rest of the address reads from right to left. For example, in the URL **http://www.whitehouse.gov**, **.gov** stands for government, **whitehouse** stands for Whitehouse, and **www** stands for World Wide Web. Addresses that end in **.edu** are for pages at educational institutions. Addresses that end in **.com** are for commercial institutions.

All you really have to know about a URL is that if you want to use one, type the URL *exactly* as you see it. Type the periods as shown, use forward slashes, and follow the capitalization of the URL. If you make any typos, a message appears indicating that the page doesn't exist or that the browser will load the wrong page. If a URL ends in .com, you can usually omit the **www** at the beginning of the URL and the **.com** from the end. For example, instead of typing **www.yahoo.com**, simply type **yahoo** and press **Enter**.

Type the URL of the page you
want to visit and press Enter.

*If you know the
address of a page,
you can go directly
to it.*

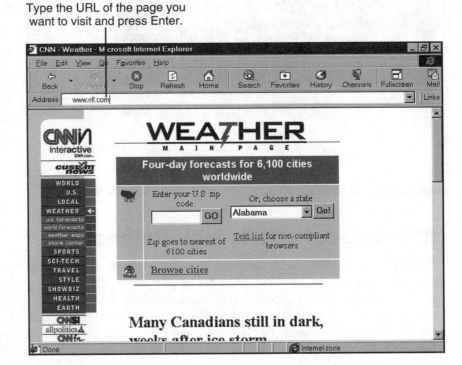

Using Internet Search Tools

How do you find information on the Web? Many Web sites have search tools that filter through an index of Internet resources to help you find what you're looking for. You simply connect to a site that has a search tool, type a couple words that specify what you're looking for, and click the **Search** button. The following are the URLs (addresses) of some popular search tools on the Web:

http://www.yahoo.com

http://www.lycos.com

http://www.infoseek.com

http://www.altavista.com

http://www.webcrawler.com

Most Web browsers now have a Search button that connects you to various Internet search tools. For example, if you click **Search** in Internet Explorer, you connect to Microsoft's search page, which offers links to a half dozen search tools. The cool thing about the Search button is that it opens a separate pane that displays the search results. You can then click links in the left pane to open pages in the right pane without having to click the Back button to return to the search results.

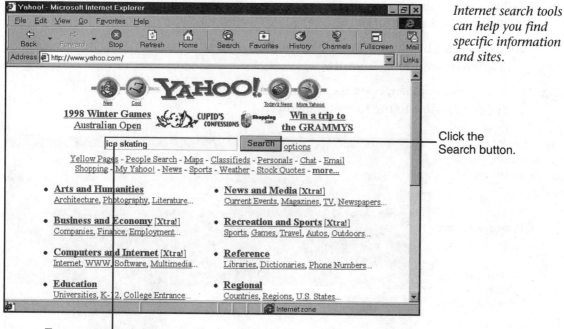

Internet search tools can help you find specific information and sites.

Click the
Search button.

Type your search phrase.

You can also use special search tools to find long lost relatives and friends on the Internet. These search tools are like electronic telephone directories that can help you find mailing addresses, phone numbers, and even email addresses. To search for people, check out the following sites:

www.four11.com

www.bigfoot.com

www.whowhere.com

www.infospace.com

Tagging and Flagging Your Favorite Pages

As you wander the Web, you stumble upon pages that you want to revisit—maybe the home page of your favorite actress or a Web site that lists the mutual funds that you invest in. In such cases, you can mark these pages and add them to a menu—typically called a Bookmark or Favorites menu. The next time you want to pull up the page, you simply select it from your customized menu. You can mark pages several ways, depending on the Web browser that you are using. In Netscape and Internet Explorer, the easiest methods are

➤ In Navigator, drag the little icon that's next to the **Location** text box over the **Bookmarks** icon and release the mouse button. This places the page name on the Bookmarks menu. You can also drag links over the Bookmarks icon.

➤ Right-click a blank area on the current page or right-click a link and choose **Add Bookmark** or **Add to Favorites**.

➤ In Internet Explorer, open the **Favorites** menu and click **Add to Favorites** to add the page's name to the Favorites menu.

In Netscape Navigator, you can use drag-and-drop to bookmark pages.

Bookmarks icon—

Drag the Location icon over the Bookmarks icon.

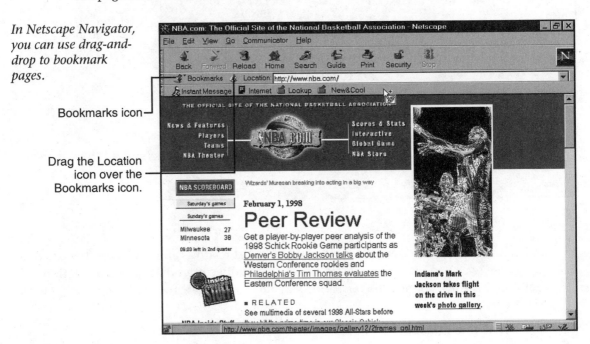

Having Pages Delivered to You

Several companies, including Microsoft, have been busy working on ways to speed up the Internet by improving hardware—cables, modems, satellites, and so on. Other companies have looked at the problem from a software standpoint and have developed the clever notion of *push content*. With push content, you subscribe to sites and have the Web sites broadcast updated content to your computer while you are working or sleeping. You can then disconnect from the Internet and view your pages offline.

> **Make Your Own Submenus** You can get fancy with Favorites and Bookmarks by creating submenus. In Navigator, open the **Bookmarks** menu and select **Edit Bookmarks**. In Internet Explorer, open the **Favorites** menu and select **Organize Favorites**. In either program, you get a window that enables you to rearrange your bookmarks or favorites, create submenus (folders), and perform other feats of magic.

The best time to set up a site subscription in Internet Explorer is when you mark the site as a favorite. In the dialog box that appears when you choose Add to Favorites, click **Yes, Notify Me of Updates and Download the Page for Offline Viewing**. You can then click the **Customize** button to run the Subscription Wizard. The wizard prompts you to enter your preferences, such as whether you want additional pages (pages linked to this page) downloaded and when you want the page(s) downloaded. Internet Explorer downloads subscribed pages at the specified time (typically in the early morning when the Internet is not so busy).

To open the pages without connecting to the Internet, simply run Internet Explorer without establishing your Internet connection. Or, open the **File** menu, choose **Work Offline**, and then disconnect from the Internet. You can then open pages as you normally would, by selecting pages from the Favorites menu, entering page addresses, and clicking links. Instead of opening the pages from the Web, Internet Explorer opens them from a temporary storage area on your hard disk called the *cache*. If you move the mouse pointer over a link that points to a page that is not in the cache, a NOT sign (circle with a bar through it) appears next to the mouse pointer, indicating that you cannot view the linked page offline. If you click the link anyway or enter the address of an uncached page, a dialog box appears asking whether you want to go online. You can then establish your Internet connection and load the page.

> **What About Subscribing in Navigator?** Navigator's bookmarks do not enable you to subscribe to pages. Netscape Communicator, however, comes with a program, called Netcaster, which enables you to take advantage of push technology, as explained in the following section.

Channel Surf the Web

In a concerted effort to transform your computer monitor into a TV set, Web developers have come up with some innovative tools. Microsoft's entry into this wave of the future is the Channels feature, a tool that enables you to create your own channel changer for the Web. Netscape has its own control, called Netcaster, which is included with Netscape Communicator. The following sections introduce you to these clever controls.

Flipping Channels with Netcaster

Netcaster transforms your desktop into a Webtop, where you can view Web sites that offer high-quality content. To run Netcaster, choose **Start**, **Programs**, **Netscape Communicator**, **Netscape Netcaster**. (The following figure gives you an aerial shot and brief tour of Netcaster.) On the left side of the Netcaster window is a tab with an N on it. Click the tab to hide the window; click the tab again to bring the window back into view. (The tab stays on top of your other windows.) To completely exit Netcaster, click **Exit** near the bottom of the window.

Netcaster provides the buttons you need to navigate and control your Webtop.

Click a channel to preview it.

Click the tab to hide or display the Netcaster window.

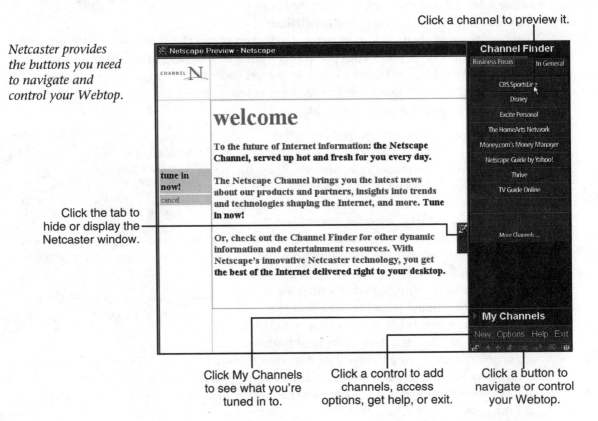

Click My Channels to see what you're tuned in to.

Click a control to add channels, access options, get help, or exit.

Click a button to navigate or control your Webtop.

Changing Channels with Microsoft's Channels

With Channels, you can tune in to the best sites the Web has to offer. Channel Guide comes with a Channel Finder that enables you to select from popular sites and then place those sites on the channel changer. To view a site, you simply click a button on the channel changer; it's just like flipping channels on your TV set! To use Channels, click the **Channels** button on Internet Explorer's toolbar or use the Channel bar on the Windows desktop.

The best way to get a feel for the Channel bar is to use it. Click the Channel Guide button at the top of the bar and follow the onscreen instructions to add buttons for the desired sites. You're then ready to start channel surfing. The following figure shows you what to expect.

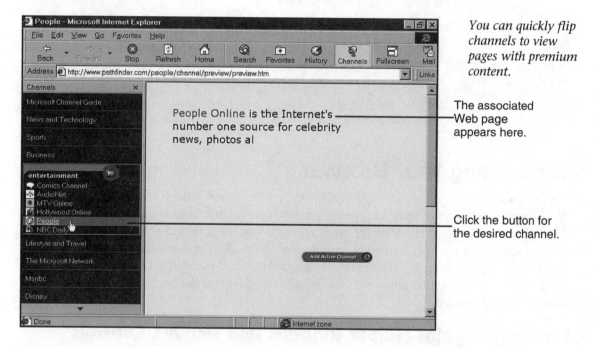

You can quickly flip channels to view pages with premium content.

The associated Web page appears here.

Click the button for the desired channel.

Copying (Downloading) Files from the Internet

The Internet is chock-full of files that you can download (copy to your computer) and use. You can download pictures, sounds, video clips, shareware (play-before-you-pay) programs, software updates, and other free stuff.

In the past, you needed a special program to connect to FTP (File Transfer Protocol) sites and download files. Although you can still use these specialized programs, it's much easier to download files with your Web browser by using the following steps:

➤ In Internet Explorer, right-click a link for the file that you want to download, and click **Save Target As**. Use the Save As dialog box to name the file and select a folder in which you want to save it.

➤ In Netscape Navigator, right-click a link for the file, and click **Save Link As**. Again, use the Save As dialog box to name the file and select a folder in which to store it.

As your Web browser downloads the file, it displays a dialog box showing the progress. The time it takes to download the file depends on the file's size, the speed of your connection, and on how busy the site is.

Dealing with Compressed Files

Most sites store compressed files, so they take up less disk space and travel across the Internet faster. If you are lucky, you get self-extracting compressed files; you double-click the file, and it decompresses itself. In other cases, you need a special decompression program, such as WinZip, which can extract the files for you. You can get WinZip at **www.winzip.com**. It extracts files that have the ZIP extension.

Accessorizing Your Browser

Web browsers are designed to open and display Web pages. Most browsers are also capable of displaying common types of graphic files (pictures) and playing some sounds. To play file types that the browser cannot handle—some graphic file types, audio clips, and video clips, for instance—Web browsers need the help of specialized applications. Internet Explorer mainly uses *ActiveX controls*, which add capability to the browser itself. Netscape Navigator primarily uses *plug-ins*, which Navigator automatically calls into action when needed.

Obtaining Popular Helper Plug-Ins and ActiveX Controls

Fortunately, your Web browser can help you find the most popular plug-ins and ActiveX controls on the Internet. In most cases, you can carelessly click links. Whenever you click a link for a file that the browser cannot play, the browser checks to see if it has the plug-in or ActiveX control that it needs. If the plug-in or control is not available, the browser prompts you to download and install it or displays a page with links to various add-ons that can do the job. You simply follow the onscreen instructions.

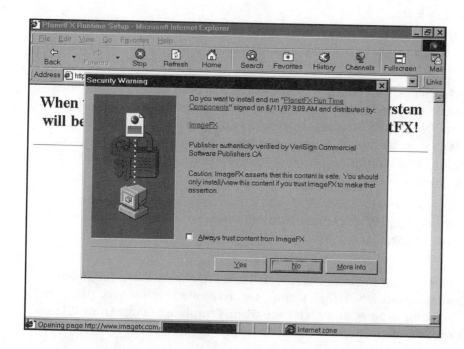

When you need an ActiveX control, Internet Explorer lets you know, and leads you through the installation.

Locating Popular Plug-Ins and ActiveX Controls

If the browser doesn't know what to do (sometimes it can't figure out which file type you are trying to play), it displays a dialog box asking you either to pick the program that you want to use to open the file or to save the file to your hard disk so that you can play it later. For now, save the file to your hard disk so that you can go in search of the program you need to play it.

Various sites on the Internet serve as repositories of plug-ins and ActiveX controls, along with various product reviews. When you need to find a plug-in or ActiveX control, try the following sites:

Stroud's: **cws.internet.com**

TUCOWS: **www.tucows.com**

ACTIVEX.COM: **www.activex.com**

BROWSERS.COM: **www.browsers.com**

Most of these sites provide a description of each add-on program and indicate whether it is an ActiveX control (for Internet Explorer) or plug-in (for Navigator). Make sure that you get the version of the add-on designed for your browser. The reviews of these add-on programs typically contain links to the developer's home page where you can obtain additional information.

After you've pulled up a few Web pages, you may find the urge to make your presence known on the Web. You can do this by creating and *publishing* your own Web page. Both Internet Explorer and Netscape Communicator come with their own page-layout programs that make Web page creation as easy as creating a document in a word-processing or desktop publishing program. The following lists the browsers with their respective steps for Web-page layout:

➤ Internet Explorer features FrontPage Express. To run it, choose **Start**, **Programs**, **Internet Explorer**, **FrontPage Express**. You can then create a simple Web page using a template or wizard. Open the **File** menu, select **New**, and follow the onscreen instructions.

➤ Netscape Communicator includes Composer. To run it, choose **Start**, **Programs**, **Netscape Communicator**, **Netscape Composer**. To create a simple Web page, open the **File** menu, point to **New**, and click **Page from Template** or **Page from Wizard**. Follow the onscreen instructions to create the page.

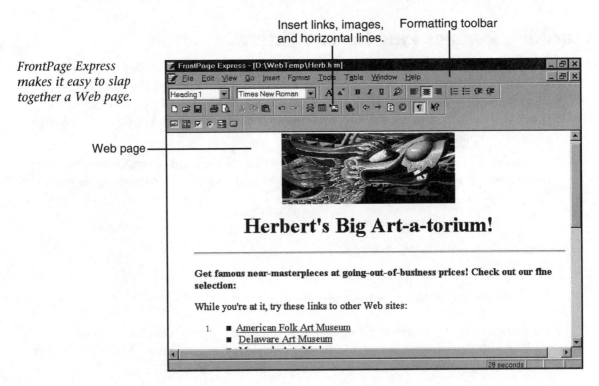

FrontPage Express makes it easy to slap together a Web page.

Insert links, images, and horizontal lines.

Formatting toolbar

Web page

With a page-layout program, you can format text, insert bulleted and numbered lists, add images, and even create your own links. The menus and toolbars contain many of the same formatting commands that you find in a standard word-processing program. The following are a few tips:

➤ To create a link, highlight the text or image that you want to appear as the link, click the button for inserting a link, and then specify the address to which you want the link to point. When typing a Web page address, add **http://** at the beginning of the address.

➤ Save your Web page and all graphic, audio, and video files in a single folder. This makes it easier to place the page on the Web.

➤ To simplify page layout, create a table and insert text and images in the table's cells. This makes it much easier to align text and graphics on your page.

➤ Check the Format menu for additional options, such as picking a page background and specifying text color and the color of links.

➤ Check the Insert menu for options that enable you to insert additional objects, including horizontal lines, links, video clips, and animated text.

After you create your Web page, you can publish it by placing it on the Web. Find out from your Internet service provider what you must do to publish your Web page. (If you use a commercial online service, such as America Online, check the help system.) You must know the address of the FTP or Web server on which the service provider wants you to place your files, the directory or folder on that server, and the address of your Web page so that you can check it out after posting it. Most service providers also give you a limited amount of storage space; know the limit.

FrontPage Express and Netscape Navigator have tools to help you copy (upload) your Web page to the specified server:

➤ In FrontPage Express, you can use the File, Save As command to run Web Post, but it's pretty complicated. Instead, save your Web page, close FrontPage Express, and use the Web Publishing Wizard. Choose **Start, Programs, Internet Explorer, Web Publishing Wizard**. Follow the onscreen instructions.

Free Web Page Homes Fire up your Web browser and use your favorite Web search tool to look for sites that allow users to publish their Web pages for free. Also, try GeoCities at **www.geocities.com**, a popular place for vagrant pages to hang out. When you find a home for your page, read the instructions carefully. Some sites have convoluted procedures for posting Web pages.

➤ In Netscape Composer, open the **File** menu and choose **Publish**. The Publish dialog box prompts you to enter a page title, the address of the FTP or Web server, and your username and password. Enter the requested information and click **OK**. (If you are uploading to an FTP server, type **ftp://** before its address; use **http://** for a Web server.)

Tech Check

The Web can be a very scary place, especially if you try to do too much with your Web browser. To live through your first encounter, stick with Internet Explorer, and make sure you can do the following:

➤ Run your Web browser.

➤ Navigate the Web with links and the Back and Forward button.

➤ Open a specific Web page by entering its address.

➤ Find information using an Internet search tool.

➤ Find yourself or someone else on the Web.

➤ Mark a page as a favorite.

➤ Subscribe to a Web site and view its content offline.

➤ Channel surf the Web.

Chapter 22

Email: Postage Free, Same-Day Delivery

In This Chapter

➤ Send email messages to your friends and relatives

➤ Read and reply to incoming email messages

➤ Attach files to outgoing messages

➤ Follow proper email etiquette

Over the last 10 years, the United States Postal Service has taken some lumps. Criticized for slow delivery and high rates, the postal service has lost ground to competitors such as UPS and Federal Express. It has tried to battle back by charging less (for packages, anyway), improving service, and airing corny commercials on TV and radio.

The postal service cannot, however, battle its fiercest and most silent competitor, email. Email enables anyone with an Internet connection to send a message anywhere in the world and have it reach its destination in a matter of seconds or minutes, instead of days. Sure, you still need the postal service to haul your other parcels, but for typed messages and computer files, email can run circles around any postal service on the planet. It's a lot cheaper, too.

In this chapter, you learn how to use an email program to quickly send, receive, and read email messages.

Ugh! Setting Up Your Email Program

Which Email Program? This chapter focuses on Outlook Express, the email program included with Internet Explorer 4, and Netscape Messenger, which is included with Netscape Communicator 4. If you are using a different version of one of these programs or a different email program, some of the options described in this chapter may differ; however, the steps for sending and receiving email are similar for most email programs.

The hardest part about email is getting your email program to connect to your Internet service provider's email server, which acts as an electronic post office. If you are using one of the major commercial online services, such as America Online or CompuServe, you can relax—the installation program took care of all the details for you. You simply click the email button and start using it.

If you have a local service provider, however, and are using a dedicated email program, such as Microsoft's Outlook Express or Netscape Messenger, then you must first enter information telling your email program how to connect to the mail server. Make sure that you have the following information from your service provider:

Email Address Your email address is usually all lowercase and starts with your first initial and last name (for example, **jsmith@iway.com**). If, however, your name is John Smith (or Jill Smith), you might have to use something more unique, such as **JohnHubertSmith@iway.com**.

Outgoing Mail (SMTP) Short for Simple Mail Transfer Protocol, the SMTP server is the mailbox into which you drop your outgoing messages. It's actually your Internet service provider's computer. The address usually starts with mail (for example, **mail.iway.com** or **smtp.iway.com**).

Incoming Mail (POP3) Short for Post Office Protocol, the POP server is like your neighborhood post office. It receives incoming messages and places them in your personal mailbox. The address usually starts with pop (for example, **pop.iway.com**).

Account This one is tricky; it could be your username—the name you use to log in to your service provider (for example, **jsmith**), or something entirely different.

Password Typically, you use the same password for logging on and for checking email. I can't help you here; you picked the password.

After you have the information, you must enter it into your email program. The following sections show you how to enter email connection settings in Outlook Express and Netscape Messenger.

Entering Email Settings in Outlook Express

Before you can enter connection settings, you must run Outlook Express. Click the **Outlook Express** icon on the Windows desktop or in the Quick Launch toolbar, or run the program from the **Start**, **Programs**, **Internet Explorer** menu.

When you first run Outlook Express, the Internet Connection Wizard starts and steps you through the process of entering the required information. Just follow the onscreen instructions. If the Internet Connection Wizard does not start, or you need to enter information for a different email account, open the **Tools** menu and select **Accounts**. Click the **Add** button and choose **Mail**.

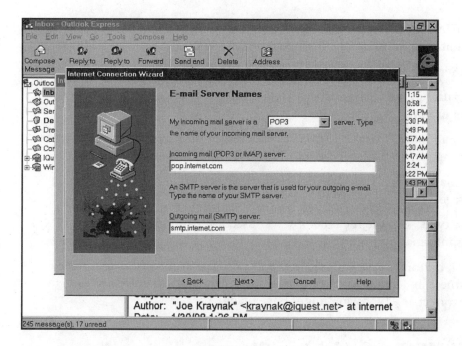

Before you can use Outlook Express, you must enter connection settings.

Entering Email Settings in Netscape Messenger

To enter the connection settings in Netscape Messenger, first run the program. Click **Start**, **Programs**, **Netscape Communicator**, **Netscape Messenger**. You can also run Messenger from Navigator by opening the **Communicator** menu and choosing **Messenger Mailbox**. After it's running, take the following steps to enter the settings for your mail server:

1. Open the **Edit** menu and select **Preferences**.

2. Click the plus sign next to **Mail & Groups** to display a list of categories.

255

3. Click **Identity**, and enter the following information in the Identity panel:

    Your name   This is your legal name or nickname (for example, **Nyce&EZ**).

    Email address   This is the address people use to write to you or to respond to your messages.

    Reply-to address   If you want people to reply to an email address other than the email address you entered above (for instance, if you have two email accounts), enter the preferred email address here.

    Organization   If you work for a company or run your own business, you can enter its name here.

    Signature File   A signature is a file you create (typically in a text editor) that includes additional information about you, or a clever quote. You can skip this.

4. Click **Mail Server** and enter the following information in the Mail Server panel:

    Mail server user name   This is the username you use to log on to your Internet account (for example, **jsmith**).

    Outgoing mail (SMTP) server   This is the address of the server in charge of handling outgoing mail.

    Incoming mail server   This is the address of the server that handles incoming email messages.

    Mail Server type   Choose the type of server used for incoming mail—POP or IMAP. Obtain this information from your service provider.

5. Click the **OK** button to save your settings and close the dialog box. If you have trouble connecting to your mail server later, perform these same steps to change settings or correct any typos you might have made.

Sending Mail Without Licking Stamps

The procedure for sending messages over the Internet varies, depending on the email program or online service that you're using. In most cases, you first enter a command for composing a new message. For example, in Outlook Express, you click the **New Message** button. A dialog box or window appears, prompting you to compose your message.

You type the person's email address, a brief description of the message, and the contents of the message in the appropriate text boxes. You can then click the **Send** button. Some email programs immediately send the message. Other programs place the messages you send in a temporary outbox; you must then enter another Send command to actually send the messages. For example, in Outlook Express, you click the **Send and Receive** button. Outlook Express then sends all messages from the Outbox and checks for incoming messages.

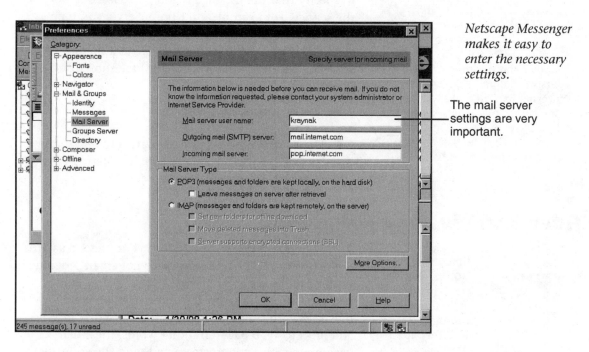

Netscape Messenger makes it easy to enter the necessary settings.

The mail server settings are very important.

Click here to send the message.   Type the person's email address here.

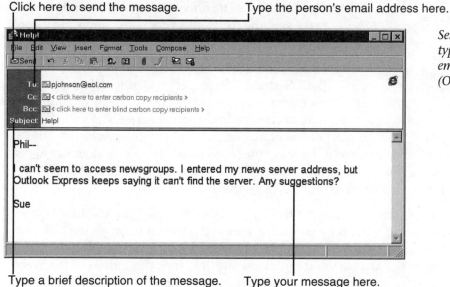

Sending mail with a typical Internet email program (Outlook Express).

Type a brief description of the message.   Type your message here.

257

Email Address Links On many Web pages, the creator may place a link at the bottom of the page that enables you to quickly send the person an email message. In Internet Explorer and Netscape Navigator, if you click such a link, the email program starts automatically and displays the window for composing a message. It even inserts the person's email address for you.

If you're sending messages from a commercial online service, such as Prodigy or America Online, you have to specify that the message is going to someone outside the service. For example, on CompuServe, you type **INTERNET:** before the email address. If you were sending a message from CompuServe to a member of America Online, the address might look something like this:

INTERNET: jsmith@aol.com

Check your online service's help system to determine whether there's anything quirky about entering email addresses.

Advanced Message Formatting

Email Address Books Most email programs, including Outlook Express and Netscape Messenger, include email address books. Instead of typing the person's email address, you simply select it from a list. To quickly display the address book, press **Ctrl+Shift+B** in Outlook Express or **Ctrl+Shift+2** in Messenger.

Although you rarely need to adorn your messages with fancy text or pictures, the new breed of email programs enable you to use special type styles and sizes, add backgrounds, insert pictures, and embellish your messages with other formatting options. You can even add links to Web pages! In other words, the email program enables you to create and send the equivalent of a Web page. The only trouble is that you have to make sure the recipient's email program is capable of displaying the formats that you add; otherwise, the person may receive a message packed with funky codes.

Both Netscape Messenger and Outlook Express offer a toolbar that contains buttons for the most common enhancements. In Outlook Express, shown below, you can use the toolbar to make text bold or italic, add bulleted and numbered lists, and insert pictures, horizontal lines, links, and other objects. (If the toolbar does not appear, check the format menu for an HTML option. HTML stands for *HyperText Markup Language*, the coding system used to format Web pages.)

You may have used similar formatting tools in Chapter 11, "Sprucing Up Your Documents with Formatting." The only new thing here is the button for inserting links. To insert a link that points to a Web page, you drag over the text that you want to appear as the link. You then click the button for inserting the link, type the address of the Web page to which you want it to point, and click **OK**. You can also drag links from a Web page into the message area and plop them right down in the message area.

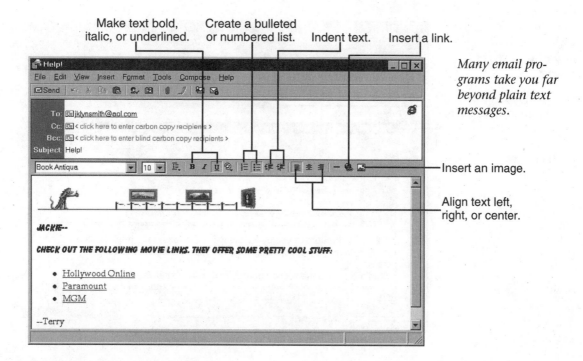

Make text bold, italic, or underlined.

Create a bulleted or numbered list.

Indent text.

Insert a link.

Many email programs take you far beyond plain text messages.

Insert an image.

Align text left, right, or center.

Checking Your Inbox

Whenever someone sends you an email message, it doesn't just pop up on your screen. The message sits on your service provider's mail server until you connect and retrieve your messages. There's no trick to connecting to the mail server, as long as you entered the connection information correctly. Most programs check for messages automatically on start up or display a button that you can click to fetch your mail. The program retrieves your mail and then displays a list of message descriptions. To read a message, you click its description. In most programs, you can double-click a message description to view the message in its own window.

To reply to a message in most email programs, you click the **Reply** or **Respond To** button. This opens a window that automatically inserts the person's email address and a description of the message. Many email programs also quote the contents of the previous message, so the recipient can easily follow the conversation. To indicate that text has been quoted, email programs typically add a right angle bracket (>) at the beginning of each quoted line. To respond, type your message in the message area, and then click the **Send** button.

*You can quickly
display the contents
of messages you
receive.*

Double-click the
message description.

The message appears
in its own window.

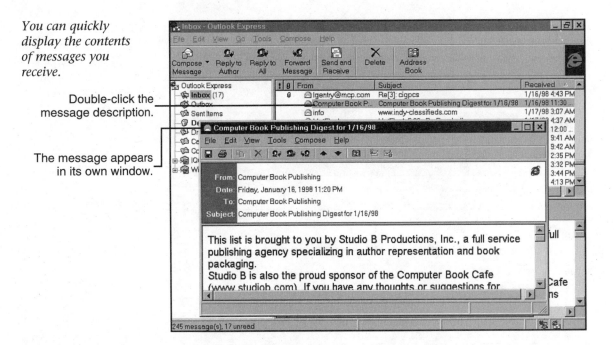

Exchanging Files via Email

Most email messages are nothing more than three or four lines of text saying very little. People shoot these terse missives back and forth like volleys of buckshot. Sometimes, however, you want to send something more substantial, perhaps an outline for a book, a graphic image of yourself, or a copy of an article you found on the Web. Whatever the case, you can send files along with your messages by creating *attachments*. The process is fairly simple, but the steps vary depending on which email program you use. In most email programs, you perform the same steps that you take for composing and addressing the message. You then click a button (for example, Attach or Insert File). This displays a dialog box that enables you to select the file that you want to send. The dialog box looks just like the dialog box you use to open files. Change to the folder that contains the file you want to send and then double-click the file's name. (In some programs, you can attach more than one file.) When you are ready to send the message, along with the attachment, simply click the **Send** button.

If you receive a message that contains an attached file, your email program usually displays some indication that a file is attached. For example, Outlook Express displays a paper clip icon. If you double-click the message (to display it in its own window), an icon appears at the bottom of the window. You can double-click the icon to open the file, or right-click and choose **Save** to save the file to a separate folder on your hard drive.

Virus Concerns

If you receive a program file from someone you don't know, be careful about running the program; it might contain a virus. If you want to run the program file, be sure to check it first with an anti-virus program. (See Chapter 25, "Online Security Issues" for details.)

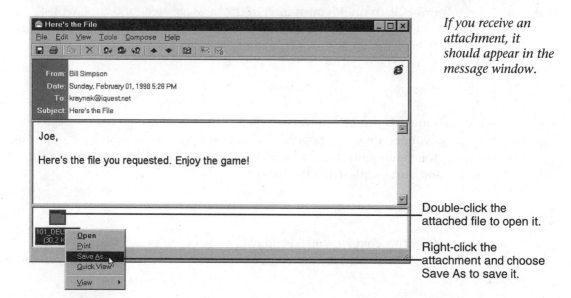

If you receive an attachment, it should appear in the message window.

Double-click the attached file to open it.

Right-click the attachment and choose Save As to save it.

Putting Your Name on a Listserv Mailing List

Many professional organizations, clubs, and special interest groups communicate using automated mailing lists, called *listservs*. On a listserv, a member sends an email message to the listserv, which automatically compiles all the messages it receives and then distributes the compilation to all members of the listserv. (The listserv may be moderated to screen out some messages, making it less automated.)

To find a listserv that interests you, fire up your Web browser and open a Web search tool (for example, **www.lycos.com**). Type a word or two that describes your interest and then tack on **listserv**, **mailing list**, or **mail**. For example, you might type **dog listserv**. Click the **Search** or **Find** button. The results should provide plenty of links to appropriate listservs.

Many listservs have their own special instructions for subscribing and unsubscribing. If you have the instructions, read and follow them. You should also write them down, print them, or save them to your disk so that you know how to unsubscribe later. If you don't have instructions, you can usually perform the following steps to subscribe to an automated listserv:

1. Compose a new email message addressed to the listserv. (Most listservs have a subscription address and a posting address. Be sure to use the subscription address.)

2. Leave the Subject or message description text box blank.

3. Type **subscribe [listname] [yourname]** in the message area (of course, replace [listname] with the name of the mailing list and [yourname] with your name, no brackets). If the listserv has only one mailing list, you may be able to omit the listname.

4. Send the message.

You receive mailing lists just as you receive email messages, although the message contents are typically much longer. A popular mailing list may contain hundreds of postings. In many cases, the mailing list itself includes instructions at the top or bottom on how to post messages and unsubscribe from the list.

Tech Check

As you have seen in this chapter, email is probably one of the easiest features of the Internet to master. Before you become too overconfident, however, make sure you can do the following:

➤ Enter the settings that your email program requires in order to connect to your email server.

➤ Send an email message to someone, assuming you know the person's email address.

➤ Retrieve email messages and display their contents.

➤ Quickly reply to a message you received.

➤ Attach a file to an outgoing message.

➤ Save a file that's attached to a message you received.

➤ Find a mailing list that interests you and subscribe to it.

Chapter 23

Passing Notes in Newsgroups

In This Chapter

➤ Tell the difference between a newsgroup and a coffee klatch with Connie Chung, Dan Rather, and Tom Brokaw

➤ View a list of more than 20,000 newsgroups

➤ Figure out what's in a newsgroup by looking at its name

➤ Connect to and read messages in at least five newsgroups

You would think that a newsgroup would consist of a bunch of guys with typewriters sitting around smoking cigars and typing news stories. Well, newsgroups aren't quite like that. A newsgroup is more like a bulletin board where people can share ideas, post questions and answers, and support one another. They're more like *discussion groups*, and people are beginning to call them that.

The Internet has thousands of these newsgroups, covering topics that range from computer programming to cooking, from horses to cars, from politics to tattoos. With your Internet connection and a newsreader, you have access to newsgroups 24 hours a day, 7 days a week. In this chapter, you learn how to connect to these newsgroups, subscribe to the newsgroups that interest you, and read and post newsgroup messages.

Setting Up Your Newsreader

Usenet If you've ever heard the term *Usenet* bandied about and were curious, it's the formal name of the network used to exchange messages in newsgroups. Usenet is short for user's network.

You can't read newsgroup messages with your Web browser. You need a program called a newsreader, whose sole purpose is to connect to newsgroups and display messages. This chapter focuses on Outlook Express, the email program included with Internet Explorer 4, and Netscape Collabra, included with Netscape Communicator 4. If you are using a different version of one of these programs or a different newsreader, some of the options described in this chapter may differ.

To access newsgroups, you must first set up your newsreader to connect to your service provider's news server. This consists of entering the news server's address, as explained in the following sections.

Entering Connection Settings in Outlook Express

You may have already encountered Outlook Express in the preceding chapter. This program also moonlights as a newsreader. To run it, click its icon on the Windows desktop or in the Quick Launch bar, or choose **Start**, **Programs**, **Internet Explorer**, **Outlook Express**.

The first time you start Outlook Express, it displays the Internet Connection Wizard. This wizard leads you step-by-step through the process of connecting you to your service provider's news server, the computer that shovels newsgroup messages into your computer. Follow the instructions to specify the address of your service provider's news server. If you don't know the address, stick **news** at the beginning of your service provider's domain name. For example, if your service provider's domain name is **internet.com**, the news server address would likely be **news.internet.com**. If the Internet Connection Wizard does not start, or you need to enter information for a different email account, open the **Tools** menu and select **Accounts**. Click the **Add** button and choose **News**.

Although the wizard takes care of most of the details for you, check your news account settings. Open the **Tools** menu, select **Accounts**, click the **News** tab, and double-click your news server. Check your user information on the **General** tab. Also check the **Server Timeouts** setting on the **Advanced** tab. You usually need to crank up the Timeouts setting to two minutes; otherwise, Outlook Express has trouble staying connected to the news server when it's getting the list of available newsgroups.

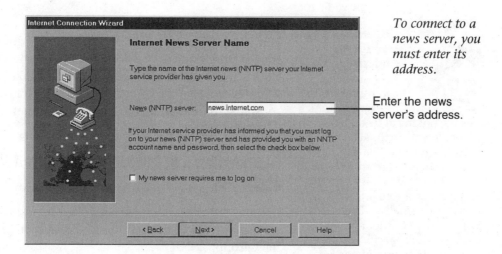

To connect to a news server, you must enter its address.

Enter the news server's address.

Entering Connection Settings in Netscape Collabra

To enter connection settings in Netscape Messenger, first run the program. Choose **Start**, **Programs**, **Netscape Communicator**, **Netscape Collabra**. You can also run Messenger from Navigator by opening the **Communicator** menu and choosing **Collabra Discussion Groups**. After it's running, take the following steps to specify the news server you want to use:

1. Open the **Edit** menu and select **Preferences**.

2. Click the plus sign next to **Mail & Groups** to expand the list of preferences, if necessary.

3. Click **Groups Server**.

4. Double-click the **Discussion Groups (News) Server** text box, and type the address of your news server (for example, **news.internet.com**).

5. Click the **OK** button to save your settings and close the dialog box. If you have trouble connecting to your news server later, perform these same steps to change settings or correct any typos that you might have made.

Accessing Newsgroups from Your Web Browser In Netscape Navigator or Internet Explorer, if you click a link to a newsgroup or type its address (for example, **news// :alt.binaries.raccoons**), the Web browser automatically runs the newsreader and connects you to that newsgroup.

Subscribing to Newsgroups (It's Free!)

Before you can start reading messages about do-it-yourself tattoos or other topics of interest, you must download a list of the newsgroups that are available on your news

Check This Out...

Dissecting Newsgroup Addresses You can usually determine a newsgroup's focus by looking at its address. Most addresses are made up of two or three parts. The first part indicates the newsgroup's overall subject area; for example, **rec** is for recreation, and **alt** stands for alternative. The second part of the address indicates, more specifically, what the newsgroup offers. For example, **rec.arts** is about the arts. If the address has a third part (most do), it focuses even more sharply. For example, **rec.arts.bodyart** discusses the art of tattoos and other body decorations.

server and subscribe to the newsgroups that interest you. Your newsreader might automatically download the list the first time you connect. Be patient: Even over a fairly quick modem connection, it may take several minutes to download this very long list. You can then subscribe to newsgroups to create a list of newsgroups that interest you.

Subscribe to Newsgroups in Outlook Express

If you're using Outlook Express, take the following steps to display a list of newsgroups and to subscribe to a newsgroup:

1. At the bottom of the folder list (left pane), click the name of your news server.

2. Click the **Newsgroups** button in the toolbar. The Newsgroups dialog box appears, displaying a list of available newsgroups. (You can update the list at any time by clicking the **Reset List** button.)

3. In the **Display Newsgroups Which Contain** text box, type a topic (for example, **cats**). This filters the list to show only those newsgroups that have cats in their name.

4. Double-click the name of the newsgroup to which you want to subscribe. A newspaper icon appears next to the name. (You can unsubscribe by double-clicking the newsgroup's name again.)

5. Repeat steps 3 and 4 to subscribe to additional newsgroups and then click the **OK** button.

6. In the folder list (left pane), click the plus sign next to your news server to display a list of subscribed newsgroups.

7. Click the newsgroup's name to display a list of posted messages in the upper-right pane.

Subscribe to Newsgroups in Netscape Collabra

If Netscape Collabra is your newsreader of choice, take the following steps to download a list of available newsgroups and to subscribe to the ones that interest you:

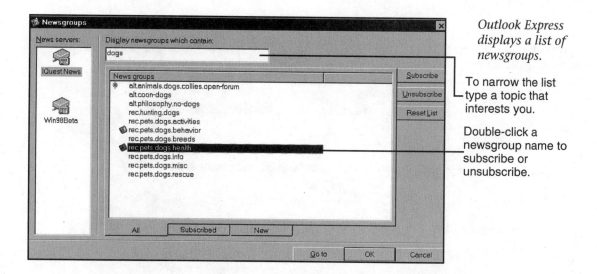

Outlook Express displays a list of newsgroups.

To narrow the list type a topic that interests you.

Double-click a newsgroup name to subscribe or unsubscribe.

1. Click the **Subscribe** button in Collabra's toolbar. The Subscribe to Discussion Groups dialog box appears, and Collabra starts to download newsgroup names from your news server. This process may take several minutes. (You might have to click the **Get Groups** button to prompt Collabra to start downloading the list of newsgroups.)

2. If a newsgroup has a plus sign next to its name, you can click the plus sign to display additional newsgroups under this heading. You can display all the subgroups by clicking the **Expand All** button. (Note that Collabra displays a number next to each newsgroup indicating the number of messages in the newsgroup.)

3. Click the name of the newsgroup to which you want to subscribe, and click the **Subscribe** button or the dot in the Subscribe column next to the desired newsgroup. The dot changes into a check mark, indicating that you have subscribed to the newsgroup.

4. Click the **OK** button to return to the Message Center window.

5. Click the plus sign next to your news server. The Message Center displays the names of all the newsgroups to which you subscribed.

6. Double-click a newsgroup's name to display a list of messages posted in that newsgroup.

Click the dot to subscribe.

You can subscribe to newsgroups to make them more accessible.

Click a plus sign to view subgroups.

Click a minus sign to hide the list of subgroups.

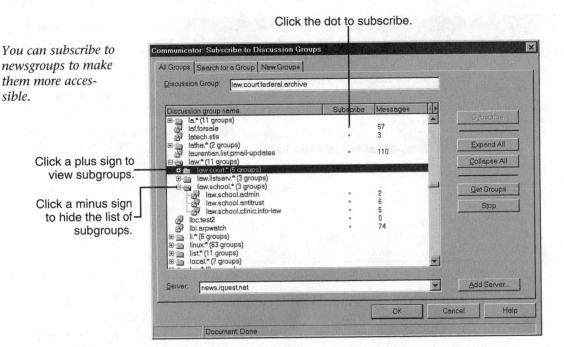

Reading and Responding to Posted Messages

Although the names of newsgroups can provide hours of entertainment by themselves, you didn't connect to a news server just to chuckle at the weirdos (well, maybe you did). You connected to read what people have to say and to post your own messages. If you used Outlook Express or Netscape Messenger to read email messages in the previous chapter, you find that the steps for reading newsgroup postings are similar:

1. Click the plus sign next to your news server's name to display a list of subscribed newsgroups.

2. Click or double-click the name of the desired newsgroup. Descriptions of posted messages appear.

3. Click a description to display the message contents in the message pane, or double-click the message to display it in its own window.

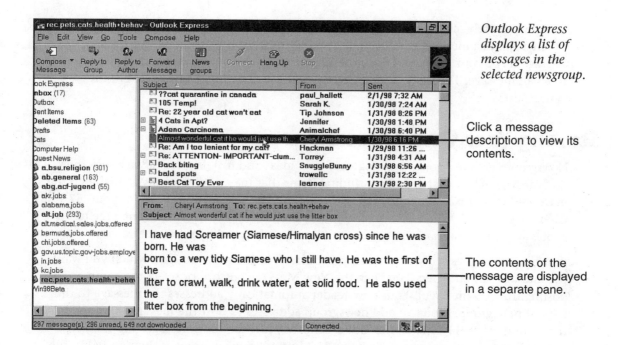

Outlook Express displays a list of messages in the selected newsgroup.

Click a message description to view its contents.

The contents of the message are displayed in a separate pane.

Following a Meandering Discussion

As people post messages and replies, they end up creating discussions. Most newsreaders are capable of displaying related messages as *threads*, so you can follow the discussion from its beginning to its end. If you see a message that has a plus sign next to it, you can click the plus sign to view a list of replies to the original message. You can then click the reply descriptions to view the contents of the replies.

Replying Publicly and Privately

When you read a message that inspires you to write a reply, you have two choices: You can reply to the group by posting your reply in the newsgroup, or you can reply to the individual via email. Some people request that you reply via email for privacy or just because they're too lazy to check for replies in the newsgroup itself.

In Outlook Express, you can reply to the group by clicking the **Reply to Group** button. This displays a window that addresses the message to the current newsgroup and to any other newsgroups in which the original message was posted. It also quotes the contents of the original message. (If the original message was long, you should delete some of the quoted material.) Type your reply, and click the **Post Message** button.

To reply privately, click the **Reply to Author** button. This starts your email program, which displays a message window addressed to the person who posted the original message. Type your reply, and click the **Send** button, as you would normally do to send an email message. The reply is sent directly to the author and is not posted in the newsgroup.

Starting Your Own Discussions

Newsgroups are great for expressing your own ideas and insights, for having your questions answered by experts, and for finding items that may not be readily available in the mass market (for example, books that are no longer in publication, parts for your '57 Chevy, and so on). When you need help, or you just feel the overwhelming urge to express yourself, you can start your own discussion by posting a message.

Posting a message is fairly easy: First, you connect to the newsgroup in which you want the message posted. Then, you click the **New Message** button (or select the command for posting the new message). Your newsreader automatically addresses the message to the current newsgroup. (You can add newsgroup addresses to post the message in other newsgroups as well.) Type a brief, but descriptive, title for your message, and then type the contents of your message. Click the **Post** button. Your message is then posted in the newsgroup, where anyone can read it. It may take awhile for people to reply, so check back every couple of days for responses. (Sometimes, nobody responds, so don't expect too much.)

You can start a discussion by posting your own message.

The newsreader addresses the message to the current newsgroup.

Type a brief description here.

Type the contents of the message.

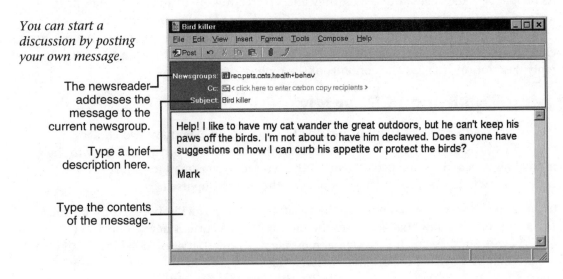

270

Tech Check

Hanging out in newsgroups can be fun. You get to see what everyone is talking about without having to watch "Oprah." To take advantage of newsgroups, you must be able to do the following:

➤ Set up your newsreader to connect to a news server.

➤ Download a list of newsgroups.

➤ Subscribe to newsgroups that interest you.

➤ Display the contents of a message posted to a newsgroup.

➤ Reply to a message publicly or privately.

➤ Start your own newsgroup discussion.

Attaching Files Most newsreaders enable you to attach files to your messages. Although most messages consist of simple text, people post graphics in some newsgroups, such as **hk.binaries.portrait.photography**. (For details on how to work with file attachments, refer to Chapter 22, "Email: Postage Free, Same-Day Delivery.")

Chapter 24

Reaching Out with Chat and Internet Phone

In This Chapter

➤ Type messages back and forth with people you've never met

➤ Prowl cyberrooms when you can't sleep

➤ Chat on the Web

➤ Use special chat programs

➤ Pretend you're someone you're not to someone else who's pretending, too

The Internet has revolutionized the way that we communicate. We correspond with email, hang messages in newsgroups, and read magazines on the Web. But that's just the standard fare. The Internet also offers more dynamic and immediate forms of communication through online chat, Internet phone, and collaboration tools (for holding virtual meetings). This chapter provides a tour of these innovative tools and shows you how to start using them.

Chatting on the Web

Many companies on the Internet have realized that chat sells. If you set up a wide selection of high-quality chat rooms, people gather to hang out and jabber. They are then more likely to visit other areas of the Web site, where they learn more about the company's products and services, and possibly buy something—or so goes the theory.

Chatting It Up at Yahoo!

What's Java? Java is a programming language that makes it possible for Web developers to create programs that run on Web pages. What has made Java so popular is that the same Java program runs on any computer (for instance, a PC or a Macintosh). All the computer needs is a Java-enabled Web browser to interpret the programming code.

Yahoo! has always been considered a premier Internet search site. Now, Yahoo! has injected its power and simplicity into Internet chat. All you need to access Yahoo! Chat is a Web browser that supports Java (most Web browsers do).

To sign up for Yahoo! Chat, use Internet Explorer to pull up Yahoo!'s home page at **www.yahoo.com**, and then click the **Chat** link near the top of the page. Onscreen instructions walk you through the process of registering and entering a chat room on the Yahoo! chat site.

After you are in a chat room, you can start chatting. The ongoing discussion is displayed in the large frame in the upper left. To send a message to the other chatters, click inside the Chat text box just below the ongoing discussion, type your message, and press **Enter**. When you tire of this simple banter, try the following:

Yahoo! Chat brings chat to the Web.

Messages from all chatters appear here.

Type your messages here and press Enter.

Yahoo! Chat toolbar

List of people in the chat room

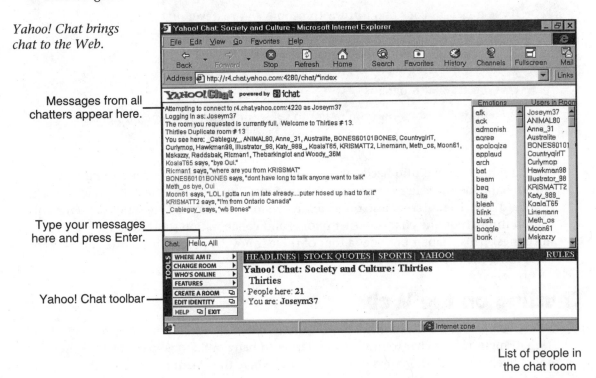

➤ Double-click an emotion in the pane just to the right of the discussion pane. This sends a text description of your gesture.

➤ Click the name of someone in the room. This displays a dialog box, which enables you to find out more about the person, send the person a private message or a file, start following the person (if the person changes rooms), or ignore the person (prevent the person's messages from appearing on your screen). "afk" means away from keyboard.

➤ In the lower-left corner of the window is a list of tools. Click a tool to change to a different chat room, find out who's online, create your own room (public or private), edit your identity, get help, or exit. (You can edit your identity to provide additional information about yourself. Other chatters then see this information if they check your profile.)

> **Going Private** If you hit it off with someone online or just want to chat with a friend or relative in private, you can create a private room, whose name does not appear in the Yahoo! rooms list. To enter the room, someone who knows your chat name has to follow you into the room. If you are invited to a private room, here's what you do to go there: Type **goto roomname** in the text box where you type messages, and press **Enter**. A room ceases to exist as soon as everyone leaves—no post-party cleanup!

Other Web Chat Areas

Although Yahoo! is on the cutting edge of Web chat, you can try some other Web chat services. Most of these services offer access via Java, an ActiveX control, or a plug-in. The following list provides an overview of some of these chat areas, along with a page address showing where to go for additional information:

talk.com (www.hotwired.com/talk) is a place where the Internet elite and anyone else who wants some edgy chat can gather to gab. This chat area has been set up by *HotWired* magazine, one of the best Internet/computer magazines around, providing honest insights into the computer industry, complete with a healthy dose of skepticism. When you connect, you are prompted to load the ActiveX control. After doing so, double-click **Enter** to log in and start chatting.

WorldVillage Chat (www.worldvillage.com/wv/chat/html/chat2.htm) is a family-oriented chat area that offers access via IRC (discussed later in this chapter) on the Web. You find that it is very similar to Yahoo! Chat. After connecting, make sure that you select the **JavaChat** option. It takes about two to three minutes to download the required Java applet.

Check This Out...

Find More Chat Rooms You can find more places to chat on the Web at Yahoo!. Search Yahoo! for **web chat**, and then select the Web Chat category. You find more than a hundred chat offerings, each offering a wide selection of chat rooms. Some of the chat screens that you find, however, are not the best.

Chat Planet (www.chatplanet.com) is one of the largest chat areas on the Web. You have to follow a trail of links to the chat room that you want to enter. After you get there, the chat screen itself is fairly easy to navigate, but not very high-tech.

Using Special Chat Programs

Although Web chat is becoming more popular, you find more people chatting with specialized chat programs to access IRC (Internet Relay Chat). The following is a list of some of the better chat programs and information on where you can get them:

Microsoft Chat comes with Internet Explorer. To run it, choose **Start**, **Programs**, **Internet Explorer**, **Microsoft Chat**. Microsoft Chat displays each person as a character in a comic strip, which makes it a bit difficult to follow the conversation. Fortunately, you can turn off the comic strip view to display normal text messages.

mIRC is one of the most popular shareware IRC programs around, because it is so easy to use. It even comes with its own IRC primer to help new users get up to speed in a hurry. You can visit the mIRC home page at **www.geocities.com/ SiliconValley/Park/6000/index.html**, where you find a link for downloading it. (The file is self-extracting, so just double-click its icon after downloading it.)

Visual IRC is one of the best IRC programs around. It offers a basic chat screen that is easy to navigate and powerful features that you typically find only in an Internet phone program, including voice chat. You can download a free copy of Visual IRC and obtain additional information at **virc.melnibone.org**. (The program is in a compressed format, and you need WinZip to decompress it. You can get WinZip at **www.winzip.com**.)

After you install a chat program, establish your Internet connection and then run the chat program. You must then use the program to connect to a chat server and pick the desired chat room. The following sections show you what to expect.

Connecting to a Chat Server

Before you can start chatting, you must connect to a *chat server* (a computer on the Internet specialized for handling IRC). The chat server to which you connect is connected to other chat servers to form a *network* (such as EFnet or Undernet). The chat rooms on a particular network are available to everyone who connected to that network, even if they are connected to different servers.

Most IRC programs prompt you to select a server on startup. A dialog box appears, typically offering a drop-down list of available servers. You select the desired server from the list, enter your name, email address, and other information, and then click the **OK** or **Connect** button to connect to the server. If the IRC program does not prompt you to choose an IRC server, scan the button bar or the menu system for the required command.

Don't be surprised if you can't connect to the first server you choose. Most Internet servers don't mind your flipping through Web pages and purloining the occasional file, but they don't like to devote their resources to a bunch of chatty slackers. If you can't connect to a particular server, try a different one.

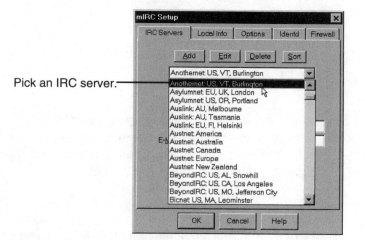

Pick an IRC server.

Most IRC programs prompt you to select a server at startup.

Entering and Leaving Chat Rooms

As soon as you connect to a chat server, your chat program downloads a list of the available chat rooms (sometimes called *channels*) and prompts you to pick one. If the list doesn't pop up on your screen, check the button bar or menu system for the command to display the list of available rooms.

In most cases, the list displays the room name and the number of people in that room, to give you some idea of how popular it is. The list may also include a description of each room, if the person who created the room added a description. Simply

Switch Chat Servers If a chat server is on a network that does not provide the types of rooms that interest you, you can disconnect from the chat server and try one on a different network. The program's toolbar or menu system should have a command for disconnecting from the chat server.

double-click the desired room name or click the name and click the button for entering or joining the room.

The IRC program displays a list of available chat rooms or channels.

Pick a room.━

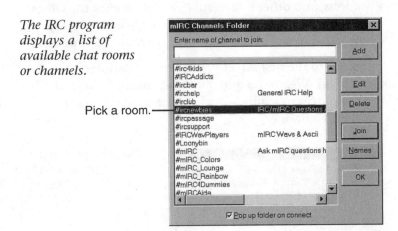

If you find that the current discussion doesn't appeal to you, you can leave the chat room. Check the toolbar or menu system for an Exit Room or comparable command, or click the chat window's Close (X) button. To enter a different room, enter the command to display the list of available rooms and then select the desired room.

Chat Away!

This is where the fun starts. In a room that's populated with talkative typists, messages scroll at a frenetic pace. The room may take on a party atmosphere, where two or three people in the room are carrying on their own conversation, completely oblivious to everyone else in the room. Just hang out for a while and watch the comments scroll past.

When you get a feel for the room, look for a text box for sending your own messages. The box is typically right below the area where the running discussion is displayed. Type your message and click the **Send** button or press **Enter**. Your message appears on your screen and on the screens of all the other people in the room.

The chat window displays a list of people currently in the chat room. In most cases, you can view information that the person entered about himself, send the person a private message or a file, or choose to ignore the person. Try right-clicking the person's name to view a context menu with the available options. If that doesn't work, try double-clicking the person's name. In most cases, double-clicking displays a dialog box for sending the person a private message.

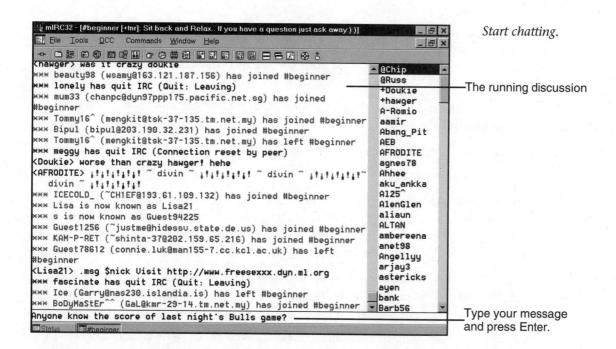

Start chatting.

The running discussion

Type your message and press Enter.

Free Long-Distance Calls with Internet Phone

The phone companies have been overcharging us for years, but they're starting to run scared. With the new Internet phone programs, you can place a long-distance call to anywhere in the world over your Internet connection for a lot less than a dime a minute.

What's the catch? Well, you can't just plug your phone into your modem and dial the number; you must have a special Internet phone program. You also need a sound card, speakers, a microphone, and the person you're calling must have a similar setup and be waiting for your call. You can't just place a call to a regular phone, unless you have access to a special server that enables this.

Assuming you have Internet Explorer or Netscape Communicator and the right hardware, you're all set to place some calls. Internet Explorer comes with an Internet phone program called NetMeeting, and Netscape Communicator includes Netscape Conference. If you don't have anyone to call, don't worry; you will find plenty of people on the Internet trying out this Internet phone thing who will answer your call, or even call you!

Placing a Call with NetMeeting

Run NetMeeting (choose **Start, Programs, Internet Explorer, Microsoft NetMeeting**). The first time you run NetMeeting, it runs a setup routine that asks you a series of questions, makes sure your sound card and microphone are operating properly, and enables you to enter additional settings. The setup routine asks whether you want your name listed on a user location server (ULS) so your friends and colleagues can figure out how to call you. If you know the ULS server that your friends and colleagues use, select it when prompted.

After you have configured NetMeeting for your system and selected a ULS server, take the following steps to call someone:

1. Establish your Internet connection and run NetMeeting.

2. Click the **Directory** tab.

3. Open the **Server** drop-down list, and select the ULS you want to use. NetMeeting logs on to the server and displays a list of all the people on the server. If a red asterisk appears in the left column, the person is already participating in a call. Additional icons indicate whether the person is using an audio or video connection.

4. To filter the list, you can choose an option from the Category drop-down list. For example, you can choose to view a list of only those people not participating in a call.

5. Scroll down the list, and double-click the person's name or right-click the person's name and select **Call**.

NetMeeting displays the names of people you can call.

Double-click the name of the person you want to call.

When you place a call, a dialog box pops up on the screen of the person that you called, and his or her computer rings. Assuming that the person you called wants to talk with you, he or she clicks the **Accept** button, and you can start talking. When you are done talking, click the **Hang Up** button on the toolbar.

Placing a Call with Conference

To run Conference, choose **Start, Programs, Netscape Communicator, Netscape Conference**. This starts Conference and runs the Setup Wizard, which leads you through the process of configuring Conference to work with your sound card, speakers, microphone, and modem. This is a one-time deal, so don't fret. Just follow the onscreen instructions, and keep clicking the **Next>** button.

Check This Out...

Dialing a Person's Email Address If the person is not logged on to the same ULS, you can search for the person via the person's email address. Open the **Call** menu and select **New Call**. In the **Address** text box, type the person's email address, and click the **Call** button.

To run Conference, follow these steps:

1. Connect to the Internet, and run Conference.

2. In the **Type in Email Address** text box, type the email address of the person you want to call. For example, you might type **jsmith@internet.com**. (If you don't have anyone to call, click the **Web Phonebook** button, choose a name from the Web page that appears, and skip the next step.)

3. Click the **Dial** button. Conference attempts to locate the person online and checks to determine whether the person has a compatible Internet phone program running. If the person is available, Conference displays an invitation on that person's screen.

4. If the person accepts your invitation and starts talking into her microphone, you are able to hear her voice. (At this point, the main Conference window is displayed on both your screen and the other person's screen.)

5. You can start talking, and he or she is able to hear your voice.

6. When you're ready to hang up, open the **Call** menu and click **Hang Up**.

If you have trouble hearing the other person (or if the other person has trouble hearing you), you can crank up the volume. To adjust the microphone volume, drag the little red dot under Microphone to the right to increase volume or to the left to decrease it. To adjust the volume of the other person's voice, drag the dot under Speaker.

Tech Check

You may not want to sell your telephone in a garage sale just yet, but this chapter showed you several phoneless ways to talk to your friends and relatives. You should be able to do the following:

➤ Connect to Yahoo! and start chatting without installing any additional programs.

➤ Find other places to chat on the Web.

➤ Download a specialized IRC program.

➤ Connect to a chat server.

➤ Enter a chat room or join a channel.

➤ Send a private message to a person in a chat room.

➤ Use NetMeeting or Conference to place a phone call over the Internet.

Online Security Issues

The Internet is no place for the paranoid. Files that you download and run could infect your system with a virus. Information that you enter on a form could be intercepted and read by some whiz-kid computer hacker, who might decide to make your life miserable. Your kids could just happen upon the Porn Central Web site.

Yes, all that is possible, but if you worry about all the things that could possibly go wrong, you never experience anything. The trick is to proceed with caution. In this chapter you learn how to enable a few safeguards to protect your data, your system, and your kids on the Internet so that you can experience the Internet completely and without worrying too much.

What Are the Risks of Going Online?

Can someone break into your computer, peek at your documents, read your email, and poke around in your financial records when you're wandering the Internet? Probably not, but the following are a few other things that you should look out for:

➤ **Forms**   Most forms that request sensitive data, such as a credit card number, are stored on secure Web servers. You can safely submit data using a secure form. (You learn later in this chapter how to determine whether a form is secure.)

➤ **Viruses**   A virus is programming code that either acts as a harmless prank or destroys data on your computer. Although ActiveX controls and Java applets are potential virus carriers, the most serious risk is posed by program files that you download, especially if you run a file that someone sent to you via email. (You learn some virus-prevention tactics later in this chapter.)

➤ **Offensive Material**   For the most part, the Internet is pretty clean; however, it does have its seedy side. If you have kids or a classroom of students, you can block access to the naughty stuff. (You learn how in this chapter.)

The Internet poses other security risks that you don't have much control over. For example, if your credit card company doesn't have a secure system, someone could break into the system and get information about you. Of course, people can get a lot of information about you by digging through your trash, listening in on your cellular phone calls, and posing as market researchers.

Can Someone Connect to My Computer?

People can connect to your computer in a couple of ways. If you set up your computer to answer the phone so that you can access it via modem from a remote location, someone else can call your computer, too. (You learn about remote computing in Chapter 29, "Life on the Run: Laptop Computing.") If the person can guess your password, he's in. Your computer may also be vulnerable if you are having an online conference with a program such as NetMeeting (covered in the previous chapter). NetMeeting has a program-sharing feature. If you allow someone to take control of your program during a conference, the person could delete files on your system.

Safely Exchanging Information on the Web

The biggest security worry on the Internet is the result of one of the biggest improvements on the Web—forms. Forms, such as the search forms used in Yahoo! or other search programs, enable you to enter information and receive feedback. They also enable you to order products, register your software, join clubs, and even play interactive games.

The problem with entering any personal information (including credit card numbers) on a form is that the information is not sent directly to the server where that information is used. Instead, the information bounces around from one server to another until it finds its destination. At any point in this little adventure, someone with the proper know-how can read the information. How often this happens, no one really knows, but it *can* happen, and that's the concern.

Most Web browsers, including Internet Explorer and Netscape Navigator, have warning messages that pop up whenever you are about to submit information using an insecure form. You can then cancel the operation before sending sensitive information. If you're just submitting a search phrase, you can cancel the warning and go ahead with the operation.

If you tire of these warning messages popping up on your screen, and you don't enter any sensitive information, you can deactivate the warnings. In most browsers, the warning dialog box contains an option for preventing the warning from appearing again. Even if you deactivate the warning messages, you have the following ways to determine whether you are using a secure form:

➤ If the Web page address starts with https instead of http, the site is secure.

➤ In Internet Explorer, look at the right end of the status bar at the bottom of the window. If you see a padlock icon, the site is secure.

➤ In Netscape Navigator, look at the lower-left corner of the window for a key icon. A broken key indicates that the site is not secure. A solid key with three teeth indicates a very secure site. A solid key with two teeth indicates that the site is fairly secure.

Credit Card Caution Anyone can stick a Visa or Mastercard logo on his Web page and pretend to be a legitimate business. Be careful when placing credit card orders. Restrict your purchases to brand-name sites until the credit card companies come up with some way to ensure security.

Preventing Viruses from Entering Your System

Picking up a virus on the Internet is like coming home from vacation and finding that someone has broken into your house and trashed it. You were having so much fun; how could this happen, and how can you prevent it from happening again? First, follow a few simple rules:

You can deactivate the warnings and still determine whether a site is secure.

https indicates that the site is secure.

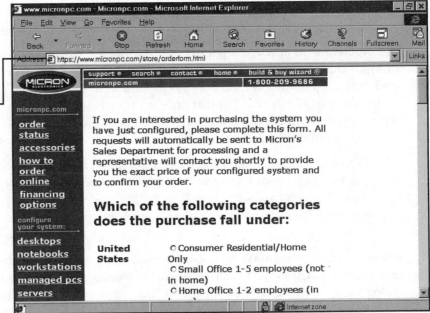

Look for the padlock icon.

➤ Download programs only from reputable and known sites. If you know the company that created the program, go to its Web page or FTP server and download the file from there. Most reputable sites regularly scan their systems to detect and eliminate viruses.

➤ Don't accept copies of a program from another person (for example, by email). Although the program may not have contained a virus when the other person downloaded it, the other person's computer may have a virus that infected the program. Ask the person where he or she got the file and then download the file from its original location yourself.

➤ Use your Web browser's security features, as explained in the following sections. Your Web browser can warn you if you are about to receive a component that could potentially contain a virus.

➤ Run an anti-virus program on a regular basis. By identifying and eliminating a virus early, you prevent it from causing additional damage. One of the best anti-virus programs on the market is McAfee VirusScan; you can download a trial version at **www.nai.com**. Symantec also offers an anti-virus program that works right alongside your Web browser, called Norton Safe on the Web. Go to **www.symantec.com** for details.

286

Running an infected program is the most common way you can introduce a virus into your system; however, the Internet poses some additional threats through programmed objects, such as Java applets and ActiveX components. Java is a more secure programming language than ActiveX, because it has built-in security features that prevent Java applets from performing destructive acts, such as deleting system files and reformatting your hard drive; however, clever hackers have proven that Java is not completely safe.

ActiveX is less secure because it places the security burden on you and relies on a system of certificates to help you determine whether the ActiveX component is safe. ActiveX components have no built-in security features that prevent the component from performing destructive acts. This makes ActiveX components powerful, but poses greater risks. Before downloading and installing an ActiveX component, your Web browser displays a dialog box indicating whether the component has been certified or not. If the component has not been certified, it's up to you to cancel the download.

Zoning In on Security in Internet Explorer

As you send data and receive active content on the Web, Internet Explorer supervises both your actions and the actions of the remote server and warns you of any risky activity. You can control these warnings by using Internet Explorer's security zones. Each zone has different security settings, enabling you to relax the security settings for sites that you trust and tighten security settings for untested sites or those that you don't trust. Internet Explorer offers the following four security zones:

➤ *Local intranet* enables your network administrator to set up a list of restricted Internet sites and enter security settings to prevent users throughout your company from accessing risky content.

➤ *Trusted sites* enables you to deactivate the security warnings for sites you trust. This prevents you from being inundated with warning messages at the sites you visit most frequently.

➤ *Internet* enables you to specify security settings for untested sites. When you wander off to sites that you do not frequent, you may want to tighten security.

➤ *Restricted sites* enables you to create a list of sites that you do not trust and tighten security for those sites. For example, you may want to prevent a particular site from automatically installing and running programs on your computer.

You can add sites to every zone except the Internet zone. To add a site to a zone, open the **View** menu, select **Internet Options**, and click the **Security** tab. Open the **Zone** drop-down list and choose the desired zone. Click the **Add Sites** button and enter the desired addresses. Click **OK** as needed to save your changes and close the dialog boxes.

You can select a
different security level
for each zone.

View a list of
security zones.

You can pick a
different security
level for each zone.

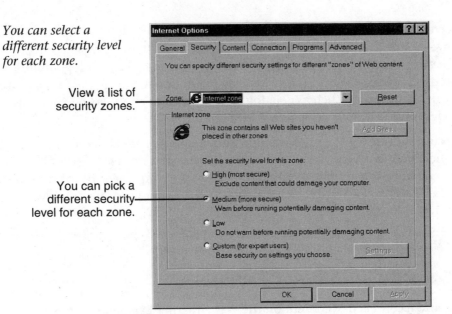

To specify a security level for a zone, open the **View** menu, select **Internet Options**, and click the **Security** tab. Open the **Zone** drop-down list, select the zone whose security level you want to change, and then select one of the following levels:

➤ **High** This prevents you from submitting any information by way of form, even a search form. If you complete a form and click the button to submit it, nothing happens. In addition, Internet Explorer won't play Java applets, download ActiveX controls, or transfer any other potentially harmful programs or scripts to your computer. The High setting is useful for sites that you place on the Restricted sites list.

➤ **Medium** This turns on prompts, so Internet Explorer displays dialog boxes whenever you attempt to send data or download scripts or other active content. The Medium setting is useful for the Internet zone, where you may want to be prompted before doing anything risky.

➤ **Low** Deactivates the prompts, allowing you to submit information using a form, and allowing sites to send you active content. The Low setting is good for trusted sites, where you are fairly certain that nothing bad is going to happen.

➤ **Custom** Allows you to enter specific security settings. For example, you may want to prevent active content from being automatically downloaded to your computer, but you don't want a dialog box popping up on your screen every time you fill out a form. If you select Custom, you can click the **Settings** button to enter your preferences.

Configuring Security Settings in Netscape Navigator

Navigator (Netscape Communicator's Web browser) stores its security settings in two places. To enter security settings for submitting information securely on the Web, click the **Security** button on the Navigation toolbar. Click **Navigator**. You can then select any of the following options to activate or deactivate them:

➤ **Entering an Encrypted Site**   Displays a warning whenever you view a Web page that complies with the latest security standards. Why would you activate this, I wonder?

➤ **Leaving an Encrypted Site**   This is another warning you can deactivate. If you're leaving, why do you care whether it's secure?

➤ **Viewing a Page with an Encrypted/Unencrypted Mix**   If part of the page is secure and another part isn't, you want to know about it. Activate this option.

➤ **Sending Unencrypted Information to a Site**   This is the option that makes the security warning pop up on your screen all the time. If you don't trust yourself, leave it activated.

➤ **Enable SSL v2**   Activates data encryption for Web pages protected with the Secure Sockets Layer (version 2) standard. Keep this activated so that when you do enter information on secure Web pages, that information is encoded.

➤ **Enable SSL v3**   Activates data encryption for Web pages protected with the Secure Sockets Layer (version 3) standard. Keep this option activated, too. This is the latest security standard from Netscape.

Security warning options

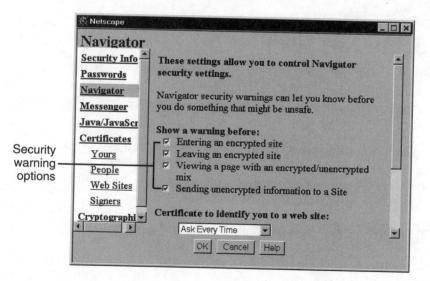

You can activate or deactivate the security warnings.

If desired, you can also disable Java and prevent Navigator from downloading and installing plug-ins automatically. Open the **Edit** menu, choose **Preferences**, and click **Advanced** (at the bottom of the left column). You can then uncheck any of the following options to disable active content:

Enable Java   Removing the check mark prevents Navigator from playing Java applets.

Enable JavaScript   Deactivating this prevents Navigator from playing JavaScripts embedded on Web pages. Although JavaScript is less likely to delete or damage files on your system, it can make your system susceptible to online snoops.

Enable AutoInstall   Deactivating this option prevents Navigator from automatically downloading and installing plug-ins for playing media files that Navigator itself cannot play.

Cookies   Cookies are like tokens that a Web page hands you when you connect to the page or enter information. These cookies stay with Navigator so that the next time you visit the site, or visit another area at the site, the Web server can identify you or keep track of items you have ordered. You can disable cookies to prevent Navigator from accepting them, or you can have Navigator display a warning whenever a site tries to send you a cookie.

> **Check This Out...**
>
> **How Risky Can a Cookie Be?**   Most cookies are designed to make your Web browsing experience more productive and enjoyable. However, sites can use cookies to track your Web-browsing habits. Although cookies typically do not store your name and email address, they can track you by using your computer's IP address, assigned to you by your service provider. If you are concerned about this, disable cookies.

Censoring Naughty Net Sites

The Internet is a virtual world, providing access to the best that our society has to offer: literature, music, creative arts, museums, movies, and medicine. Like the rest of the world, however, the Internet has its share of pornography, obscenity, and violence, not to mention rude and obnoxious behavior.

Over the years, people have debated whether the government should exercise some censorship over the Internet. As society wrestles with this issue, offensive material remains readily available. In the following sections, you learn what you can do on your end to prevent this material from reaching you or your children.

Enabling and Disabling Internet Explorer's Censor

Before you can censor with Internet Explorer, you have to activate the Ratings feature. Open the **View** menu, select **Internet Options**, and click the **Content** tab. Under Ratings, click the **Enable** button. The Create Supervisor Password dialog box appears. Type a password in both text boxes that you'll remember but that your kids will have a tough time guessing. Keep clicking **OK** to save your changes and close the dialog boxes.

Now, don't set the kiddies in front of the screen just yet. Test your setup first. Try going to **www.playboy.com**. If you see some scantily clad maidens, Ratings isn't on. Close Internet Explorer, run it again, and then try going to the nudie page. You should see the Content Advisor dialog box, as shown here, displaying a list of reasons you have been denied access to this site (as if you didn't know). Click **OK**.

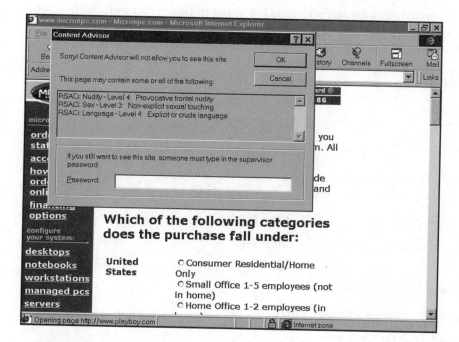

The Content Advisor tells you why you can't visit this site.

Censoring the Web in Navigator

Netscape Navigator does not have any built-in features that you can use to censor the Internet. Several specialized programs are available, however, that can work along with Navigator to block access to objectionable Web pages and Internet newsgroups. The following is a list of some of the better censoring programs along with addresses for the Web pages where you can find out more about them and download shareware versions:

Change the Ratings To relax the ratings, you can change the settings. Open the **View** menu, select **Internet Options**, and click the **Content** tab. Click Settings, enter your password, and enter your preferences.

➤ **Cyber Patrol** (at **www.cyberpatrol.com**)   The most popular censoring program. It enables you to set security levels, prevent Internet access during certain hours, and prevent access to specific sites. Passwords enable you to set access levels for different users.

➤ **CYBERsitter** (at **www.solidoak.com**)   Another fine censoring program. Although a little less strict than Cyber Patrol, CYBERsitter is easier to use and configure. CYBERsitter has a unique filtering system that judges words in context, so it won't block access to inoffensive sites, such as the Anne Sexton home page.

➤ **Net Nanny** (at **www.netnanny.com**)   This is unique in that it can punish the user for typing URLs of offensive sites or for typing any word on the no-no list. If a user types a prohibited word or URL, Net Nanny can shut down the application and record the offense, forcing your student or child to come up with an excuse. To make the most of Net Nanny, however, you're going to have to spend a bit of time configuring it.

Tech Check

If you weren't afraid of using the Internet before reading this chapter, you probably are now. My advice is not to worry too much and make sure that you can do the following:

➤ Name the three biggest security risks that the Internet poses.

➤ Determine if a form that you are filling out is secure.

➤ Deactivate the security warnings in Internet Explorer or Netscape Navigator and still determine whether a form is secure.

➤ Configure security zones in Internet Explorer.

➤ Disable Java in Netscape Navigator.

➤ Deactivate Internet Explorer's online censor.

➤ Find a censoring program on the Web.

Part 5
Guerrilla Computing

You know the basics. You can survive with any program, rearrange your files, and even connect to the Internet. You can use your computer to perform specific tasks and have some fun.

But if you must buy a new computer, do you know what to look for? If your computer is running out of memory and disk space, do you know what to do? Can you tune up your computer to make it run at optimum speed? Do you know how to use the portable computing features in Windows?

In this part, you'll learn how to survive in the trenches. You'll learn some savvy tips for buying a new computer, how to upgrade it, and how to fine-tune it to make it the best it can be.

Chapter 26

Savvy Consumer Guide to Buying a Computer

In This Chapter

➤ Buy a computer that won't be obsolete in a year

➤ Pick the fastest and the most affordable chip

➤ Get a hard disk drive that's big enough and fast enough

➤ List five important things to look for in a laptop computer

If you already bought your dream computer, reading this chapter may be hazardous to your mental health. You may find out that the computer you have is already obsolete. (I know mine is.) Maybe you should have gotten 64MB of RAM instead of 32. Maybe the slimline (space-saving) case wasn't the best choice, and you really should have shelled out a couple hundred extra for AGP graphics (whatever that is). But chasing after the great American techno-dream can only make you bitter and broke, so skip ahead to the next chapter and retain your blissful ignorance.

For the rest of you, you chronic procrastinators who have put off buying a computer, read on. These pages show you that although you really can't afford the ideal computer, you can make the right trade-offs to get the best computer for your budget.

Desktop or Notebook?

The question of whether you should buy a notebook computer boils down to one main question: Is it worth double the money to be able to carry your computer on a plane? That's at least how much extra a notebook computer costs over a comparably equipped desktop model. The following are some other drawbacks to notebook computers:

➤ The keyboard's dinky, and if you spill something on it, you risk ruining the entire system.

➤ The screen is dinky. (If you want a bigger screen, it's going to cost big bucks.)

➤ The screen is slow. (Your mouse pointer disappears as you move it.)

➤ The CD-ROM drive is as fragile as a crystal wineglass.

➤ The speakers and microphone are lousy.

➤ No mouse, although you can connect one.

➤ Limited expandability. (Adding a hard drive or memory is a pain.)

➤ They're hot (at least mine is). The Pentium processor, which puts out a lot of heat, is right under the heel of my hand. That's what I get for going mail order.

➤ They're real easy to steal (not that I ever stole one).

So, why would anyone even consider buying a notebook? The following are several good reasons:

Check This Out...

Laptop? Notebook? Subnotebook? The laptop computer got its name because it's small enough to set on your lap. Notebooks are small enough to fit in a briefcase (if you don't need to stick anything else in the briefcase) and weigh in at less than six pounds. Subnotebooks are even smaller and lighter. (In this book, I use laptop and notebook interchangeably.)

➤ Because you have to. (If you need to work on the road, you don't have a choice.)

➤ Because you want to. (You can work and play anywhere.)

➤ You have lots of money and you want to look cool. (You even have enough money to buy a docking station, so you can connect your notebook computer to a real monitor, keyboard, and speakers.)

➤ Your desk is already too cluttered.

➤ It's easy to add stuff. (Although adding a hard drive or memory is tough, PCMCIA slots make it easy to add a modem, network card, or other peripherals.)

So, what have you decided? Notebook or desktop? After you've made that decision, you've narrowed the field quite a bit. You're ready to move on to some real issues.

Computer Buyer's Checklists

After deciding whether to go with a notebook or desktop PC, the first thing you should do is go to your local computer store and check out what's available. Leave your credit card, cash, and checkbook at home so that you won't buy something impulsively. Read the system descriptions next to each computer, play with the keyboard and mouse, open the CD-ROM drive, and so on. Pretend that you're taking the computer for a test drive.

After you have done that, read some computer ads and reviews in magazines, such as *PC Computing* and *Computer Shopper*. This gives you some insight into prices, known problems with existing brands, and any late-breaking technologies of which you should be aware.

To make sure you're considering the most important shopping issues, use the following buyer's guide checklists for desktop and notebook computers. These tables list the most important considerations and favor power over price. If you're on a strict budget, you can make a few trade-offs. Don't let the techno-terms baffle you, just flip to the glossary at the back of this book.

Desktop Computer Shopping List

Component	Minimum Requirements
Processor (CPU)	Pentium II or better, 300MHz or faster. Pentium II has built-in MMX technology, which improves multimedia performance.
Cache	512K L2 pipeline burst cache. Cache improves the overall speed of the processor. Don't settle for 256K, and make sure it's L2 or better.
RAM	32MB (or more) SDRAM or EDO RAM. SDRAM is twice as fast as EDO. Make sure you can add another 32MB of RAM without removing existing RAM chips.
Hard Drive	4GB drive with access times ranging from 8-12 ms (milliseconds)—the lower the number the better.
USB Ports	Two USB ports. The next breed of add-on equipment will be USB compatible, making it easy to add components to your system.

continues

297

Desktop Computer Shopping List   Continued

Component	Minimum Requirements
Monitor	SVGA, non-interlaced, 15-inch or 17-inch monitor with a dot pitch of .28 or less, 1024×768 resolution. (The smaller the dot pitch, the greater the screen definition.)
Display Card	AGP graphics card with 4MB of RAM. AGP provides superior support for three-dimensional graphics and games.
Floppy Drive	3 1/2-inch floppy disk drive.
CD-ROM/DVD	12X CD-ROM drive, or one of the new DVD drives (make sure it can play CDs).
Backup Drive	At least half the capacity of your hard disk drive. You don't want to have to back up your system to floppy disks.
Audio	32-bit, wavetable sound card, speakers, and a good microphone. 64-bit sound cards are better. Don't settle for a 16-bit sound card: they're on their way out.
Game Port	If your sound card does not have a game port, make sure there is a separate game port on the back of the system unit.
Modem	56K data transfer, 14.4Kbps fax transfer, plus voice support. If you want a faster connection, check into ISDN modems or satellite PC support.

Notebook PC Buyer's Checklist

Feature	Minimum Requirements
Processor (CPU)	Pentium MMX, 166MHz. Newer notebooks may offer the Pentium II, but these are top-of-the-line notebooks.
Cache	512K L2 pipeline burst cache. Cache improves the overall speed of the processor. Don't settle for 256K.
RAM	32MB SDRAM or EDO RAM. SDRAM is twice as fast as EDO. You can get by with 16MB, but not if you expect your notebook to hold its own against a desktop model. Make sure you can upgrade to 64MB.
Weight	4–8 pounds. Keep in mind that you are toting this thing around with you. In the notebook arena, the lightweights win.
Display	12.1-inch Active matrix TFT 800×600 resolution or better, 75 Hertz or faster. Compare displays before you buy.
Hard Drive	2GB or larger. Hard drives on notebook computers are usually smaller than those on desktops.

Feature	Minimum Requirements
Battery	Lithium-ion or better. Find out how long it takes to charge the battery, how many hours you can operate the notebook between charges, and how many times you can charge the battery. Don't trust what the manufacturer says: read product reviews.
Keyboard	Roomy. Make sure the keys aren't too close together for your fingers.
Touchpad	Yes. I know I knocked touchpads in Chapter 1, but they're still the best pointing device on notebooks. Just make sure that it has a free serial port for connecting a mouse.
Floppy Drive	Yes. On many notebooks, you can plug the floppy drive into the parallel port, so you don't have to lug it around all the time.
CD-ROM/DVD	Yes. Most programs come on CDs. Don't settle for an external CD-ROM drive. Make sure it's built in and is at least 12X or faster. Also, make sure you can upgrade to DVD later.
Audio	16-bit stereo or better. Make sure the notebook has input and output jacks for connecting a real pair of speakers and a high-quality microphone.
Game Port	Most notebooks don't have a game port. If you want to use a joystick, find out what it takes to add a game port.
PCMCIA Slots	Two PCMCIA slots. These slots enable you to insert credit-card sized expansion boards into the system to add devices such as a fax/modem, CD-ROM drive connection, network card, game port, or even a hard disk drive. You simply pop one card out and another one in, depending on what you want to do.
USB Ports	Two USB ports. With USB, you have nearly unlimited expansion capabilities, and installing add-ons is easy.
Infrared Port	Maybe. To quickly connect your computer to another computer, printer, keyboard, or other device, without a cable, you need an infrared port. Although most notebooks have infrared ports, most people don't use them.
Modem	33.6Kbps or faster with fax. You need a modem to connect to the Internet, even if you don't plan on traveling much.
Docking Station	Available? You may not need one now, but if you decide to get one later, make sure that you can. Docking stations are typically manufactured to work with only one type of notebook. You can actually damage your notebook by using a docking station that's not designed for it, and if you do, your warranty won't cover the repair bills.

Planning for Future Expansion

When you're buying a computer for $2,000, the last thing you want to think about is shelling out more money for additional equipment. If you don't think about the future now, however, you won't be able to upgrade your computer later. Check for the following:

➤ **USB Ports** Enable you to add up to 127 USB compatible devices to your computer without turning off the computer, opening the system unit, installing special software, or worrying that one device might conflict with another.

➤ **ZIF CPU Socket** (ZIF is short for zero insertion force). With a ZIF socket, you can plug in a faster processor later without much trouble. ZIF sockets are standard on newer PCs.

➤ **Open Drive Bays** Enable you to add a hard disk, DVD, or backup drive to your computer later. The system unit should have two open (unoccupied) drive bays.

➤ **Expansion Slots** (Three open PCI slots and two open ISA slots). These may become less important as the computer industry moves to USB, but for now, if you want to plug in extras (a sound card, external drive, scanner, or TV card), you need some open expansion slots. PCI slots handle newer cards, but some sound cards and other cards still use ISA slots.

➤ **Plug-and-Play** Enables you to insert plug-and-play devices without having to configure settings on the expansion card. Windows detects the device automatically when you install it, changes the settings (to avoid conflicts with other devices), and installs the necessary driver.

➤ **Expandable Memory** Expandable to 128MB or more. Make sure you can add memory modules without removing the existing modules. If the computer comes installed with 32MB of RAM, which occupy all the RAM slots, you have to remove modules and pitch them or try to resell them.

Buying the Perfect Printer

I've made some mistakes in purchasing printers. First, I bought a black-and-white printer and had to listen to my kids complain about it for two years. Then, I bought a color printer with no scanner/fax/copy features, because I really didn't need them at the time. Now, I have to buy a new printer or purchase a separate fax machine and scanner. So, to avoid the mistakes I've made, use the following checklist.

Printer Purchase Checklist

Feature	What You Should Consider
Laser	Fast, but expensive, if you have the money, go with a laser printer.
Inkjet	Less expensive, but the print quality rivals that of a laser printer.
Color	Don't buy a black-and-white printer. Even if you think you don't need color, you find that you can't live without color for occasional greeting cards, photos, and similar publications. If you're buying an inkjet printer, make sure the color and black ink cartridges are separate, so you won't waste the color ink when you run out of black. Color laser printers are still too pricey for most budgets.
Quality	600 dpi (dots per inch) or higher. If you need photo-quality output, go with 1200 dpi.
Speed	4–8 ppm (pages per minute) or faster for monochrome, 2–4 ppm for color. Otherwise, you're twiddling your thumbs waiting for the printer to spit out the last page.
Price	$500 for a good inkjet. $1,000 for a laser. If you want a combination fax, copier, scanner, inkjet printer, expect to pay $1,000.
Consumables	Expect to pay 3–10 cents per page to print. How much do the print cartridges cost and how many pages can each one print? Do you need to print on special paper?
Envelope Feed	The paper tray should have an easy way to feed business envelopes into the printer.
Fax	300 dpi, 14.4Kbps transmission, auto-redial, speed dial numbers, page memory to store received faxes if the printer runs out of paper.
Scanner	TWAIN compatible color flatbed scanner that can handle 8 1/2-by 11-inch pages and scans at 600 dpi or better. 24-bit color, 8-bit grayscale. TWAIN enables you to quickly import scanned images into your documents.
Copier	600×300 dpi, multiple copies.

Scanners, Digital Cameras, TV Cards, and Other Toys

The PC has made great strides in restitching our social and economic fabric. We can chat with anyone in the world without leaving our homes, publish our own documents, avoid long-distance phone bills, do our own taxes, and even shop from our homes (or was that the Home Shopping Network that did that?). With the new toys available, PCs are now threatening the very existence of TVs, PhotoMarts, and video arcades. When you're out shopping for a computer, be sure to check out the latest gadgets:

➤ **TV Tuners**   Many home PCs come with a TV tuner that enables your computer to double as a TV set. You plug in the cable or TV antenna and you can pretend you're working as you watch the ball game. If you already have a computer without a TV tuner, you can purchase one separately; just make sure you have an open expansion slot in your system unit.

➤ **Scanners**   The scanner market is crammed with a wide range of products: black-and-white, color, handheld models, business card scanners, sheet-fed, flatbed, and even photo scanners (to transform 35mm negatives into printed pictures). When shopping for a scanner, consider quality first. If you want photo-quality scans, don't settle for less than 1200 dpi color, although 600 dpi is sufficient for most uses. Make sure that the scanner is TWAIN compatible so that you can scan pictures into your documents and that the scanner comes with good OCR (optical character recognition) software so that you can scan text. Before you buy, read some reviews.

➤ **Digital Cameras**   The latest popular toy is the digital camera, which stores your pictures on floppy disks or special memory cards. Quality and price vary greatly. When you're out camera shopping, check the maximum resolution of the photos (don't settle for less than 640×480) and the number of photos you can store on a disk or card. Find out how much additional disks or cards cost. If you're looking for a bargain, and you don't need to take the camera with you, you can get digital cameras that plug right into the system unit for a lot less money, because they use your computer's resources for storage and display.

➤ **Graphics Tablets**   Feeling artistic? For a few hundred bucks, you can purchase a graphics tablet that transforms your hand-drawn sketches, notes, and doodles into something you can pull up on your monitor.

➤ **Video Modems**   Are standard phone calls starting to bore you? If so, you can install a video modem, stick a digital video camera on your monitor, and talk face to face over the phone, assuming, of course, that the other person has a video modem.

➤ **Palmtop Computers**   If a notebook PC is still too bulky, and you don't really need to type a lot on the road, consider a palmtop computer. Many of the new palmtops come with a scaled down version of Windows, called Windows CE, which makes the transition from your desktop PC much easier. Weighing in at about a pound, a palmtop has a miniature screen, a tiny keyboard, and just enough RAM to perform basic tasks (usually about 4MB). Most palmtops also have modem and fax capabilities, although wandering the Web on a palmtop is no vacation.

Buyer Beware: Slick Sales Tricks

The computer market is very competitive, which makes computers much more affordable, but also forces manufacturers and dealers to cut corners. Their ads focus on all the positive aspects of their products but say nothing about how they are able to offer their computers to you for hundreds of dollars less than their competitors. The following is a list of some of the shady practices for which you should watch out:

➤ **Free Software**   Don't buy a computer solely for the software that comes with it. Some manufacturers bundle lots of software with the computer to try to empty its stock of obsolete computers. Home PC buyers, dazzled by the long list of free games and programs, end up with anemic computers.

➤ **All RAM Slots Occupied**   Most computers have four slots for installing RAM chips. If you buy a computer with 32 megabytes of RAM and the manufacturer used four 8MB chips, all the slots are occupied. Request that the dealer install two 16MB chips. That leaves you two slots open, enabling you to easily upgrade by adding two more 16MB or 32MB chips later (you typically must install RAM chips in pairs).

➤ **All Expansion Slots Occupied**   Although the computer has plenty of expansion slots, the manufacturer installed something in every slot, so there are none left to expand in the future.

➤ **EDO RAM**   Who cares what kind of RAM you get, as long as you get a lot of it, right? Wrong. Get SDRAM or better. EDO RAM can't keep up with your speedy processor.

➤ **No L2 Pipeline Burst Cache**   L2 (Level 2) cache makes your system scream by placing the cache right on the CPU chip on Pentium Pro and Pentium II systems. Without L2 cache, your powerful chip has to wait for instructions.

➤ **Second-Rate Power Supply**   The power supply feeds juice to all the computer components, including the motherboard and drives. Make sure the computer has at least a 300-watt power supply so that it has enough juice for future upgrades.

➤ **Slimline Case**   A slimline case sounds good if you have a small work area; however, slimline cases don't offer you the expansion options you get with a standard case or mini-tower.

➤ **Old BIOS**   Manufacturers may try to cut corners by installing an outdated BIOS or going with the cheapest BIOS available.

➤ **Cheap Video Card**   You won't notice anything until your kid installs DOOM and then hollers that something is wrong with the computer.

➤ **Off-Brand Modem**   Slow modem, no fax capabilities, no voice capabilities, and no driver for it in Windows. Make sure the modem has a quality brand name and that the speed is up to the current standard.

➤ **Monitor Sold Separately**   This is the mother of all slick gimmicks. You're comparing prices between two systems and grab for the lower price only to learn that you have to shell out another 400 bucks for a monitor.

Shopping on the Internet

You can walk into Best Buy or CompUSA and purchase a pretty good computer for a pretty good price. You can, however, usually get more power and higher quality for the same price by shopping through a mail-order company, such as Gateway 2000, Micron Electronics, or Dell. All these companies have Web sites, where you can check out their current products without having to deal with a salesperson, and if you have a credit card that's not maxed out, you can even order your computer online. Or, if you like to talk to salespeople, you can call them using a toll-free number. The following is a list of popular mail-order companies, along with information on how to contact them:

Check This Out...

Go Cheap
Many of the companies listed here offer reconditioned computers at greatly reduced prices. If you simply can't afford a top-of-the-line PC, buy a used one. Of course, after drooling all over this chapter, a used PC is probably out of the question.

Micron   **www.micronpc.com** or **800-326-7309** (Micron is good at offering its customers the latest technology available, although their computers cost a little more.)

NEC   **www.necnow.com** or **1-888-863-2669** (Powerful computers, but expect to pay more.)

Dell   **www.dell.com** or **800-626-4382** (Great prices and a wide selection.)

Gateway   **www.gw2k.com** or **800-216-2793** (Gateway provides excellent technical support after the purchase.)

Tech Check

If you can keep all this information in your head as you're shopping, bully for you. If not, just make sure you can do the following:

➤ Decide which is better for you: a desktop or notebook PC.

➤ Write down everything that you want in a desktop PC.

➤ Write down everything that you want in a notebook PC.

➤ List five things a computer should have to enable expansion.

➤ Set two printers side by side and decide which one is better.

➤ Come up with a list of toys that you want to buy when you win the lottery.

➤ Read a computer ad and figure out where the dealer has skimped to reduce the price.

Chapter 27

Upgrading Your Computer to Make It the Best It Can Be

In This Chapter

➤ Follow the proper safety precautions for all upgrades

➤ Add a modem, sound card, or other expansion board to your PC

➤ Jack up performance with a fast processor and more memory

➤ Install a new hard disk drive, or at least know what it involves

➤ Install a joystick

Like a house, a computer can be a money pit. One month, you decide you need a new hard disk. The next month, you just have to have a CD-ROM drive and a sound card, and you always need more memory. By the time you're done, you're a thousand bucks poorer, and you have a computer packed with fancy new equipment yoked to your incredibly slow 486 CPU.

To prevent this from happening to you, make a list of all the upgrades that your current computer needs to make it what you want it to be. Add up the costs for the items, and then compare the total cost to what it would cost for a brand-spanking new computer that has everything you want. Chances are, there won't be much difference. On the other hand, if you have a good computer that just needs a memory boost or a sound card or modem, upgrading is the best, and cheapest, solution.

Smart Shopping for Upgrades

The best place to start shopping for upgrades is through the dealer from which you purchased your computer. I'm not saying that this is the best place to *buy* upgrade components, but it is the best place to begin. You can pick the dealer's brain to find out which components you need and the types of components that are compatible with your system, and you can get a price to use for comparison purposes (the price is usually too high).

After you have the information in hand (tell the person you'll call back later), get a copy of a computer magazine (any PC magazine will do), and flip to the back to search through the ads for mail-order companies. In case you don't have a computer magazine handy, the following are a few companies to try:

USA Flex at **800-723-0334** or **www.usaflex.com** is a good place to shop for printers, graphics cards, CD-ROM drives, scanners, and modems.

First Source at **800-468-9866** or **www.firstsource.com** is an excellent place to buy memory and processor upgrades. They offer quality products at reasonable prices, and their sales staff can help you figure out what you need for your particular system.

Will You Void the Warranty? Before going mail order, check your computer's warranty. Many manufacturers specify that if you install add-ons from anyone else but them, your warranty is void. If the warranty is expired, you're not going to lose anything going with a mail order company.

Computer Discount Warehouse at **800-886-4239** or **www.cdw.com** offers a wide selection of software, multimedia and processor upgrades, monitors, and input devices.

Just because these are mail-order companies, don't assume that they ignore you when you run into trouble. Their upgrades come with complete instructions that are at least as good as the instructions you receive from the original manufacturer. The products are high-quality, and most mail-order companies have their own tech support line that you can call for help.

Safety Precautions for All Upgrades

Before you start poking around under the hood of your system unit, you should be aware of some safety precautions. Because so many delicate electrical components reside there, you have to be careful. Follow these standard precautions:

➤ Make sure all the parts of your computer are turned off and unplugged.

➤ Before you start, touch a metal part of the system unit to discharge any static electricity from your body. Better yet, go to an electronics store and buy a grounding strap. Attach the strap to yourself (usually to your wrist) and to ground (a metal part of your computer will work).

➤ New computer parts usually come in anti-static bags. Before handling a part, touch a metal part of the system unit case to discharge static electricity from your body.

➤ Keep parts in their anti-static bags (not on top of the bags) until you are ready to use them.

➤ If the parts have warranty seals, be careful not to break them. Breaking a seal invalidates the warranty.

➤ Hold parts by their edges and mounting brackets. Avoid touching any components or solder on the parts.

➤ Never slide parts over your work surface. This can build up a static charge in the part.

➤ Keep plastic, vinyl, furs, and Styrofoam out of your work area. And don't rub your stocking feet over a vinyl carpet either.

➤ If your new toy arrives on a cold day, let it warm to room temperature before installing it. Any condensation on the new part could damage your system.

➤ If you drop a stray screw inside the system unit, stick some tape on a pencil and try to fish out the screw; don't use your fingers or a magnet.

➤ When removing the cover from your system unit, make sure that you don't bump any cables loose or pinch them when you replace the cover.

➤ When working inside the system unit, try not to brush against circuit boards. (Once, I knocked a jumper off my sound card and had to work in silence for a couple days until I realized what I had done.)

Slapping In an Expansion Board

Nine out of ten upgrades require you to install an expansion board (also called a *card*). An expansion board is an integrated circuit board that plugs into the main circuit board (the *motherboard*) inside your system unit. An internal modem is an expansion board. A sound card is an expansion board. In some cases, you might even have to install a card to add a floppy drive, CD-ROM drive, or hard drive to your system.

The Tricky Part: Addresses and Interrupts

In case you haven't heard, Windows 95 has ushered in the era of plug-and-play expansion boards. You simply plug the expansion board into an expansion slot on the motherboard (see "Rock the Board in Place," next), boot up with Windows 95, and follow the onscreen instructions to set up your new device. USB promises to make upgrading even easier.

Some expansion boards on the market, however, do not conform to the rules of plug-and-play. With these types of boards, you have to make sure that the new board does not use the same settings as an existing board. Typically, you need to worry about the following three settings:

➤ **IRQ**   This stands for *interrupt request* and is a number that enables a device to demand attention from the central processing unit. If two devices have the same IRQ, they demand attention at the same time, confusing the CPU.

➤ **DMA Channel**   A path to your computer's RAM. Most computers have eight DMA (Direct Memory Access) channels. If two devices have the same DMA channel, usually only one device gains access to RAM. The other device simply won't work.

➤ **I/O Port Address**   A designation that enables a device to take input and output information at a certain location. As with IRQs and DMAs, if two devices use the same I/O setting, problems occur.

Try installing the expansion board with the factory settings (don't change anything). If the card doesn't work, then you can try changing the settings, as explained in the documentation. (Change only one setting at a time.) You change these settings on the expansion board by flipping tiny switches or by sliding jumpers over or off wire posts on the card. Draw a picture of the current switch or jumper settings before you start messing with the card.

Rock the Board in Place

To install an expansion board, first remove the system unit cover. The expansion slots are on the motherboard, near the back of the system unit (where your printer and monitor plug in). Find an expansion slot that matches the size of the board that you need to plug in. If you're installing an expansion board that requires an external connection (such as an internal modem or sound card), remove the metal cover plate near the expansion slot, as shown in the next figure.

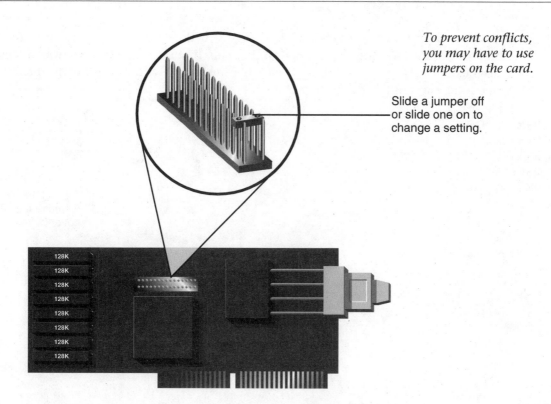

*To prevent conflicts,
you may have to use
jumpers on the card.*

Slide a jumper off
or slide one on to
change a setting.

To install the expansion board, insert the contacts at the bottom of the board into one of the expansion slots, and then press down on the card while rocking it *gently* back and forth in the direction that the slot runs. Expect the fit to be snug, but don't push so hard that you crack the board. Make sure the board is seated securely in the socket, and that it is not leaning against any other boards (this could cause the board to short circuit). Secure the board in place using the screw that you removed from the cover plate. (A good sign that the board is properly seated is that the plate fits snugly over the opening in the back of the system unit.)

When you're done, don't replace the system unit cover. If the expansion board does not work, you have to get inside the system unit again and play with the jumpers. Your computer works fine with the cover off, just don't touch anything inside the computer while it's on.

Run the Setup Program

Many expansion boards come with their own software (on disks) that you need to install. The software tells your computer how to work with the expansion board, and tells the expansion board how to do its job. Follow the instructions that came with your expansion board to run the setup or installation program. (In many cases, the software includes a diagnostic utility that can determine whether the board is installed properly and help you resolve any conflicts with other boards.)

If the expansion board connects to something outside the system unit, remove the cover plate.

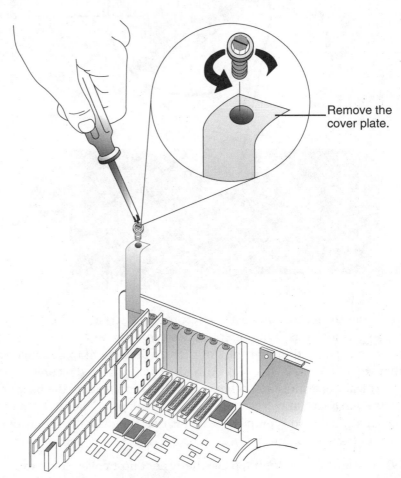

Remove the cover plate.

Adding New Hardware in Windows

Windows 95 and later versions come with a utility called the Add New Hardware Wizard that searches for new components and leads you through the process of installing the necessary software (driver). To run the Add New Hardware Wizard, take the following steps:

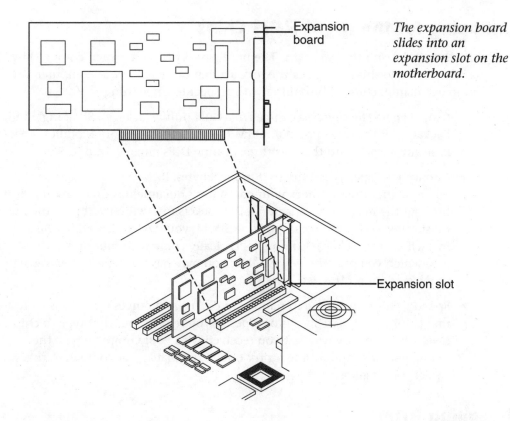

Expansion board

The expansion board slides into an expansion slot on the motherboard.

Expansion slot

1. Exit all running programs. This prevents you from losing any data in case Windows locks up during the process.

2. Click the **Start** button.

3. Move the mouse pointer over **Settings**, and then click **Control Panel**. The Control Panel window appears.

4. Double-click the **Add New Hardware** icon. The Add New Hardware Wizard appears, informing you about what the wizard does.

5. Follow the onscreen instructions to complete the installation. You may have to insert the Windows CD or a disk that came with the board.

Cramming In the RAM

If you're working in Windows, and you want to surf the Internet, run a few applications, and answer your email—all at the same time—chances are you need at least 32MB of memory. If your computer system lacks that muscle power, this section can help you beef it up.

Shopping for the Right RAM Chips

Installing RAM isn't the hard part. The hard part is deciding which chips to buy. The easiest way to do this is to check the invoice that came with your computer or call the computer manufacturer. Chips differ with respect to three things:

➤ **Chip Type**   The *chip type* can be DIP (Dual Inline Package), SIP (Single Inline Package), or the more popular SIMM (Single Inline Memory Module). A SIMM is basically a small card that has three or nine DIPs plugged into it.

➤ **Capacity**   Capacity is expressed in megabytes. RAM typically comes in units of 4, 8, 16, or 32 megabytes. Check your computer's documentation or ask the dealer to find out the maximum capacity of the sockets into which you plug the memory. In most cases, you can't install just one SIMM; you have to install SIMMs in pairs (one in each of two sockets). Computers typically come with four or more SIMM sockets into which you plug the new SIMMs. You may have to remove low-capacity SIMMS to make room for the new ones.

➤ **Speed**   This is measured in nanoseconds (ns) and ranges from 50ns to 120ns. Don't mix chips of different speeds or types. If you're not sure what type of chips you need, check the invoice that you received with your computer, call the manufacturer's support line, or try one of the mail-order companies that I listed earlier. Don't guess.

Installing RAM

After you have the additional memory, how do you install it? The answer is that it depends. With most computers, you add memory by inserting SIMMs into the SIMM sockets. Other computers require a special memory board. The board contains the RAM chips. You insert the board into one of the expansion slots inside the system unit (see "Slapping In an Expansion Board," earlier in this chapter). To install SIMMs, take the following steps:

1. Turn off the computer, unplug it, and remove the cover from the system unit.

2. Touch the system unit case to discharge any static electricity from your body. A small zap can damage the SIMM or other sensitive components.

3. Locate the SIMM sockets. Refer to your computer's documentation; these sockets can be anywhere on the motherboard. (Two of mine were hiding under my hard drive, so be prepared to pull out a drive or anything else that might be in the way.)

4. If you need to remove SIMMs, gently pull them from their sockets. Each SIMM socket may have two clips to hold the SIMM in place. You may have to gently pry them away from the SIMM as you lift or before you lift.

5. Insert the new SIMMs into the empty sockets with a gentle rocking motion. SIMM pins can be very fragile and may insert on an angle, so be careful. Make sure that they are well seated, and if the socket has clips, make sure that the clips are secure.

6. Replace the system unit cover.

Most computers automatically detect the new memory on startup. Turn on the computer, and watch the monitor. It should show the total amount of memory in your computer. Other computers may require you to run a setup program. You can usually run this program by pressing a special key (such as F1) while your computer is booting or by entering **setup** at the DOS prompt. Watch the screen on startup or check your computer documentation to find which key to press.

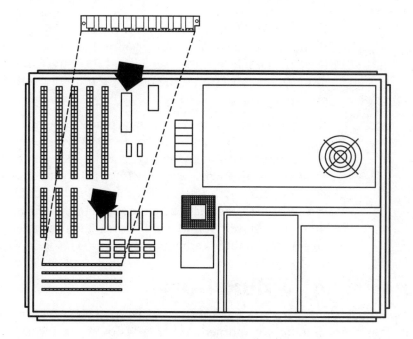

You can plug SIMMs directly into SIMM sockets on the motherboard.

Replacing Your Computer's Processor

Although additional RAM is the easiest, and usually best, way to increase the overall speed of your PC, a new processing chip can give you a (nearly) new computer. For instance, if you have a slow Pentium processor, say 75MHz, you can install a 150Mhz MMX chip that can double its speed.

Before you run out and buy an overdrive processor, make sure that your system can handle it. You can't just slap any processor onto any motherboard and expect it to work.

Call the computer manufacturer and ask about the best available upgrades. If you currently have a Pentium processor, check **www.intel.com** for additional information.

After you've found the right processor, installing the new processor is fairly easy, assuming that you can locate the old processor on the motherboard and dislodge it from its den. If you're lucky, you are able to see the chip's label. Otherwise, you have to refer to the pictures in your computer documentation. If it's a Pentium chip you're searching for, look for a fan; the chip should be near a fan or have a fan right on top of it.

What's with the Fan? Pentium processors are hot (not just popular, but physically hot). They need some way to cool themselves or they fry in their own juice. To keep them cool, they either use passive cooling devices (they look like tiny cooling towers), or active devices—fans. Some fans you have to plug in, but with more advanced designs, the fan draws current from the socket itself, so you don't have to plug it in.

After you have located the processor, hope that it is a ZIF processor. ZIF is short for Zero Insertion Force (meaning that this is going to be easy). If you have a non-ZIF processor, you need a special tool to pull the processor from its socket; don't try to do it with a butter knife. If the processor is clamped into place (most ZIF processors are clamped), you must loosen the clamp. Then look for a lever on the side of the socket and lift it gently; this should dislodge the processor. If the processor has a fan with a plug on it, unplug the fan.

Now you're ready to insert the new processor, which should fit into the socket only one way. Align the pins on the processor with the holes in the socket (you should be good at this by now), and gently (very gently if you have a ZIF processor), push the processor into the socket. If the processor has a fan that you have to plug in, insert the plug that you removed from the old socket. Then, lower the lever that you lifted earlier to lock the processor in place.

Replacing (or Adding) a Hard Drive

Before you run out and buy a new hard drive, you should ask yourself a few questions, such as is there room in your computer for another hard drive? Look at the documentation or call the computer manufacturer, and find out the following information:

➤ Do you have an open drive bay? You can figure this out by opening the system unit and looking inside. Look for an opening around your existing drives.

If you don't have an open bay, you have two choices. You can purchase an external hard drive that connects to the system unit with a cable, or you can replace the current drive with one that stores more. No novice should attempt the second option, because you have to transfer data from the old drive to the new drive. Hire a qualified technician to replace the drive for you.

➤ Is the drive bay half-height or full-height? A full-height hard drive won't fit in a half-height bay, even with a crowbar.

➤ Do you need a hard drive controller card? If your current hard drive is connected with an IDE or SCSI (pronounced scuzzy) cable, the cable should have another outlet into which you can plug your new hard drive. If not, you may have to plug a controller card into an expansion slot, and then plug the drive into that board.

➤ What kind of hard drive do you need? Do you need a SCSI drive or IDE (or EIDE)? If your current drive is an IDE drive, your new drive should be IDE (or EIDE), too. Likewise with SCSI drives.

➤ Does the power supply have an open outlet? Your hard drive needs electricity (from the power supply). Most power supplies have several unused outlets. If yours doesn't have an extra outlet, you need an adapter that enables two devices to plug into the same outlet (or you need a new power supply).

➤ Does the new hard disk drive have a *cache* or *buffer*? The cache is built-in memory that stores often-used data electronically so that the computer can get it quickly. The cache size should be anywhere from 64K to 256K—the more the better.

➤ Make sure that the drive comes with the mounting brackets and cables you need. In many cases, you don't need special mounting brackets or an extra cable.

The UPS guy shows up with your new hard drive. Now what? Reread the safety precautions given earlier, and then take the following steps:

1. Pop off the top of your system unit.

2. Attach the mounting bracket to the hard drive (if required), and lay the drive inside the drive bay. Don't mount the drive to the bay just yet; you may have to jiggle things around to connect the cables.

3. If you need to install a hard drive controller board, skip back to the section called "Slapping in an Expansion Board," to find out what to do.

4. If you have an existing IDE or SCSI drive that has a data cable (a wide, flat cable, typically gray) with an open plug on it, plug it into the data outlet on the new drive. Otherwise, connect the hard drive to the hard drive controller board using the data cable that came with the drive.

5. Connect the hard drive to the power supply. (In most cases, you simply insert a plug from the power supply into the outlet on the hard drive.)

6. Now, secure the hard drive to the drive bay using the mounting screws and replace the system unit cover.

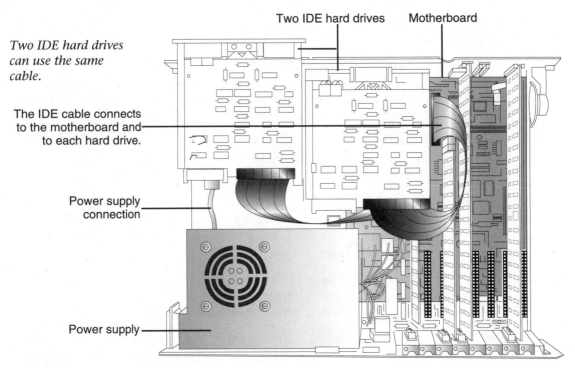

Two IDE hard drives   Motherboard

Two IDE hard drives can use the same cable.

The IDE cable connects to the motherboard and to each hard drive.

Power supply connection

Power supply

Check This Out...

Do You Have an Auto Detect Option? If your setup program has an Auto Detect option for a drive, select it. You can then save the settings, exit the setup program, and restart your computer. Your computer automatically finds the new hard drive and enters the required hard drive settings for you.

The hard drive is in your computer, but the computer doesn't know that. Run your computer's setup program (the procedure varies from one computer to another, so refer to your computer's documentation or watch the screen on startup). You get a screen that enables you to set up various devices. Select a drive that's marked as not installed (usually drive D or E, if you have a CD-ROM drive), and enter settings for the drive as specified by the hard drive manufacturer.

You may also have to use the FDISK and FORMAT commands on the new drive. Check the documentation to be sure. When formatting, make sure that you enter the FORMAT command with the letter of the *NEW* drive. If you use the letter of an existing drive, you destroy all the information on that drive.

Installing a CD-ROM or Floppy Drive

The procedure for installing a CD-ROM drive or another floppy disk drive is very similar to that of installing another hard drive. You must find an open drive bay and use mounting brackets to secure the drive inside the bay. You must then connect the drive to the motherboard or to a drive controller card, using a special cable, and plug the drive into the power supply. (Of course, if you purchase an external drive, you can just plug it in to the required port.) After you've installed a drive, you must run your computer's setup program (for a floppy drive), or install special software (for a CD-ROM drive).

Game Cards and Joysticks

Before you run out and buy a joystick and game card, spin your system unit around and look to see whether you have a game port on the back. Some computers have a built-in game port. If you have a sound card, it probably has a game port as well. In either case, you can buy a joystick and connect it to this port without having to purchase a game card. If you don't have a game port, you have to buy a game card and a joystick.

When shopping for a joystick, don't just look at the price tag. I bought a joystick for twenty bucks, but its movement was so jerky that I couldn't fly my spaceship a nautical mile without getting shot down. Look for a joystick that uses both analog (for older games) and digital (for newer games) technology. In addition to providing greater control, digital joysticks calibrate themselves.

> **Check This Out...**
>
> **Calibrating a Joystick** If your joystick doesn't work correctly, you may have to calibrate it. You can do this in most games that use the joystick. If you have Windows, double-click the **Joystick** or **Game Controllers** icon in the Control Panel. In the dialog box that appears, click the **Calibrate** button, and follow the onscreen instructions to calibrate your joystick.

If your computer doesn't have a game port, first install the game card for your joystick. (See "Slapping In an Expansion Board," earlier in this chapter for details.) Turn off your computer. Then, simply plug your joystick into the game port.

Tech Check

If this chapter merely whets your appetite for upgrade information, you can purchase another book called *The Complete Idiot's Guide to Upgrading and Repairing PCs* that contains scads of information about upgrading. Until then, just make sure that you can do the following, or at least have a general understanding of what's involved:

➤ Determine whether it would be better to buy a new computer.

➤ Recite a list of the standard safety precautions for all upgrades.

➤ Find an expansion slot inside your computer, and plug in an expansion board.

➤ Make sure the RAM chips that you get are the type, capacity, and speed that your computer can use.

➤ Replace a ZIF CPU.

➤ Add a new hard drive to your system.

➤ Plug in a joystick.

Chapter 28

Do-It-Yourself Computer Tune-Ups

In This Chapter

➤ Run the Windows Tune-Up Wizard (Windows 98 only)

➤ Clear useless files off your hard disk

➤ Speed up your hard disk in Windows

➤ Double your disk space without installing a new drive

➤ Give your programs more memory without installing more RAM

Your computer is like a car. You might be able to use it without ever tuning it up or changing the oil, but it probably won't last as long or run as well. In this chapter, you learn some basic computer maintenance that helps keep your computer running trouble-free and at peak performance.

If you don't feel comfortable with some of the performance-boosting tips covered in this chapter, just skip them. The tips aren't mandatory, but they do help you squeeze the maximum performance out of your PC.

Running the Windows Tune-Up Wizard (Windows 98 Only)

As you install programs, wander the Web, and create documents, your system continually becomes slower and less efficient. If a program's installation utility automatically adds the program to the StartUp menu, Windows starts more slowly. When you wander the Web, your Web browser saves files to your hard disk without asking you, cutting down on available space. When you create and edit documents, programs often place temporary files on your disk that remain there until you delete them. And files on your hard disk continually become more and more fragmented as parts of files are stored on separate areas of the disk.

The Windows Tune-Up Wizard (included in the Windows 98 prerelease we looked at) can help you keep your computer in tip-top condition. It automatically performs a series of tests and corrections at a scheduled time to check for problems on your hard disk, defragment files, delete temporary files, remove programs from the StartUp menu, and optimize your hard disk. With the Windows Tune-Up Wizard, you rarely have to go behind-the-scenes with Windows to perform these tasks manually. (If you don't have Windows 98, later sections in this chapter show you how to use Windows 95 tools to optimize your system.)

To run the Wizard, take the following steps:

1. Click the **Start** button, point to **Programs**, **Accessories**, **System Tools**, and click **Windows Tune-Up**.

2. Choose **Express** and click **Next**. Express tells the Wizard to delete temporary files and Web files from your hard disk, optimize your hard disk, and check it for errors, but Express does not tell the wizard to remove programs from the StartUp menu.

3. Choose the desired time (a time when you normally have your computer on but are not using it) and click **Next**.

4. The Wizard displays a list of optimization activities it performs at the scheduled time(s). To have the Wizard perform these activities now, choose **When I Click Finish**....

5. Click the **Finish** button. Be sure to leave your computer on at the scheduled time so that Windows can perform the optimization activities at the scheduled time(s).

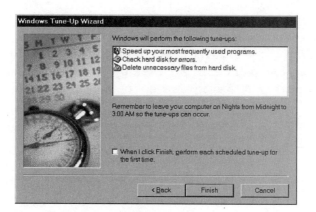

The Windows Tune-Up Wizard optimizes your system on schedule.

Making Windows Start Faster

Windows is a slow starter, even on a quick machine. If you have some power-saving features on your computer, you can make Windows start a lot faster. Instead of turning your PC off and on, use the **Power** or **Power Management** icon in the Control Panel to have Windows put your PC in sleep mode when you're not using it. Then, you can quickly restart by pressing **Enter** or rolling the mouse around.

If you need to turn your computer completely off, or you just like to, try the following to reduce the startup time:

➤ To prevent Windows from running programs on the StartUp menu, hold down the **Shift** key right after you log on to Windows. If you don't log on to Windows, press and hold **Shift** when you see the Windows *splash* screen (the screen that appears before you get to the desktop).

➤ To remove programs from the StartUp menu, right-click the taskbar, click **Properties**, click the **Start Menu Programs** tab, click the **Remove** button, and click the plus sign next to **StartUp**. Click the program you want to remove and click the **Remove** button. (Careful, if you have an anti-virus program that runs on startup, you may want to keep it on the StartUp menu.)

➤ To quickly restart Windows without restarting your computer, click **Start**, **Shut Down**, and click **Restart**. Hold down the **Shift** key while clicking **Yes** or **OK**.

> **Check This Out...**
>
> **Other Delays** Windows has some built-in delays to give you time to press keys during startup and choose startup options. For example, you can press **F8** before Windows starts to display startup options. You can edit out these delays by editing some of your system files; however, this is risky business, and I'm not about to tell you how to get yourself into trouble.

323

If you have Internet Explorer 4 on your computer, and you have your Windows desktop displayed as a Web page, the active desktop components can add a lot of time to the Windows startup. If you don't use the desktop components, turn them off. Right-click a blank area of the desktop, point to **Active Desktop**, and choose **Customize My Desktop**. Remove the check mark next to every desktop component and click **OK**.

Cleaning Your Hard Disk Without the Tune-Up Wizard

Your hard disk probably contains temporary and backup files that your programs create without telling you. These files can quickly clutter your hard disk drive, taking room that you need for new programs or new data files that you create. You can easily delete most of these files yourself.

The first candidates for removal are temporary (.TMP) files. These are files that your programs create but often forget to delete. You can safely delete all temporary files from your hard drive. Click the Windows **Start** button, point to **Find**, and click **Files or Folders**. Type *.tmp and press **Enter**. Press **Ctrl+A** to select all the files, and then press the **Delete** key. Gone! You should now have an extra megabyte or more of disk space. (Windows may not be able to delete some .TMP files that it is currently using.)

Check This Out...

Deleting Backup Files

When you save a file that you created, most programs create a backup file that contains the previous version of the file. These files typically have the .BAK extension. If you mess up a file, you can open the backup file instead. Before deleting backup files, make sure that you don't want the previous versions of your files.

To remove temporary files that your Web browser saves, clear the disk cache in your browser. To clear the disk cache in Internet Explorer 4, open the **View** menu and select **Internet Options**. Under Temporary Internet Files, click the **Delete Files** button. In Navigator 4, open the **Edit** menu, select **Preferences**, click the plus sign next to **Advanced**, click **Cache**, and click the **Clear Disk Cache** button.

While you're at it, open your email program and delete any email messages that you no longer need. When you delete email messages, some email programs, such as Outlook Express, stick the deleted messages in a separate folder (called Deleted Items in Outlook Express); be sure to delete the messages from that folder, as well.

Now, most of the stuff you deleted is sitting in the Recycle Bin, where it is still hogging disk space. First, open the Recycle Bin, and scroll down the list of deleted files to make sure that you will never ever again need anything in the Bin. If you find a file that you might need, drag it onto the Windows desktop for safekeeping. Now, open the **File** menu and choose **Empty Recycle Bin.**

Speeding Up Your CD-ROM and Hard Drive

Although your computer's hard drive and CD-ROM drive are good at storing data permanently, they are slow compared to RAM. To help increase their speed, Windows enables you to use a *read-ahead buffer.* Windows reads data off the hard drive or CD and stores it in memory (the *RAM cache*) before that data is actually needed. When Windows needs the data, Windows can then access it quickly from RAM.

You can increase the size of the read-ahead buffer to increase the speed of your hard disk or CD-ROM drive, but this takes memory away from your applications. If you have a lot of physical memory (more than 32MB), try increasing the size of the read-ahead buffer. If your system is low on memory, or you rarely use your CD-ROM drive, try decreasing the size.

To increase the read-ahead buffer for your hard drive or CD-ROM drive, right-click **My Computer** and choose **Properties.** Click the **Performance** tab, and click the **File System** button. Click the **Hard Disk** tab, and drag the Read-ahead optimization slider to **Full.**

Click the **CD-ROM** tab. Open the **Optimize access pattern for** drop-down list, and click the speed of your CD-ROM drive. Drag the **Supplemental cache size slider** to the desired setting: Increase the cache size if you frequently use the CD-ROM drive, or decrease the cache size if you rarely use it. Click **OK** when you're done.

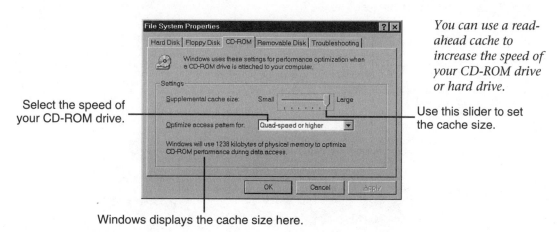

Select the speed of your CD-ROM drive.

Use this slider to set the cache size.

Windows displays the cache size here.

You can use a read-ahead cache to increase the speed of your CD-ROM drive or hard drive.

325

Refreshing and Repairing Disks with ScanDisk

Windows comes with a utility called ScanDisk that can test a disk (hard or floppy), repair most problems on a disk, and refresh the disk, if needed. What kind of problems? ScanDisk can find defective areas on a disk and block them out to prevent your computer from using defective storage areas. ScanDisk can also find and delete misplaced (usually useless) file fragments that may be causing your computer to crash.

ScanDisk on Startup? If you shut down Windows improperly (pressing the power button on your system unit before Windows is ready), later versions of Windows runs ScanDisk automatically when you restart your computer.

You should run ScanDisk regularly (at least once every month) and whenever your computer seems to be acting up (crashing for no apparent reason). Also, if you have a floppy disk that your computer cannot read, ScanDisk may be able to repair the disk and recover any data from it. To run ScanDisk, take the following steps:

1. Choose **Start**, select **Programs, Accessories,** and **System Tools,** and then click **ScanDisk.** The ScanDisk window appears.

2. Click the letter of the drive that you want to check.

3. To check for and repair only file and folder errors, click the **Standard** option; to check the disk for defects (in addition to file and folder errors), click **Thorough.** (Thorough can take hours; select it only if you're on your way to bed.)

4. If you want ScanDisk to fix any errors without asking for your confirmation, make sure that **Automatically fix errors** is checked. (I always choose this option and have never encountered problems with ScanDisk doing something it was not supposed to do.)

5. Click the **Start** button.

ScanDisk can repair most disk problems.

Pick the disk that you want to check.

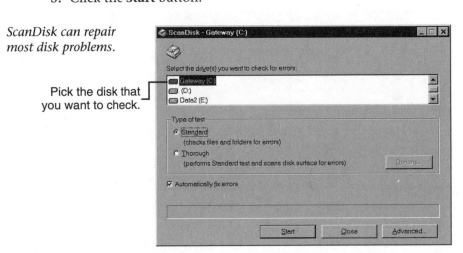

Defragmenting Files on Your Hard Disk

Whenever you delete a file from your hard disk, you leave a space where another file can be stored. When you save a file, your computer stores as much of the file as possible in that empty space, and the rest of the file in other empty spaces. The file is then said to be *fragmented*, because its parts are stored in different locations on the disk. This slows down your disk drive and makes it more likely that a file will be lost or damaged.

Caution If you have an older version of Windows 95, you might have the DOS version of Defragmenter on your computer. Never use the DOS Defragmenter program. It can't handle the long filenames that Windows 95 allows for. It might also destroy some of your files. Run Disk Defragmenter from the Start menu only.

Every month or so, you should run a defragmentation program to determine the fragmentation percent and to defragment your files, if necessary. If you ran the Tune-Up Wizard, as explained earlier in this chapter, Windows Disk Defragmenter automatically performs the operation at the scheduled time. If you did not run the Tune-Up Wizard, you can run Disk Defragmenter yourself.

To have Disk Defragmenter defragment your files, take the following steps:

1. Choose **Start**, select **Programs**, **Accessories**, **System Tools**, and click **Disk Defragmenter**. A dialog box appears, asking which disk drive you want to defragment.

2. Open the **Which drive do you want to defragment?** drop-down list, and click the desired disk. You can defragment all your disks by clicking **All Hard Drives**. (You don't need to defragment floppy disks.)

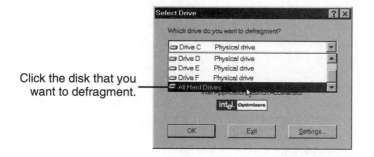

Click the disk that you want to defragment.

You can defragment any or all your disks.

3. Click **OK**. Another dialog box appears, indicating both the percent of file fragmentation on the disk and whether or not you need to defragment the disk.

4. Click the **Start** button. Defragmenter starts to defragment the files on the disk.

5. Wait until the defragmentation is complete. It's best to leave your computer alone during the process; don't run any programs or play any computer games.

Doubling Your Disk Space

As computers become more complex, program and document files are becoming larger and larger. Five years ago, a typical program would take up a couple megabytes of disk space. Nowadays, each program can consume 10 megabytes or more. In addition, as you explore the Internet, you commonly encounter graphics and audio and video clips that are over 1 megabyte!

As files become larger and as your own thirst for the latest programs and media increases, your hard disk quickly becomes packed. To help, Windows offers a couple utilities that can make your hard drive use its storage space more efficiently: Drive Converter (available only in later versions of Windows) and DriveSpace. (Drive Converter may be called FAT32 Converter in your version of Windows.)

To understand Drive Converter, you must first understand how older hard disk drives stored data in the past. If you have a hard drive larger than 500 megabytes, older operating systems (using FAT16) would use 32 kilobytes of hard drive space to store every file 32 kilobytes or less of data. For example, a 2-kilobyte file would still take up 32 kilobytes of disk space. You could partition your hard disk drive into units smaller than 500 megabytes to make the operating system store files in 4K chunks instead, saving you up to 40 percent of wasted space. Partitioning the hard disk drive, however, destroys any data that it contains. Drive Converter can perform the optimization without destroying data.

The only problem with Drive Converter is that doesn't help much on smaller hard disks. If you have a 500 megabyte, or smaller, hard disk, you can use a different utility—DriveSpace. DriveSpace compresses the files on the hard drive, so they take up less space when not in use. When you run a compressed program or open a compressed file, DriveSpace automatically decompresses it. Because DriveSpace must decompress files when you run a program or open a document, it decreases overall system performance.

To use Drive Converter (or find out if it can even help), take the following steps (the conversion may take more than one hour):

1. Choose **Start**, select **Programs**, **Accessories**, **System Tools**, and click **Drive Converter** or **FAT32 Converter**.

2. Click **Next**. Drive Converter analyzes your hard disk drive(s) to determine which drive(s) are currently using FAT16.

3. Click the drive that you want to optimize. Drive Converter displays a warning indicating that you are not able to access the converted drive using a previous version of Windows, MS-DOS, or Windows NT.

4. Click **OK**. Drive Converter checks for any running programs that might interfere with its operation and displays a list of them.

5. Close any of these programs and click **Next**. Drive Converter prompts you to back up the files on your hard disk before continuing.

6. Click **Create Backup**, and refer to Chapter 31, "Backing Up for the Inevitable Crash," for details on how to proceed.

7. When you return to Drive Converter, click **Next**. Drive Converter indicates that it must restart your computer in MS-DOS mode.

8. Close any programs that are currently running and click **Next**.

If you cannot use Drive Converter on your hard drives, or if you need additional storage space, take the following steps to run DriveSpace (this can take a long time, too):

1. Back up all files on the hard disk drive that you want to compress, as explained in Chapter 31.

2. Choose **Start**, select **Programs**, **Accessories**, **System Tools**, and click **DriveSpace**.

3. Select the disk drive that you want to compress.

4. Open the **Drive** menu and select **Compress**. The Compress a Drive dialog box displays a graph of how much free space the drive currently has and how much it will have after compression.

5. Click the **Start** button. A confirmation dialog box appears, prompting you to create or update your Windows StartUp disk before proceeding.

6. Click **Yes** and follow the onscreen instructions to create a StartUp disk. Another confirmation dialog box appears, prompting you to back up your files before proceeding, which you should have done in step 1.

7. Click **Compress Now**. Wait until the compression is complete. This can take from several minutes to several hours depending on the size of the hard disk.

DriveSpace displays pie charts to illustrate how much disk space it can save you.

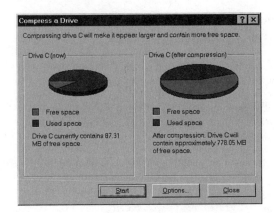

If, after compressing a drive, you have trouble running a particular application, you can uncompress the drive, and return your system to normal (open the **Drive** menu and select **Uncompress**). In such a case, you can leave your original drive uncompressed, and create a new, compressed drive for storing your data files or any new programs that you install. To create a separate compressed drive, run DriveSpace, open the **Advanced** menu, and select **Create Empty**.

Making the Most of Your Computer's Memory

Your computer can't do anything without memory, and it can't do anything very well or very quickly if it doesn't have enough memory. Windows does a pretty good job of managing memory for you and of using your hard disk for additional memory (called *virtual memory*). Although virtual memory is slower than real memory, it can help you avoid getting **Insufficient Memory** error messages when you try to load large programs or run several programs at one time.

If you are receiving **Insufficient Memory** messages on a regular basis, or if you have more than one hard disk drive, you should check the virtual memory settings. Open the **Control Panel**, and double-click the **System** icon. Click the **Performance** tab, and click the **Virtual Memory** button. Check for the following:

➤ Make sure that **Let Windows Manage My Virtual Memory Settings** is selected.

➤ Make sure that you have at least 30MB of free space on the disk drive that Windows is using for virtual memory. (If the space dips below that, clear files from your hard disk, as explained earlier in this chapter.)

➤ If you have more than one hard disk drive installed, click **Let Me Specify My Own Virtual Memory Settings**, and choose your fastest hard disk drive that has the most free space from the **Hard Disk** drop-down list. Click **OK**, and then click the **Virtual**

Memory button again. Click **Let Windows Manage My Virtual Memory Settings** and click **OK**. This enables Windows to manage the settings on the disk that you chose.

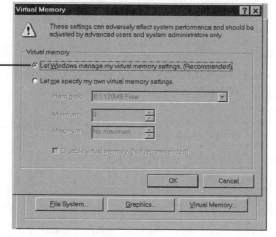

Make sure that Windows is naming the virtual memory.

Windows 95 does a fine job of managing the virtual memory.

Speeding Up the Video

Windows 95 and later versions offer much improved video support over Windows 3.1, but you can still wring some more speed out of your video. If video clips on the Web or in your multimedia programs seem clunky and choppy, try setting the video resolution no higher than 800-by-600 and the colors to 256. Your display card and Windows must work much harder to render screens at higher resolutions and color depths, and you won't notice much of a dip in quality on most of your video clips and graphics. Take the following steps:

1. Right-click a blank area of the Windows desktop and choose **Properties**.

2. Click the **Settings** tab.

3. Open the **Colors** drop-down list and choose **256**. Don't go any lower, or your graphics look lousy.

4. Drag the **Screen Area** slider to set the area at 800-by-600. You can try 640-by-480 to speed things up even faster, but if you don't like it, change back to 800-by-600.

Check the Start Menu Your display card may have its own control panel for additional performance settings. Check the Start, Programs menu for a program group or icon for running the display card's control panel.

5. Click the **Advanced** button to see what's available. You may see a dialog box with hardware acceleration settings and screen refresh rate settings that you can use to increase the display performance even more. Click **OK** when you're done.

6. Click **OK** to save your settings. Windows may prompt you to restart.

Tech Check

As you can see, you can do a lot to keep your computer tuned; however, if you like to do as little as necessary to keep your computer in shape, make sure you do the following regularly:

➤ Use the Windows Tune-Up Wizard to schedule regular tune ups, if you have it.

➤ Take programs you don't use off the StartUp menu.

➤ Defragment files on your hard disk, if needed.

➤ Determine whether the read-ahead buffer is optimized for your hard disk and CD-ROM drive.

➤ Check a disk with ScanDisk.

➤ Double your disk space.

Chapter 29

Life on the Run: Laptop Computing

In This Chapter

➤ Take your show on the road with a laptop or notebook PC

➤ Go further on a single battery

➤ Stick PC cards in the little slots and get them to work

➤ Dock with the mothership (docking stations)

➤ Phone home to connect when you're on the road

In the past, portable computing meant that you had to use a computer so feeble that it could barely keep up with your typing, let alone Windows and your mouse. The new portable PCs, however, are powerhouses. Many come with 200MHz Pentium MMx CPUs, 4GB hard drives, CD-ROM, speakers, a microphone, and a lot of RAM. The screens are still

Windows Components Installed? Many of the features described in this chapter are not installed during a typical Windows installation. If the option is not available, refer to Chapter 5, "Windows Tips, Tricks, and Traps," to install the missing Windows components.

tiny, but the typical notebook PC can hold its own against a comparable desktop model.

Going portable, however, introduces you to several issues that you may not have faced with your stationary desktop PC. You need to know how to transfer files from your notebook to your desktop PC, connect to your company's network, insert and remove PCMCIA (PC) cards, and conserve battery power when you're trying to meet a deadline on the road. Fortunately, Windows provides the tools that you need to deal with these issues.

Taking Your Work on the Road with My Briefcase

If you have both a notebook and desktop computer, you probably need to transfer files from your desktop computer to your notebook computer to take work with you on trips. If you edit the files on your notebook computer, you must then copy them back to the desktop computer to ensure that you have the most recent versions on both computers. Of course, you can simply copy the files to a floppy disk using My Computer or Windows Explorer, but you then run the risk of replacing the new versions of your documents with older ones. Fortunately, Windows offers a convenient tool for safely transferring files between computers: *Briefcase*. Briefcase helps you decide which files should be replaced.

Take the following steps to use Briefcase:

1. On your desktop computer, drag files from My Computer or Windows Explorer over the My Briefcase icon on the Windows desktop and release the mouse button.

More Briefcases To avoid replacing the wrong files, keep each group of files in its own briefcase. To create a new briefcase, right-click the Windows desktop, point to **New**, and choose **Briefcase**. Give each briefcase a unique name.

2. Insert a blank floppy disk and drag the **My Briefcase** icon over the floppy disk icon in My Computer.

3. Take the floppy disk home or on the road and edit the files on your notebook computer. (Open them from the floppy disk and save them to the floppy disk.)

4. When you return, insert the floppy disk into your desktop computer's floppy disk drive.

5. Run My Computer, double-click the floppy disk drive icon, and double-click **My Briefcase**. A window appears, displaying the files and indicating whether they are up-to-date or need updating. If the files are not displayed as shown in the figure, open the **View** menu and choose **Details**.

6. To update all the files with their newer versions, click the **Update All** button in the toolbar. To update only some files, first select the files that you want to update (the files marked Needs Updating) and click the **Update Selection** button.

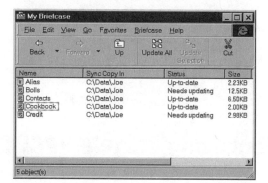

My Briefcase helps you decide which files to update.

Conserving Battery Power

With a fully charged battery, a notebook computer can operate for about three hours. That's not much time if you are putting in a full day's work on the road. Fortunately, Windows has some advanced power-saving features designed specifically for notebook computers. These features can double the life of your battery by powering down your monitor and hard disk drive after a specified amount of time. You can even activate warnings to have Windows notify you when the battery is running down, so you can save your work and shut down Windows before the battery goes dead.

Built-In Power-Saving Features? Many notebook PCs have built-in power-saving features that may conflict with those that Windows offers. Check your notebook PC's documentation to determine whether it is okay to use the Windows features.

To change any of the power-saving settings in Windows, double-click the **Power** or **Power Management** icon in the Windows Control Panel. Enter the desired settings and click **OK**. When your notebook is running on battery power, the system tray on the right end of the taskbar displays a battery icon. Point to the icon to see how much battery power is left, or right-click the icon and choose **Open Battery Meter**.

*Windows can help
you conserve power.*

Enter the desired
power-saving settings.

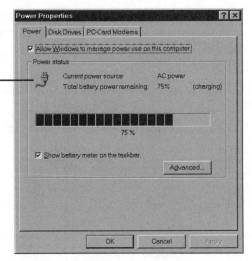

Adding and Removing PCMCIA (PC) Cards

**Conserve
Desktop PC
Power, Too!**
Newer desktop
PCs have built-
in power-saving
features similar to those on
notebook PCs. If you're using a
desktop PC, the Power Management utility may be able to help
you trim your electric bill.

Most newer notebook computers make it much easier to
upgrade memory, drives, modems, and so on, by using
PCMCIA cards (or PC cards). (PCMCIA is short for *Personal
Computer Memory Card International Association*). PC cards
are small devices that plug directly into expansion slots on
the *outside* of the computer. These cards are about the size
of credit cards, and you can insert them when the power is
on. It's a little like inserting a diskette in a floppy disk
drive.

When you are shopping for a PCMCIA card, you should
keep in mind that there are three types of cards. They are
all the same length and width, but their thicknesses vary:

➤ Type I cards (up to 3.3mm thick) are used primarily for adding memory to a computer.

➤ Type II cards (up to 5.5mm thick) are typically used to add a fax modem, network
adapter, or CD-ROM drive. (The drive is connected to the PCMCIA card with a
cable.)

➤ Type III cards (up to 10.5mm thick) are usually used for adding a hard disk drive.

Your notebook computer should have one or more PCMCIA slots. These slots also come
in three types:

➤ Type I slots can use only one Type I card.

➤ Type II slots can use one Type I card or two Type II cards.

➤ Type III slots can use one Type III card or one Type I card and a Type II card.

You can insert the card with the power on or off. When you insert the card with the power on, Windows automatically detects it, sounds a two-toned beep, and runs the Add New Hardware Wizard, which leads you through the process of installing a driver for the card. (The next time you insert the card, Windows remembers it, so you don't have to reinstall the driver.) To remove the PC card, take the following steps:

Playing the Slot Machine The PCMCIA slots are typically numbered 0 and 1. Insert your first card in the 0 slot and the second one in the 1 slot; otherwise, the cards may not work properly. Check your computer's documentation to determine which slot is which.

1. Click the **PC Card (PCMCIA)** Status icon in the system tray and select the **Stop** option for the card that you want to remove. A dialog box appears, indicating that it is safe to remove the card.

2. Click **OK**.

3. Press the **Eject** button next to the PCMCIA card. The card pops out of the slot, and Windows emits a two-toned beep (high tone followed by a medium tone). Pull the card out of the slot.

Going Full-Featured with a Docking Station

A docking station or *port replicator* provides the portability of a notebook PC with the advanced features of a desktop PC. The docking station is a unit that contains ports for a monitor, printer, keyboard, mouse, speakers, and other devices. You turn off your notebook computer, insert it into the docking station, and pretend that it's a big, powerful computer.

The trouble with docking stations is that your notebook is set up to use its built-in monitor, keyboard, and speakers. It is not set up to use the hardware that's connected to the docking station. If your notebook is plug-and-play compatible, you won't have any problem. Just connect it to the docking station, and Windows takes care of the details. (A few notebook computers enable you to dock without turning off the power.)

No Docking Station? If you don't have a docking station, you may still be able to connect your notebook PC to a standard monitor, keyboard, mouse, and speakers. Check the back and sides of your notebook PC for additional ports.

If your notebook PC is not plug-and-play compatible, connect it to the docking station, make sure all docking station devices are turned on, and then turn on your notebook. Windows detects new non-plug-and-play devices and runs the Add New Hardware Wizard to lead you through the process of installing the drivers. If Windows does not detect a device, run the Add New Hardware Wizard to install the driver (as explained in Chapter 27, "Upgrading Your Computer to Make It the Best It Can Be.")

After you install the necessary drivers, you have a driver for each device on your notebook and each device connected to the docking station. These drivers may conflict, and Windows chooses which one it wants to use. To solve this problem, create two separate *hardware profiles* to deal with the docked and undocked configurations. You can then disable devices in each profile.

Take the following steps to create a new hardware profile and disable devices:

1. Right-click **My Computer** and select **Properties**.

Don't Disable the Wrong Devices Before disabling devices, make sure that you have a recent Windows Start Up diskette. If you disable the wrong device, use your Windows Startup diskette to start your computer, and then reenable the device. (See Chapter 32, "Do-It-Yourself Fixes to Common Ailments," to learn how to create a startup diskette.)

2. Click the **Hardware Profiles** tab. If your notebook is plug-and-play compatible, you should see two options—Docked and Undocked. Click **OK** and skip the remaining steps.

3. If you see only one option, Original Configuration, click it and click the **Copy**.

4. Type **Docked** as the name of your new configuration and click **OK**. The Docked configuration is selected, so you can disable notebook devices when the notebook is docked.

5. Click the **Device Manager** tab.

6. Click the plus sign next to one of the notebook devices that you want to disable when the notebook is docked.

7. Double-click the name of the device that you want to disable.

8. Click **Disable in This Hardware Profile**, and click **OK**.

9. Repeat steps 6 and 8 to disable additional devices.

10. Click the **Hardware Profiles** tab and choose **Original Configuration**.

11. Click the **Device Manager** tab, and click the plus sign next to one of the docking station devices that you want to disable when the notebook is undocked.

12. Complete steps 6 to 9 to disable all docking station devices, and then click **OK**.

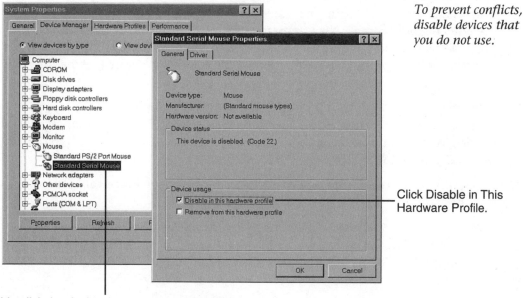

To prevent conflicts, disable devices that you do not use.

Click Disable in This Hardware Profile.

Double-click the device that you want to disable.

Whenever you start your notebook, Windows attempts to determine which configuration to use. If Windows can't make this determination, it displays a list of available configurations—Original Configuration and Docked. Type the number next to the configuration that you want to use.

Linking Your Notebook and Desktop Computers

Windows includes a feature called *Direct Cable Connection*, which enables you to connect two computers by using a serial or parallel cable. After the computers are connected, you can use one computer to link to the other computer and use its files, programs, and printer, just as if you were typing at its keyboard. The Direct Cable Connection is especially useful if you need to transfer large amounts of data from one computer to another. You simply copy a folder from one computer, switch to the other computer, and paste the folder on the desired hard disk. You can do this between a notebook and desktop computer, between two desktop computers, or between two notebook computers.

Set Up a Connection

To set up a direct cable connection, you must first connect the serial or parallel ports on the two computers. To connect the serial ports, you must have a *serial null-modem cable* (sometimes called a *file transfer cable*), a special serial cable that is designed for direct data transfers rather than modem communications. Connecting the parallel ports is the preferred method, because they transfer data from 10 to 15 times faster than the serial ports. If you want to share a printer, and the printer is connected to the parallel port, connect the serial ports, instead. Shut down the computers before making the connection.

After you have installed the cable, you must set up one computer as the *host* and the other as the *guest*. The host is usually the more powerful of the two computers. If you are connecting a desktop and notebook computer, the desktop computer is typically the host. Take the following steps to set up the connection in Windows:

1. Turn off the two computers, connect them with the required cable, and turn them back on.

2. On the host computer, choose **Start, Programs, Accessories, Direct Cable Connection**. (If Direct Cable Connection is not listed, see "Installing and Uninstalling Windows Components," in Chapter 5, to install it.) The Direct Cable Connection Wizard appears.

3. Click **Host** and click **Next**. You are prompted to pick the port in which you plugged the cable.

4. Select the port and click **Next**.

5. (Optional) To prevent unauthorized access to your computer, choose **Use Password Protection**. Click the **Set Password** button, enter the password in the two text boxes, and click **OK**.

6. On the guest computer, choose **Start, Programs, Accessories, Direct Cable Connection**.

7. Click **Guest** and click **Next**. You are prompted to pick the port in which you plugged the cable.

8. Select the port and click **Next**.

9. Go back to the host computer and click **Finish**. The host computer displays a dialog box indicating that it is waiting for the guest computer to connect.

10. On the guest computer, click **Finish**. If you set password protection on the host computer, a dialog box appears on the guest computer, prompting you to enter the password. Type the password and click **OK**.

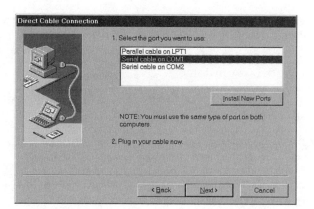

Direct Cable Connection leads you through the process of connecting your computers.

Share Resources

A direct cable connection works very much like a network connection. Before you can share files and printers over a direct cable connection, you must enter share settings for disk drives, folders, files, and printers on the host computer. For details on how to share disks, files, folders, and printers, see Chapter 17, "Networking (for Those Corporate Types)."

Calling Your Desktop Computer or Network Via Modem

If you are on the road and need to use your desktop computer or log on to your network, you can use Dial-Up Networking to place the call. You can then copy files and run programs from your desktop computer or network server. Although sharing files and programs over a modem connection provides relatively slow performance, it does give you access to resources that you would not otherwise be able to use.

To use your notebook computer to dial into your desktop computer from a remote location, you must first set up your desktop computer as a *Dial-Up Networking server* (or *Dial-Up Server*). This enables the desktop computer to answer incoming calls and establish communications with your notebook computer. Your notebook acts as the *Dial-Up Networking client*. You must create a new Dial-Up Networking connection, supplying Dial-Up Networking with your desktop computer's phone number.

Although this isn't a complicated task to pull off, it is tedious and consists of more steps than you find in the Washington Monument (898, in case you're wondering). Instead of boring you with the details, I give you the boiled-down overview:

1. Double-click the **Network** icon in the **Control Panel** and use the **Add** button to install the following network components on *both* computers: Client for Microsoft Networks, Dial-Up Adapter, and a network protocol (TCP/IP, NetBEUI, or IPX/SPX). Stay in the Network box until step 4.

2. Make sure that **Primary Network Logon** is set as **Client for Microsoft Networks**. Do this on both computers.

3. Click **File and Print Sharing** and activate all the options.

4. Still in the Network box? Double-click **File and Printer Sharing for Microsoft Networks**, select **Browse Master** and make sure its Value is set to **Automatic**. Click **OK**. You're done with the Network box, so click **OK**.

5. On the desktop computer, enter share settings for any disks or folders that you want to be able to access. See Chapter 17.

6. Set up your desktop computer to answer the phone. Run Dial-Up Networking from My Computer, open the **Connections** menu and choose **Dial-Up Server**. Enter your preferences, and be sure to require a password; otherwise, anyone with a PC, modem, and too much free time can break into your computer. A Dial-Up Server icon appears in the system tray.

Check This Out...

Problems?
Getting your Dial-Up server to work properly can be difficult. If you have problems, check out Microsoft's technical support information on the Web at **www.microsoft.com** (as explained in Chapter 33, "Help! Finding Technical Support").

7. On your notebook computer, run Dial-Up Networking from My Computer and double-click the **Make New Connection** icon. Follow the instructions to create an icon for dialing your desktop computer. (If your desktop PC is going to be outside of your destination's area code, keep that in mind when you're typing the phone number.)

Before you leave on your big trip, make sure that you turn on your desktop PC, or it won't answer the phone. When you're on the road, simply plug your notebook's modem into a phone jack, double-click the **Dial-Up Networking** icon you created, and click **Connect** to dial your desktop computer. When your desktop computer answers, double-click the **Network Neighborhood** icon on your Windows desktop to access your desktop PC's disks and folders.

Tech Check

Now that you've worked through this chapter, you should be able to take advantage of your notebook PC's unique features. Before you hit the road, make sure that you can do the following:

➤ Use My Briefcase to safely transfer files between your desktop and notebook PCs.

➤ Conserve your battery so that you can work longer.

➤ Install a fax modem or network PC card without disassembling your computer.

➤ Plug your notebook PC into a docking station and resolve any hardware conflicts.

➤ Connect your notebook and desktop PCs for fast file transfers.

➤ Give your desktop computer a jingle when you're on the road.

Part 6
"Houston, We've Got a Problem"

When everything goes right, personal computing is fairly enjoyable. Even if you're not a computer nerd, using the computer to do your work, explore your interests, or even socialize can be fun. However, when things go wrong, your computer can become your bitter enemy, offering you no clue as to what went wrong or how to fix it.

In this part, you will learn how to keep your computer in peak operating condition, protect the document files you create, and diagnose and cure common computer ailments. As for those computer problems you cannot fix on your own, this part shows you how to get technical support over the phone and on the Internet.

Free (or at Least Cheap) Computer Maintenance

When you purchased your computer, the dealer probably didn't mention that in addition to letting you run programs and play games, your computer functions as an excellent clean-air machine. Most system units have two fans, one sucking in and one blowing out, to pull all the dust and smoke from your room and deposit it on the sensitive electrical components inside your computer. In addition, the static electricity that builds up in the monitor, printer, and other devices is like a dust magnet, gathering all those tiny particles that the system unit misses.

If you don't clean this dust and gunk from your computer regularly, it builds up quickly and can cause problems. Your mouse pointer might start to skip around on the screen, you might start receiving disk errors, and the dust build-up can eventually cause your new Pentium CPU to experience a meltdown. Besides, who wants to work or play in a dustbowl? In this chapter, you learn how to keep your computer spic-and-span.

Tools of the Trade

Before you start cleaning, turn off your computer and any attached devices, and gather the following cleaning equipment:

➤ Screwdriver or wrench for taking the cover off of your system unit. (If you don't feel qualified to go inside the system unit, take your computer to a qualified technician for a thorough annual cleaning. It really does get dusty in there.)

➤ Computer vacuum. Yes, they have vacuum cleaners especially designed for computers.

➤ Can of compressed air. You can get this at a computer or electronics store. If you decide to forego the vacuum cleaner, you can use the compressed air to blow dust out of the system unit.

➤ Soft brush (a clean paintbrush with soft bristles will do). Use the brush to dislodge any stubborn dust that the vacuum won't pick up.

➤ Toothpicks (the only tool you need to clean your mouse).

➤ Cotton swabs.

➤ Paper towel.

➤ Alcohol (not the drinking kind, save that for when your hard drive crashes).

Safety Precautions If you decide to go inside the system unit, follow the same precautions listed in Chapter 27, "Upgrading Your Computer to Make It the Best It Can Be."

➤ Distilled water. (You can get special wipes for your monitor, but paper towels and water do the trick.)

➤ Radio or CD player. (When you're cleaning, you need music.)

Don't run out and buy a floppy disk or CD-ROM cleaning kit. If your drive is having trouble reading disks, then clean it.

Vacuum and Dust Your System

Work from the top down and from the outside in. Start with the monitor. (You can use your regular vacuum cleaner for this part; if you have a brush attachment, use it.) Get your vacuum hose and run it up and down all the slots at the top and sides of the monitor. This is where most of the dust settles. Work down to the tilt-swivel base and vacuum that (you may need a narrow hose extension to reach in there). Now, vacuum your printer, speakers, and any other devices. If the dust is stuck to a device, wipe it off with a damp (not soaking wet) paper towel.

Now for the system unit. When vacuuming, make sure that you vacuum all the ventilation holes. Any other openings in the case act as additional ventilation holes: the floppy disk drive, power button, CD-ROM drive, open drive bays, and so on. Vacuum these openings. If you have a CD-ROM drive, open it and vacuum the tray.

Now for the tough part—inside the system unit. Before you poke your vacuum hose in there, you should be aware of the following precautions:

➤ Use only a vacuum designed for computers or use a can of compressed air to blow out the dust. Don't use a Dust Buster, your regular vacuum cleaner, or your ShopVac. These can suck components off your circuit boards and can emit enough static electricity to fry a component. A computer vacuum is gentle and grounded.

➤ Be careful around circuit boards.

➤ Touch a metal part of the case to discharge any static electricity from your body, and keep your fingers away from the circuit boards.

Now, take the cover off the system unit and vacuum any dusty areas. Dust likes to collect around the fan, ventilation holes, and disk drives. Try to vacuum the fan blades, too. If you can't get the tip of the vacuum between the blades, gently wipe them off with a cotton swab. Some fans have a filter where the fan is mounted. If you're really ambitious, remove the fan (careful with the wires) and clean the filter.

Cheap Air Filter Some PCs have a fan that pulls air from the outside and pushes it through the ventilation holes. If the system unit case has openings near the fan, cut a square of sheer hosiery fabric, stretch it over the openings, and tape it in place with duct tape, keeping the tape away from the openings. Check the filter regularly and replace it whenever dust builds up.

Wiping Gunk Off the Monitor

If you can take the tip of your finger and write WASH ME on your monitor, it needs to be cleaned. Check the documentation that came with your computer or monitor to see whether it's okay to use window cleaner on it—the monitor may have an antiglare coating that can be damaged by alcohol- or ammonia-based cleaning solutions. (If it's not okay, use water.) Spray the window cleaner (or water) on a paper towel, just enough to make it damp, and then wipe the

Cheap Trick Don't waste your money on antistatic wipes. Wipe your monitor with a *used* dryer sheet. (A new dryer sheet might smudge the screen with fabric softener.)

screen. DON'T spray window cleaner or any other liquid directly on the monitor; you don't want moisture to seep in. You can purchase special antistatic wipes for your monitor. These not only clean your monitor safely, but they also discharge the static electricity to prevent future dust build-up.

Brushing Off the Keyboard

Your keyboard is like a big place mat, catching all the cookie crumbs and other debris that falls off your fingers while you're working. The trouble is that, unlike a place mat, the keyboard isn't flat; it's full of crannies that are impossible to reach. And the suction from a typical vacuum cleaner just isn't strong enough to pull up the dust (although you can try it).

The easiest way I've found to clean a keyboard is to turn it upside-down and shake it gently. Repeat two or three times to get any particles that fall behind the backs of the keys when you flip it over. If you don't like that idea, get your handy-dandy can of compressed air and blow between the keys.

For a more thorough cleaning, shut down your computer, and disconnect the keyboard. Dampen a cotton swab with rubbing alcohol and gently scrub the keys. Wait for the alcohol to evaporate before reconnecting the keyboard and turning on the power.

Check This Out...

Thrills and Spills

If you spill a drink on your keyboard, try to save your work and shut down the computer fast, but properly. Flip the keyboard over and turn off your computer. If you spilled water, just let the keyboard dry thoroughly. If you spilled something sticky, give your keyboard a bath or shower with lukewarm water. Take the back off of the keyboard, but DON'T flip the keyboard over with the back off or parts scurry across your desktop. Let it dry for a couple of days (don't use a blow-dryer), and put it back together. If some of the keys are still sticky, clean around them with a cotton swab dipped in rubbing alcohol. If you still have problems, buy a new keyboard; they're relatively inexpensive.

Picking Hairballs Out of Your Mouse

If you can't get your mouse pointer to move where you want it to, you can usually fix the problem by cleaning the mouse. Flip the mouse over and look for hair or other debris on the mouse ball or on your desk or mouse pad. Removing the hair or wiping off your mouse pad fixes the problem 90 percent of the time.

If that doesn't work, remove the mouse ball cover (typically, you press down on the cover and turn counterclockwise). Wipe the ball thoroughly with a moistened paper towel. Now for the fun part. Look inside the mouse (where the ball was). You should see three rollers, and each roller has a tiny ring around its middle. The ring is not supposed to be there. The easiest way I've found to remove these rings is to gently scrape them off with a toothpick. You have to spin the rollers to remove the entire ring. You may also try rubbing the rings off with a cotton swab dipped in rubbing alcohol, but these rings are pretty stubborn. When you're done, turn the mouse back over and shake it to remove the loose crumbs. Reassemble the mouse.

Basic Printer Maintenance

Printer maintenance varies widely from one printer to another. If you have a laser printer, you need to vacuum or wipe up toner dust and clean the little print wires with cotton swabs dipped in rubbing alcohol. For an inkjet printer, you may have to remove the print cartridge and wipe the print heads with a damp cotton swab. If you have a combination scanner/printer, you may have to wipe the glass on which you place your original.

You also need to be careful about the cleaning solution you use. Most printer manufacturers tell you to use only water on any of the inside parts—print rollers, print heads, and so on. In other cases, you can use a mild cleaning solution. Some manufacturers recommend rubbing alcohol on some, not all, parts.

Even with all these variables, the average user can do a few things to keep the printer in peak condition and ensure high-quality output:

➤ When turning off the printer, always use the power button on the printer (don't use the power button on your power strip). This ensures that the print head is moved to its rest position. On inkjet printers, this prevents the print head from drying out.

➤ Vacuum inside the printer. Open any doors or covers to get inside.

➤ If the ink starts to streak on your printouts (or you have frequent paper jams in a laser printer), get special printer-cleaner paper from an office supply store and follow the instructions to run the sheet through your printer a few times.

Check This Out...

Rubbing Alcohol Rule of Thumb Rubbing alcohol is an excellent cleaning solution for most electronic devices, because it cleans well and dries quickly. Use it for your keyboard, plastics, and most glass surfaces (except for some monitors). Avoid using it on rubber (for example, your mouse ball), because it tends to dry out the rubber and make it brittle.

➤ Using a damp cotton ball, wipe paper dust and any ink off the paper feed rollers. DON'T use alcohol. DON'T use a paper towel; fibers from the paper towel could stick to the wheels.

Cleaning Your Disk Drives

Don't bother cleaning your floppy or CD-ROM drives unless they're giving you trouble. If your CD-ROM drive is having trouble reading a disc, the disc is usually the cause of the problem. Clean the disc and check the bottom of the disc for scratches. If the drive has problems reading every CD you insert, try cleaning the drive using a special CD-ROM drive cleaning kit. The kit usually consists of a CD with some cleaning solution; you squirt the cleaning solution on the CD, insert it, remove it, and your job is done.

If you have a floppy disk drive that has trouble reading any disk that you insert, you can purchase a special cleaning kit that works like the CD-ROM cleaning kit. Although cleaning the disk drive may solve the problem, the problem can also be caused by a poorly aligned read/write head inside the drive, which no simple cleaning kit can correct.

Tech Check

Now that you know all about computer maintenance, you can save yourself fifty bucks on the Sears maintenance agreement. Just make sure you can do the following:

➤ Vacuum your system without knocking loose any cables or components.

➤ Find the right cleaning solution for your monitor.

➤ Clean out your keyboard.

➤ Remove those nasty mouse rings with a toothpick.

➤ Name the best way to keep an inkjet printer cartridge from drying out.

➤ Go two years without cleaning your floppy disk or CD-ROM drive.

Chapter 31

Backing Up for the Inevitable Crash

In This Chapter

➤ Stick the entire contents of your hard drive on a backup disk

➤ Back up only the data files that you have created

➤ Pick a backup plan you can live with

➤ Recover files when disaster strikes

Backing up a hard disk poses the same question that airline passengers have faced for a long time: Is safety worth the added time and inconvenience of baggage checks and metal detectors? Can your hard drive crash? Yes. Can you lose all your files? Yes. Can someone steal your computer? Yes. Are you willing to do what it takes to recover from such a disaster? Probably not.

Backing up regularly seems like nothing more than a hassle until disaster strikes. You delete a file and dump the Recycle Bin, lightning strikes and destroys your hard drive, or your computer won't start no matter what you do. In the event of such a mishap, you could probably reinstall your programs, but what about your data? Would you remember all the data that you entered in your personal finance program? Could you rewrite the diary you were keeping? Would you be able to rebuild your spreadsheets and all the other documents that you had painstakingly created? Probably not.

Back up your files regularly. Using a backup program, you can create backup copies of all the files on your hard disk. If you ever destroy a file by mistake, or lose one or more files for any reason, you simply restore the file(s) from your backups.

Backup Strategies for the Real World

Backups are worthless if you don't have a backup strategy—a plan that ensures the backup copies are up-to-date. If you restore your files from old backups, you get old files, losing any changes you've made since the last backup. Like most strategies, backup strategies vary depending on how you work and how you organize your files. The following is a list of common strategies that might help you to develop your own plan:

➤ **The "Data only, hope nothing happens" strategy** Create a DATA folder and save all the files that you create in folders under the DATA folder. Don't worry about backing up Windows or your programs; you can reinstall them. The trouble with this strategy is that you lose all your Windows and program settings if your hard drive dies, including your Internet connection settings, email messages, address book, network settings, desktop enhancements, and plenty else. (By the way, this is my strategy.)

➤ **The "I feel lucky today" strategy** This consists of backing up when you feel like it. People who follow this strategy rarely back up and are at a high risk of losing data.

➤ **The standard strategy** Back up your entire system monthly and daily back up only those files that change from day to day. This is the best strategy for making sure that you can recover everything. To do this, you perform a full backup monthly. On a daily basis, you perform an *incremental backup*, which backs up only those files that have changed since the last backup.

➤ **The "I'm special; I have a backup drive" strategy** This is for people who have a tape backup or Zip drive. You *schedule* a full backup every week and an incremental backup at the end of the day. As you're driving home from work, your backup program backs up all your files for you. Most backup programs have a built-in scheduler. In the Windows 98 prerelease, you could use Task Scheduler to schedule backups.

Backing Up in Windows

Windows comes with its own Backup utility, which can back up files using your floppy disk. It also supports many special backup drives. However, it does not support some of the newer backup drives. If your backup drive came with its own backup program, use that program instead.

354

Full and Incremental Backups

Whenever a backup program copies a file, it turns the file's *archive attribute* off, indicating that the file has been backed up. If you edit the file, your computer turns the archive attribute on, indicating that the newly edited file has not been backed up. If you then perform an incremental backup, the backup program knows that it must back up this changed file. When you perform a full backup, the backup program copies all the files, no matter what the archive attribute is set to. The backup program then turns off the archive attribute for all those files.

If you don't have a special backup program, use the Windows Backup utility. To run the Backup, choose **Start**, **Programs**, **Accessories**, **System Tools**, **Backup**. In Windows 95, Backup displays a couple of introductory dialog boxes, which you can skip with the click of a mouse. (Windows might also search for a tape drive and prompt you to test your drives.) In the Windows 98 prerelease, the Backup Wizard started (see the following section for details). Backup then displays a list of the hard disks on your system. After dealing with the preliminaries, take one of the following steps:

➤ To back up all the folders and files on a drive, check the box next to the drive's letter.

➤ To back up some (but not all) of the folders and files on a drive, click the plus sign next to the icon for the drive. You can then check the boxes next to individual folders and files to mark them for backup.

After marking your disks, folders, and files for backup, click the **Next Step** button. Backup prompts you to choose the drive that you want to use to store the backup files. Click the icon for the drive you want to use to store the backup files. This can be a floppy drive, tape backup drive, network drive, or another hard disk drive.

Check This Out...

No Windows Backup? The Backup utility is not installed during a typical Windows installation. If Backup is not listed on your menu, see "Installing and Uninstalling Windows Components," in Chapter 5, for instructions on how to install it.

Check This Out...

Weird Check Boxes To select all the folders and files on a disk, the folder list must not be expanded. If the list is expanded, checking the box selects only the files on the root directory of the disk. Collapse the folder list by clicking the minus sign next to the disk. (In the Windows 98 prerelease, this problem was fixed.) If the check box is gray with a check mark in it, some files or folders on the disk or in the selected folder are selected; others are not.

You can choose to back up
individual files and folders.

*You can back up
entire disks or
selected folders and
files.*

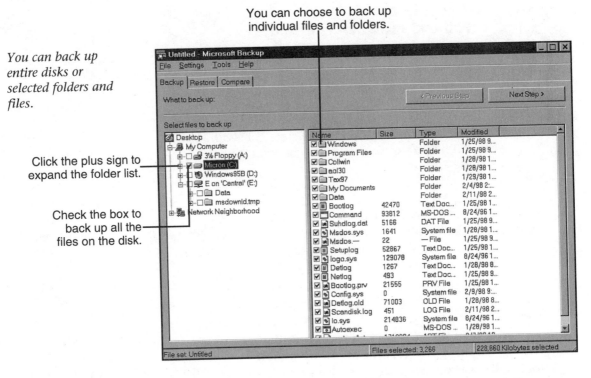

Click the plus sign to
expand the folder list.

Check the box to
back up all the
files on the disk.

If you're backing up to a floppy drive or a tape backup unit, make sure that you have a
disk or tape in the drive. Click the **Start Backup** button, type a name for this backup, and
click **OK**.

Using the Windows 98 Backup Wizard

Check This Out...

Full System-Diskettes
Many new
systems come
with nearly 1
gigabyte of
program files installed on the
hard disk. If you attempt a full
system backup to diskettes, the
backup requires over 30 blank
diskettes!

The Windows 98 prerelease, which was available at the
time this book was published, included a Backup
Wizard, which stepped you through the backup process.
To run the Wizard, choose **Start**, **Programs**, **Accessories**,
System Tools, **Backup**. Choose **Create a New Backup
Job**, click **OK**, and follow the Wizard's instructions to
complete the operation.

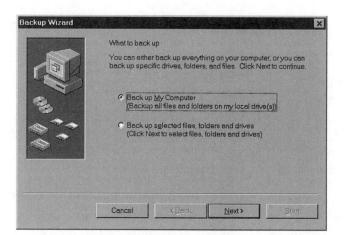

The Backup Wizard leads you through the process.

Backing Up Your Entire System

If you choose to do a full system backup using the Windows 98 Backup Wizard, Backup does a complete backup of your system, including the all-important Windows Registry file. This file contains all the settings that make Windows tick. If you choose not to use the Wizard, click the **Options** button at the bottom of the Backup Window, click the **Advanced** tab, and make sure that **Back Up Windows Registry** is checked.

> **Back Up Selected Files** To back up only selected disks, folders, and files, choose **Back Up Selected Files, Folders and Drives** in step 3. You then mark the items that you want to back up, just as in Windows 95 Backup.

In Windows 95, backing up your entire C drive omits the Windows Registry. If you restore Windows from your backup, Windows won't run. To back up your entire system in Windows 95 Backup, run Backup and then open the **File** menu and choose **Open File Set**. Click **Full System Backup** and click **Open**. Then, proceed with the backup as you normally would. (Windows Backup includes the Full System Backup *backup set*, which prompts Backup to back up *everything* on your system.)

Restoring Files from Your Backups

Rarely, if ever, do you have to restore your entire system. If you delete a file accidentally, you can usually pull it out of the Recycle Bin and be assured that you have recovered the latest version of the file. If the Windows Registry becomes corrupted, you can start your computer with an up-to-date Windows Startup diskette and restore the registry. If an error message appears indicating that a file for running one of your programs is missing, you can restore that one file from your backup disks or tapes or reinstall the program.

Techno Talk

Backup Set A backup set is a collection of saved settings that indicates to Backup which disks, files, and folders to back up and how to back them up—compressed or uncompressed, which backup drive to use, and so on. To save your backup preferences as a backup set, take the steps to back up your files, and choose a drive to back up to. Then, open the **File** menu, select **Save As**, and name and save the file. To perform the same backup later, open the **File** menu, select **Open File Set**, and choose the backup set you created. (In Windows 98, Backup refers to backup sets as *backup jobs*. The Wizard enables you to choose a backup job when you start Backup.)

In short, don't panic and restore everything when you encounter one little mishap. If your backup files are old, even a couple of days old, you could lose much of your work by restoring everything when you need only restore one or two files.

With that warning in mind, you can now proceed to restore files from your backups. The following steps lead you through the process of restoring selected files from your backups in Windows 95:

1. Choose **Start**, **Programs**, **Accessories**, **System Tools**, **Backup**.

2. Click the **Restore** tab.

3. Insert your backup tape or the last floppy disk of the backup set into the drive.

4. In the **Restore from** list, click the drive that contains the backup disk or tape.

5. In the **Backup Set** list, if there is more than one backup set listed, click the name of the backup set that you want to restore.

6. Click the **Next Step** button. A list appears, showing all the folders and files that are on the backup tape or disks.

7. Under **Select files from the backup set**, take one of the following steps:

   To select all the files in the backup, make sure that no folder names are displayed under the drive letter, and then check the box next to the drive letter. Skip to step 9.

   To restore one or two files or folders, click the plus signs to display the folder(s) or contents of the folder you want to restore. Go on to the next step.

8. To restore the contents of an entire folder, check its box. To restore selected files in a folder, click the name of the folder that contains the file(s) (not on the folder's check box), and then check the box next to each file that you want to restore.

9. Click the **Start Restore** button. If you are restoring from floppy disks, a dialog box appears, indicating which disk to insert. Follow the onscreen instructions.

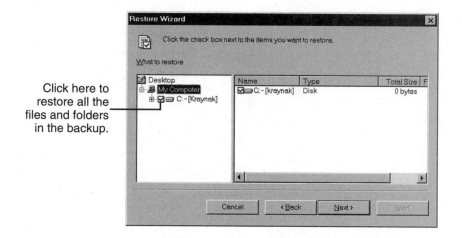

Click here to restore all the files and folders in the backup.

You can restore all the files and folders or only the ones that you specify.

In Windows 98, you can use the Backup Wizard to restore files. Run Backup, click the **Restore Backed Up Files** option, and click **OK**. Follow the onscreen instructions to restore all the files or only selected files.

Tech Check

For complete peace of mind, you should back up your files regularly and know how to restore them should disaster strike. Before you place your entire life's work on your hard disk, you should do the following:

➤ Pick a backup strategy that works for you, and follow it.

➤ Run Windows Backup.

➤ Back up selected disks, folders, and files.

➤ Back up your entire system, including the Windows Registry.

➤ Restore selected folders and files from your backups.

Check This Out...

Practice Copy two or three files to a separate folder on your hard disk and practice backing up and restoring the files until you feel comfortable working with Backup. Open the **Settings** menu and choose **Options** to view available options for backing up and restoring files.

Chapter 32

Do-It-Yourself Fixes for Common Ailments

In This Chapter

➤ Figure out what to do and not do in a crisis

➤ Sniff out the cause of a problem

➤ Recover safely when your computer locks up

➤ Get your speakers to say something

➤ Make your modem dial

With a little patience, you can solve most of your own problems (your computer problems, that is). You just have to know how to go about it—what to do and what not to do. The overall approach is twofold: You need to trace the problem to its cause, and not make the problem worse than it already is.

In this chapter, you learn how to react in a crisis and how to solve your computer woes. Although I can't cover every problem, I cover many common ones and give you some strategies for solving problems that aren't covered here.

Troubleshooting Tactics: A Pre-panic Checklist

When you run into a problem that doesn't have an obvious solution, the best course of action is inaction—that is, don't do anything. If you're fidgeting to do something, take a walk or watch Oprah. Then come back and walk through this checklist:

Are there any onscreen messages? Look at the monitor for any messages that indicate a problem. Although onscreen messages are usually very general, they provide a starting point.

Is everything plugged in and turned on? If a part of your computer is dead—no lights, no sound, no action—it probably isn't connected or isn't turned on. If everything is turned on, turn everything off and check the connections. Don't assume that just because something looks connected that it is; wiggle the plugs.

When did the problem start? Think back to what you did before the problem arose. Did you install a new program? Did you enter a command? Did you add a new device? When my speakers went mute, I realized that the problem started after I installed a new hard drive. I had knocked a tiny jumper off the sound card during the hard drive installation.

Is the problem limited to one program? If you have the same problem in every program, the problem is probably caused by your computer or Windows. If the problem occurs in only one program, focus on that program.

When did you have the file last? If you lost a file, it probably did *not* get sucked into a black hole. It is probably somewhere on your disk, in a separate directory. Open the **Start** menu, choose **Find**, and start hunting.

Realize that it's probably not the computer, and it's probably not a virus. Although the computer itself can be the cause of some major problems, it is rarely the cause of minor, everyday problems. The problem is usually in the software—Windows or one of your programs—and you should work on the assumption that the problem that you're having is not caused by a virus. Of the problems that people blame on computer viruses, 95 percent are actually bugs in the software or problems with specific device drivers (the instructions that tell your computer and Windows how to use the device).

My Computer Won't Start

A computer is a lot like a car; the most frustrating thing that can happen is not being able to even get the engine to turn over. To solve the problem, consider these questions:

Is the computer on? Are the lights on the computer lit? If so, the computer is plugged in and is on. Make sure the power switch on the system unit is turned on. Some computers have a power button that you have to press and hold for a couple of seconds. Also, check the monitor and power cables.

Is the screen completely blank? Even though the screen is completely blank, the computer may have booted; you just can't see it. If you heard the computer beep and you saw the drive lights go on and off, the computer probably booted fine. Make sure the monitor is turned on and the brightness controls are turned up. Try moving your mouse or pressing the Enter key; your computer may be in sleep mode, and this wakes it up.

> **Check This Out...**
>
> **Make a Windows Startup Disk** Windows comes with a utility that can transform a floppy disk into a Startup disk. Open the Windows Control Panel, double-click the **Add/ Remove Programs** icon, and click the **Startup Disk** tab. Click the **Create Disk** button and then follow the onscreen instructions. Of course, you can't create the disk if your computer won't boot, but after you get your computer started, make a Startup disk.

Is there a disk in drive A? If you see a message onscreen that says **Non-system disk or disk error**, you probably left a floppy disk in drive A. Remove the disk and press any key to start from the hard disk.

Can you start from a floppy disk? If you still can't get your computer to start from the hard disk, try starting from the Windows Startup disk (you do have a Windows Startup disk, don't you?). Insert the Startup disk in drive A and press **Ctrl+Alt+Del**. If you can start from a floppy, the problem is on your hard disk. You need some expert help to get out of this mess.

My Computer Locked Up

If your computer freezes (you can't move the mouse pointer, enter commands, or even exit your programs), wait three or four minutes. The computer might be too busy to handle your request. If it's still frozen, press **Ctrl+Alt+Del**. A dialog box should appear, showing you the names of the active programs. Next to the program that's causing the problem, you should see **[not responding]**. Click that program's name and click **End Task**. (You may lose data when you close a program that is not responding.) You should now be able to continue working.

If you close the errant program and Windows is still locked up, press **Ctrl+Alt+Del** again, and close any other programs that are causing problems. If you still cannot regain control of your computer, you may have to press **Ctrl+Alt+Del** again or use your computer's Reset button. Do this only as a last resort. Shutting down your system without exiting programs properly causes you to lose any work you had not saved before shutting down. (Files saved to your hard disk are safe.)

If your Windows freezes up again after you reboot, there may be an errant file fragment that's causing the problem. Try running ScanDisk, as instructed in the section "Refreshing and Repairing Disks with ScanDisk," in Chapter 28.

It Could Be a Program

Many programs, especially Web browsers and games, are buggy. They have programming code that makes the program conflict with Windows, another program, one of your hardware devices, or even your computer's memory. One common problem is that the program never frees up the memory it uses. As it runs, it takes up more and more of your computer's memory until Windows itself has no available memory to use. The program might run okay for an hour or so, and then your entire system grinds to a halt.

The only permanent solution is to install a *patch* or *bug fix* from the manufacturer, assuming a *patch* is available. This fixes the problem that causes the program to lock up your system. Contact the manufacturer's tech support department to determine whether they have a fix for the problem, as explained in Chapter 33, "Help! Finding Technical Support." For a temporary solution, use the program in spurts. Use the program for a while, save your work, exit, and restart before your computer locks up. You may also have to shut down and restart Windows.

Check Your Mouse Driver

Windows might be having a problem with the mouse driver (the instructions that tell Windows how to use your mouse). The first thing that you should do is check to make sure that you don't have two conflicting mouse drivers installed. Right-click **My Computer**, choose **Properties**, and click the **Device Manager** tab. Click the plus sign next to **Mouse**. If you have more than one mouse listed, you have more than one mouse driver installed.

Before you remove one of the mouse drivers, make a Windows Startup disk, as explained earlier. If you disable the wrong mouse driver, you're in for some heavy-duty troubleshooting. To disable a mouse driver, double-click the mouse that doesn't match the type of mouse that you have, click **Disable in This Hardware Profile**, and click **OK**. Click **OK** and restart your computer.

If that doesn't fix the problem, call the tech support department for the mouse manufacturer and ask whether they have an updated driver (they send it to you via email or on a floppy disk). In most cases, the updated driver contains the fix for the problem. (See "Updating the Software for Your Hardware" later in this chapter to learn how to install an updated driver.)

If you cannot obtain an updated mouse driver, try using one of the standard drivers that comes with Windows. Open the **Control Panel**, and then double-click the **Mouse** icon. Click the **General** tab, and then click the **Change** button. Select one of the standard mouse types, and click **OK**.

Caution If you pick the wrong mouse driver, you won't have a mouse pointer in Windows, making it tough to navigate. If you pick the wrong driver, start your computer with the Windows StartUp disk, and then you can move around to pick another driver.

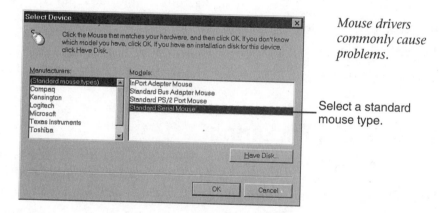

Mouse drivers commonly cause problems.

Select a standard mouse type.

Check the Windows Graphics Acceleration Setting

Windows is initially set up to exploit the full potential of your computer. Unfortunately, sometimes Windows 95 is too aggressive, especially when it comes to your system's video acceleration. Windows 95 cranks up the video acceleration rate to the maximum, which can sometimes cause your system to crash without displaying an error message. Try slowing it down:

1. Right-click the **My Computer** icon and select **Properties**.

2. Click the **Performance** tab and click the **Graphics** button.

3. Drag the **Hardware Acceleration** slider to the second or third hash mark, and click **OK**.

4. Click **Close**.

5. When asked whether you want to reboot your system, close any programs that may be running and click **Yes**.

Obtain an Updated Video Driver

Check This Out...

Reduce Colors Some programs have trouble dealing with a large number of colors. Right-click the Windows desktop, choose **Properties**, and click the **Settings** tab. Choose **256 Colors** from the **Colors** drop-down list. Don't go lower than 256; some programs do not work with a lower setting.

Hiding behind the scenes of every video card and monitor is a video driver that tells your operating system (Windows) how to use the card and monitor to display pretty pictures. Occasionally, the driver contains a bug that can lock up your system. More frequently, the driver becomes outdated, causing problems with newer programs. In either case, you should obtain an updated driver from the manufacturer of the video card. You can call the manufacturer's tech support line and have them send the driver to you on a floppy disk, or obtain the driver from the company's Web site. (See "Updating the Software for Your Hardware" later in this chapter to learn how to install an updated driver.)

My Screen Is Flickering

If your screen is flashing or turning odd colors, the plug that connects the monitor to the system unit has probably come loose. Turn everything off and then check the connection. If the plug has screws that secure it to the system unit, tighten the screws.

Magnetic fields (from speakers, phones, and other sources) can also cause your screen to freak out, just as they can cause problems with a standard TV. You may see a band of color along one edge of the screen. Move any electrical appliances away from your monitor. The problem may go away immediately or take a day or two to correct itself.

I Can't Get the Program to Run

If you try to run a program using a shortcut icon, the icon may be pointing to the wrong program. Right-click the shortcut, choose **Properties**, and check the entry in the **Target** text box. This shows the path to the program's folder followed by the name of the program file that launches the program. If the text box is blank or points to the wrong file, click the **Find Target** button and use the resulting dialog box to change to the program's folder and choose the right program file.

If the program starts and immediately closes, you may not have sufficient memory or disk space on your computer. Right-click **My Computer** and choose **Properties**. Click the **Performance** tab and click the **Virtual Memory** button. Make sure that you have at least 30 megabytes of free space on the disk that Windows is using for virtual memory. Any less, and you have to clear some files from your hard disk.

If the program still won't run, try reinstalling it. If that doesn't work, contact the program manufacturer's tech support department to determine the problem and the required fix. The program may require special hardware or additional software that is not available on your system.

I Have a Mouse, but I Can't Find the Pointer Onscreen

After you get your mouse working, you will probably never have to mess with it again (except for cleaning it, which we talked about back in Chapter 30, "Free (or at Least Cheap) Computer Maintenance"). The hard part is getting the mouse to work in the first place. If you connected a mouse to your computer and you don't see the mouse pointer onscreen, there are a few possibilities that you should investigate:

➤ **Am I in a program that uses a mouse?** Some old programs don't support a mouse, so you won't see the mouse pointer in these programs. For example, you won't see a mouse pointer at the DOS prompt or in many DOS computer games. Run a program that you know uses a mouse to see whether it works there.

➤ **Is the mouse pointer hidden?** Mouse pointers like to hide in the corners or edges of your screen. Roll the mouse on your desktop to see whether you can bring the pointer into view. (If you have a notebook computer, the mouse pointer might disappear when you move the mouse quickly.)

➤ **When you connected the mouse, did you install a mouse driver?** Connecting a mouse to your computer is not enough. You must install a program (called a *mouse driver*) that tells the computer how to use the mouse. Follow the instructions that came with the mouse to figure out how to install the program. To install one of the mouse drivers included with Windows, see the section "Adding New Hardware in Windows" in Chapter 27.

Record Your Changes Write down changes that you make to your system. It takes a little extra time, but it enables you to retrace your steps later.

I Can't Hear My Speakers!

Several things can cause your speakers to go mute. Check the following:

➤ Are your speakers turned on?

➤ Is the speaker volume control turned up?

➤ Are your speakers plugged in to the correct jacks on your sound card? Some sound cards have several jacks, and it's easy to plug the speakers into the input jacks instead of the output jacks.

➤ If you're having trouble recording sounds, make sure that your microphone is turned on and plugged in to the correct jack.

➤ Does your sound card have a volume control? Crank it all the way up.

➤ Right-click the speaker icon on the Windows taskbar and choose **Open Volume Controls**. Open the **Options** menu, choose **Properties**, and make sure that every volume control in the list at the bottom of the dialog box is checked. Click **OK**. Use the sliders to crank up the overall volume, CD volume, and Microphone volume. Make sure that the **Mute** options are *not* checked.

If you still can't get your speakers to talk, right-click **My Computer**, select **Properties**, and click the **Device Manager** tab. Scroll down the list and click the plus sign next to the **Sound...** option. If your sound card is not listed, you need to reinstall the sound card driver. If the sound card is listed but has a yellow circle with an exclamation point on it, the sound card is conflicting with another device on your system. Check your sound card's documentation to determine how to resolve hardware conflicts. This can be pretty complicated and may require you to change settings on your sound card (you may have to go inside the system unit).

I Can't Get My Modem to Work

If your modem can't dial, Windows can help you track down the problem. Double-click the **Modems** icon in the Control Panel, click the **Diagnostics** tab, and click the **Help** button. The Windows Modem Troubleshooter appears. Answer the questions to track down and correct common modem problems.

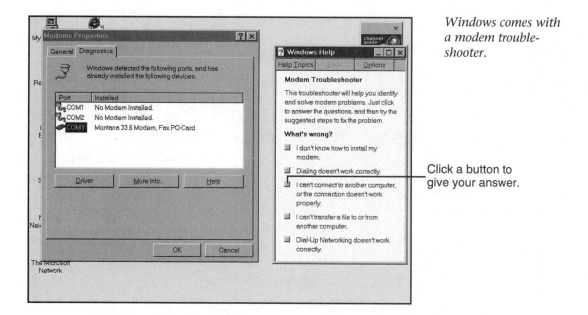

Windows comes with a modem trouble-shooter.

Click a button to give your answer.

The Computer Won't Read My Floppy Disk

Don't feel bad; it happens to everyone. You stick a floppy disk in the disk drive, close the drive door, change to the drive, and you get an error message saying basically that the disk is no good. Your computer can't read it, write to it, or even see that it's there. What happened? That depends. Check the following:

➤ **Is the disk inserted properly?** Even the most experienced computer user occasionally inserts a disk upside-down. Check to make sure that the disk is in the right slot the right way.

➤ **Is the disk drive door closed?** If the drive has a door, it must be closed. Otherwise, you get an error message saying that your computer can't read or write to the disk.

➤ **Is the disk write-protected?** If the disk is write-protected, you won't be able to save a file to the disk. For a 3 1/2" disk, slide the write-protect tab so that you can't see through the little hole. On a 5 1/4" disk, remove the write-protect sticker.

➤ **Is the disk full?** If you try to save a file to a disk and you get an **Insufficient space** message, the disk has insufficient free space to hold any more data. Use a different disk.

Check This Out...

Fixing Bad Disks If a disk is bad, you may be able to salvage it using the ScanDisk, as explained in the section "Refreshing and Repairing Disks with ScanDisk" in Chapter 28. If a drive is bad, you have to take it to a computer mechanic to get it fixed. Usually the problem is that the drive is not spinning at the right speed or that the arm that reads and writes data to the disk is not aligned properly on the disk.

➤ **Is the disk formatted?** If you buy new, unformatted disks, you must format the disks before you can use them.

➤ **Did you format the disk to the proper density?** If you format a high-density disk as a low-density disk, or vice versa, you will probably run into problems when you try to use the disk.

➤ **Is the disk bad?** Although it's rare, disks do go bad. Some disks even come bad from the manufacturer. If you get a **Sector not found** or **Data error** message, the disk may be bad. Then again, the drive might need a tune-up. Try some other disks. If you're having problems with all disks, the problem is in the drive. If you are having trouble with only one disk, it's the disk.

My Keyboard Is Wacky

If what you type replaces existing text, you switched from Insert to Overstrike mode by mistake. In most programs, you switch modes by pressing the **Ins** (Insert) key. Press the key again, and you should be back in Insert mode.

Some fancy keyboards enable you to *remap* the keys. For example, you can make the F1 key on the left side of the keyboard act like the Enter key, or you can make it perform a series of keystrokes. Advanced users like to remap keys to customize the keyboard and make it a time-saver; however, if you accidentally press the remap key and then continue typing, you may remap your entire keyboard without knowing it. You know it when you press the K key and get a Z, or you press the Spacebar and delete a paragraph. You can usually unmap the keyboard. If you have an AnyKey keyboard, you can return a key to normal by pressing the Remap key and then pressing twice the key that you want to return to normal. (If you don't have an AnyKey keyboard, consult the documentation that came with your computer.) To return all the keys on an AnyKey keyboard to normal, take the following steps:

1. Make sure that your computer is on, and then press the **Remap** key. The Program light blinks.

2. Press the **Ctrl** key twice, and then press the **Alt** key twice. This ensures that these keys are functioning properly.

3. Press the **Suspend Macro** key. The Program light stops blinking.

4. Press **Ctrl+Alt+Suspend Macro.**

My Keyboard Is Dead

If your keyboard is completely dead, or if your computer displays the message **Keyboard not found** when you boot your computer, do a quick inspection to make sure that the keyboard is plugged in and that the cord is in good shape. Also, your system unit may have a keyboard lock on it. Get the key and unlock it.

My Printer Won't Print

If you run into printer problems, you probably have to do more fiddling than Nero. Look for the following:

➤ Is your printer plugged in and turned on?

➤ Does your printer have paper? Is the paper tray inserted properly?

➤ Is the printer's On Line light on (not blinking)? If the OnLine light is off or blinking, press the **On Line** button to turn on the light.

➤ Is your program set to print to a file? Many Print dialog boxes have a **Print to File** option, which sends the document to a file on your disk instead of to the printer. Make sure that this option is NOT checked.

➤ Is the print fading? If so, your printer may need a new toner or ink cartridge. If your inkjet cartridge has plenty of ink, check your printer manual to determine how to clean the print head. Inkjet cartridges have some sensitive areas that you should never clean, so be careful.

➤ If you have an inkjet printer, check the print head and the area next to the print head for tape and remove the tape. Ink cartridges usually come with two pieces of tape on them. You must remove *both* pieces before installing the cartridge.

➤ Is your printer marked as the default printer? In My Computer, double-click the **Printers** icon. Right-click the icon for your printer and make sure that **Set as Default** is checked. If there is no check mark, select **Set as Default**.

➤ Is the printer paused? Double-click the printer icon in the taskbar, open the **Printer** menu, and make sure that **Pause Printing** is not checked. If there is a check mark, click **Pause Printing**.

➤ Is the correct printer port selected? In My Computer, double-click the **Printers** icon and double-click the icon for your printer. Click the **Details** tab and make sure that the correct printer port is selected—LPT1 in most cases.

➤ Did you get only part of a page? Laser printers are weird; they print an entire page at one time, storing the entire page in memory. If the page has a big complex graphic image or a lot of fonts, the printer may be able to store only a portion of the page. The best fix is to get more memory for your printer. The quickest fix is to use fewer fonts on the page and try using a less complex graphic image.

➤ Is it a printer problem? To determine whether the printer has a problem, go to the DOS prompt (choose **Start**, **Programs**, **MS-DOS prompt**), type **dir > lpt1**, and press **Enter**. This prints the current directory list. If it prints okay, the problem is in the Windows printer setup. If the directory does not print or prints incorrectly, the problem is probably the printer. (Many printers have a button combination that you can press to have the printer perform a *self-test*. Check your printer manual.)

➤ If error messages keep popping up on your screen, Windows may be sending print instructions to the printer faster than your printer can handle them. In My Computer, double-click the **Printers** icon, and then right-click your printer icon and choose **Properties**. Click the **Details** tab and increase the number of seconds in the **Transmission Retry** text box.

When a document fails to print, new users commonly keep entering the Print command, hoping that if they enter it enough times, the program starts printing the document. What this does is send several copies of the same document to a print queue (a waiting line). When you finally fix the problem, you end up with a hundred copies of the same document. To prevent this from happening, do one of the following:

➤ Enter the **Print** command only once. If the document doesn't print, find the problem and fix it immediately.

➤ In Windows, you can check the print queue by double-clicking the **Printer** icon on the right side of the taskbar. You can then select and cancel duplicate print jobs.

Updating the Software for Your Hardware

Computer hardware and software is in constant transition. Whenever Microsoft updates Windows, manufacturers have to ensure that the hardware they're coming out with works with the new operating system, and Microsoft does its best to ensure that the new operating system can handle most hardware devices. In this rush to get their products to market, the computer industry often releases products that contain bugs— imperfections that cause problems.

To help make up for these shortcomings, hardware manufacturers commonly release updated *drivers* for their devices. The driver works along with the operating system to control the device. You can solve many problems with your display, sound card, printer, joystick, modem, and other devices by installing an updated driver. The best way to get an updated driver is to download it from the Internet. If you don't have an Internet connection and you suspect that a device driver is causing problems, call the manufacturer's technical support line and ask whether they have an updated driver. They can send it to you on a floppy disk. (See the next chapter for details about technical support.)

Updates in Windows 98
The Windows 98 prerelease that I was using during the writing of this book contained a nifty utility that could check for updated drivers at Microsoft's Internet site and download the updated driver for you. To run it, choose **Start** and select **Windows Update** at the top of the menu.

After you have the updated driver, take the following steps to install it:

1. If you have the updated driver on a floppy disk, insert the disk.

2. Right-click **My Computer** and choose **Properties**.

3. Click the **Device Manager** tab.

4. Click the plus sign next to the type of device that requires a new driver.

5. Double-click the name of the device.

6. Click the **Driver** tab and then click the **Update Driver** button.

7. Choose the option searching for a better driver and click **Next**. If the driver is on a floppy disk, Windows finds it and prompts you to install it. Follow the onscreen instructions and skip the remaining steps.

Special Instructions
Some drivers come with their own installation program. Try changing to the disk and folder in which the driver file is stored and running the installation program.

8. If you downloaded the driver from the Internet, click the **Other Locations** button, choose the disk and folder where the driver file is stored, and click **OK**.

9. Follow the onscreen instructions to complete the installation.

Tech Check

If you don't remember all the specifics given in this chapter, don't worry. The important things to remember are how to trace a problem back to its cause. Make sure that you can do the following:

➤ Make your computer start when it tells you that it can't.

➤ Thaw your computer when it freezes.

➤ Spur a stubborn program into action.

➤ Stop your mouse pointer from skipping around on the screen.

➤ Coax your modem into dialing a number.

➤ Give your speakers a voice.

➤ Make your printer print something when it refuses to print.

Help! Finding Technical Support

You just flipped through the previous chapter and found that none of the problems described there pertained to the problem that you're having. At this point, you're probably cursing *Time*'s 1997 Man of the Year and thinking of taking a sledgehammer to your system unit.

Before you do that, try one other solution: Contact the technical support (tech support) department for the program or device that's giving you problems. In this chapter, you learn the ins and outs of tech support—what they can and cannot help you with, what to ask, what information you should have ready, and how to find answers to common questions on the Internet.

Phone Support (Feeling Lucky?)

The documentation that came with your program or hardware device usually contains a phone number in the back for contacting technical support. It's usually printed really small to discourage people from calling. Flip through your manuals to find the number you need.

Before you call, be aware that the quality of technical support over the telephone varies widely from one company to another. Most places have a computerized system that asks you to answer a series of questions, usually leading to a dead end. Other places keep you on hold until you eventually give up and call a relative or friend for help. Yet, some tech support departments provide excellent, toll-free service, enabling you to talk with a qualified technician who can walk you through the steps required to solve your problem.

Even if you get to speak with a great tech support person, you need to be prepared. No tech support person can read minds. You have to be able to describe the problem you're having in some detail. Before you call, here's what you need to do:

➤ Write down a detailed description of the problem, explaining what went wrong and what you were doing at the time. If possible, write down the steps required to cause the problem again.

➤ Write down the name, version number, and license (or registration) number of the program with which you are having trouble. You can usually get this information by opening the **Help** menu in the problem program and choosing the **About...** command.

➤ Write down any information about your computer, including the computer brand, chip type (CPU) and speed, monitor type, amount of RAM, and the amount of free disk space.

➤ Make sure that your computer is turned on. A good tech support person can talk you through most problems if you're sitting at the keyboard.

➤ Make sure you're calling the right company. If you're having trouble with your printer, don't call Microsoft. If you even get through to a Microsoft Windows tech support person, the person will tell you to call the printer manufacturer. (Although, sometimes it's tough to figure out what's causing the problem.)

➤ Don't call when you're mad. If you start screaming at the technical support person, the person is going to be less likely to offer quality help.

Finding Tech Support on the Web

Nearly every computer hardware and software company has its own Web site, where you can purchase products directly and find technical support for products that you own. If your printer is not feeding paper properly, you're having trouble installing your sound card, you keep receiving cryptic error messages in your favorite program, or you have some other computer-related problem, you can usually find the solution on the Internet.

In addition, computer and software companies often upgrade their software and post both updates and fixes on their Web sites for downloading. If you are having problems with a device, such as a printer or modem, you should check the manufacturer's Web site for updated drivers. If you run into problems with a program, check the software company's Web site for a *patch*—a program file that you install to correct the problem.

The following table provides Web page addresses of popular software and hardware manufacturers to help you in your search. Most of the home pages listed have a link for connecting to the support page. If a page does not have a link to the support page, use its search tool to locate the page. You might also see a link labeled FAQ (frequently asked questions), Common Questions, or Top Issues. This link can take you to a page that lists the most common problems other users are having and answers from the company.

Computer Hardware and Software Web Sites

Company	Web Page Address
Acer	www.acer.com
Borland	www.borland.com
Broderbund	www.broderbund.com
Brother	www.brother.com
Canon	www.ccsi.canon.com
Compaq	www.compaq.com
Corel	www.corel.com
Creative Labs	www.soundblaster.com
Dell	www.dell.com
Epson	www.epson.com
Fujitsu	www.fujitsu.com
Gateway	www.gw2k.com
Hayes	www.hayes.com

continues

Computer Hardware and Software Web Sites   Continued

Company	Web Page Address
Hewlett-Packard	www.hp.com
Hitachi	www.hitachipc.com
IBM	www.ibm.com
Intel	www.intel.com
Iomega	www.iomega.com
Lotus	www.lotus.com
Micron Electronics	www.micronpc.com
Microsoft	www.microsoft.com
Motorola	www.mot.com/MIMS/ISPD/support.html
NEC	www.nec.com
Packard Bell	www.packardbell.com
Panasonic	www.panasonic.com
Sony	www.sony.com
Toshiba	www.toshiba.com
3COM (U.S. Robotics)	www.3com.com

Check out the FAQ or Top Issues link for answers to common questions.

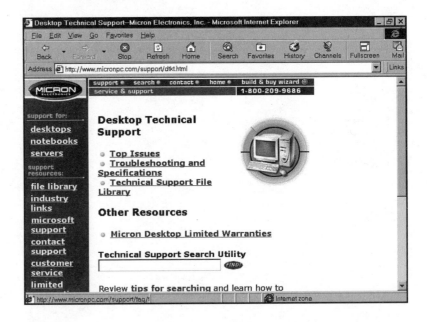

If the manufacturer you're looking for is not listed in this table, don't give up. Connect to your favorite Web search page and search for the manufacturer by name or search for the problem you're having. You should also seek help from online computer magazines. Here are some excellent resources:

> **ZDNet** at **www.zdnet.com** is the home of several quality computer magazines, including PC Computing, Windows Sources, and ComputerLife. Here you find articles on general computing, hardware and software reviews, tips, and answers to specific questions.

clnet at **www.cnet.com** is a great place if you need technical support for Internet problems. It's also a great place to check out gaming information and obtain shareware programs. Although you don't find as much information about general computing issues as you find at ZDNet, the information you do find is very useful.

Windows Magazine at **www.winmag.com** is an excellent place to find answers to your Windows questions, learn about the latest improvements, and check out software reviews.

Check the Manual
Although manufacturers like to keep the tech support phone number a secret, they want you to know their Web page address so that you can check out their other products. The Web site's technical support areas also cut down on calls to tech support.

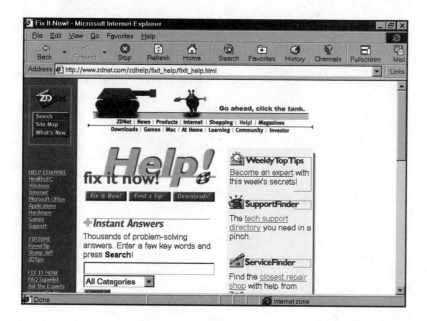

ZDNet's Help area might have just the fix you need.

Tech Check

When you can't solve your own problems, you need to know how to find help. To succeed in your search, you must be able to do the following:

➤ Prepare for a productive phone conversation with a tech support person.

➤ Check out your computer manufacturer's tech support Web page.

➤ Find technical support using computer magazines on the Web.

WHAT..?

Speak Like a Geek: The Complete Archive

The computer world is like a big exclusive club, complete with its own language. If you want to be accepted into the Royal Order of Computer Geeks, you had better learn the lingo. The following miniglossary helps you start. Keep in mind that you never achieve full geekhood by passively reading the terms and definitions. Try to say the term aloud, and then use it in a sentence. When your fellow geeks hear you reciting computer terms to yourself, they immediately accept you into their group.

ActiveX   A relatively new technology that makes it easy both to embed animated objects, data, and computer code in the documents that you create and to share those objects with others. For example, with ActiveX, you can open a file created in Microsoft Word in your Web browser (for instance, Internet Explorer) and edit it just as if you had opened it in Word.

AGP (Accelerated Graphics Port)   A display card standard that increases the speed at which display instructions travel from your system unit to the monitor. AGP is about four times faster than the previous standard display configuration.

application   Also known as *program,* a set of instructions that enable a computer to perform a specific task, such as word processing or data management. An application can also be a collection of programs, called a *suite.*

ASCII file   A file containing characters that any program on any computer can use. Sometimes called a *text file* or an *ASCII text file.* (ASCII is pronounced "ASK-key.")

BIOS (basic input-output system)   The BIOS, pronounced "BUY-ose," is the built-in set of instructions that tell the computer how to control the disk drives, keyboard, printer port, and other components that make up your computer. Think of the BIOS as the little black box inside new cars that keeps everything working in sync. The BIOS is stored on a *ROM* (read-only memory) chip. A *flash BIOS* enables you to update the BIOS by running a software program instead of replacing the ROM chip. A *PnP BIOS* supports plug-and-play components.

bit   The basic unit of data in a computer. A computer's alphabet consists of two characters—1 and 0. 1 stands for On, and 0 stands for Off. Bits are combined in sets of eight to form real characters, such as *A*, *B*, *C*, and *D*. See also *byte*.

bits per second   A unit for measuring the speed of data transmission. Remember that it takes 8 bits to make a byte (the equivalent of a single character). Modems have common bps ratings of 28,800 to 56,600.

boot   To start a computer and load its operating system software (usually Windows).

bps   See *bits per second*.

bus   A superhighway that carries information electronically from one part of the computer to another. The wider and faster (speed is measured in MHz) the bus, the faster your computer. The old ISA bus could carry 16 bits of data at a time; the newer PCI bus can carry 32 bits or 64 bits. There are three such highways:

> ➤ A *data bus* carries data back and forth between memory and the microprocessor.

> ➤ An *address bus* carries information about the locations (addresses) of specific information.

> ➤ A *control bus* carries control signals to make sure that the data traffic flows smoothly, without confusion.

byte   A group of 8 bits that usually represents a character or a digit. For example, the byte 01000001 represents the letter *A*.

cache   Pronounced "cash." A temporary storage area in memory or on disk that computer components and various programs use to quickly access data.

CD-ROM (compact disc–read-only memory)   A storage technology that uses the same kind of discs that you play in an audio CD player for mass storage of computer data. A single disc can store more than 600MB of information. Pronounced "see-dee-rahm."

cell   The box formed by the intersection of a row (1,2,3...) and column (A,B,C...) in a spreadsheet. Each cell has an *address* (such as B12) that defines its column and row. A cell may contain text, a numeric value, or a formula.

chat   To talk to another person by typing at your computer. What you type appears on the other person's screen, and what the other person types appears on your screen. You can chat on the Internet or an online service, such as Prodigy or America Online.

click   To move the mouse pointer over an object or icon and press and release the mouse button once without moving the mouse.

client   Of two computers, the computer that's being served. On the Internet or on a network, your computer is the client, and the computer to which you're connected is the *server*.

Clipboard   A temporary storage area that holds text and graphics. The Cut and Copy commands put text or graphics on the Clipboard, replacing the Clipboard's previous contents. The Paste command copies Clipboard data to a document.

CMOS (Complementary Metal-Oxide Semiconductor)   Pronounced "sea-moss," this is a battery-powered storage unit that helps your computer remember the date, time, and additional settings. If your computer starts losing track of time, it might be a sign that you need to change the battery.

COM port   Short for COMmunications port. A receptacle, usually at the back of the computer, into which you can plug a serial device such as a modem, mouse, or serial printer. If your computer has more than one COM port, the ports are numbered COM1, COM2, and so on.

command   An order that tells the computer what to do. In command-driven programs, you have to press a specific key or type the command to execute it. With menu-driven programs, you select the command from a menu.

computer   Any machine that accepts input (from IVuser), processes the input, and produces output in some form.

CPU (central processing unit)   The computer's brain. See *microprocessor*.

crash   Failure of a system or program. Usually, you realize that your system has crashed when you can't move the mouse pointer or type anything. The term *crash* is also used to refer to a *disk crash* (or *head crash*). A disk crash occurs when the read/write head in the disk drive falls on the disk. This would be like dropping a phonograph needle on a record. A disk crash can destroy any data stored where the read/write head falls on the disk.

cursor   A horizontal line that appears below characters. A cursor acts like the tip of your pencil; anything that you type appears at the cursor. See also *insertion point*.

data   The facts and figures that you enter into the computer and that are stored and used by the computer.

database   A type of computer program used for storing, organizing, and retrieving information. Popular database programs include Access, Approach, and Paradox.

density   A measure of the amount of data that can be stored per square inch of storage area on a disk.

desktop publishing (DTP)   A program that enables you to combine text and graphics on the same page and manipulate the text and graphics onscreen. Desktop publishing programs are commonly used to create newsletters, brochures, flyers, résumés, and business cards.

dialog box   An onscreen box that enables you to enter your preferences or supply additional information. You use the dialog box to carry on a "conversation" with the program.

directory   A division of a disk or CD, which contains a group of related files. Think of your disk as a filing cabinet, and think of each directory as a drawer in the cabinet. By keeping files in separate directories, it is easier to locate and work with related files. Directories are more commonly called *folders*.

disk   A round, flat, magnetic storage medium. A disk works like a cassette tape, storing files permanently so that you can play them back later. See also *floppy disk* and *hard disk*.

disk drive   A device that writes data to a magnetic disk and reads data from the disk. Think of a disk drive as a cassette recorder/player. Just as the cassette player can record sounds on a magnetic cassette tape and play back those sounds, a disk drive can record data on a magnetic disk and play back that data.

docking station   A unit that connects a portable computer to peripherals, making the portable computer act like a desktop computer. Docking stations typically enable you to connect a mouse, full-size keyboard and monitor, speakers, and a printer to your notebook computer.

DOS (disk operating system)   DOS, which rhymes with "boss," is an essential program that provides the necessary instructions for the computer's parts (keyboard, disk drive, central processing unit, display screen, printer, and so on) to function as a unit. Although Windows makes DOS nearly obsolete, you still see its name floating around in Windows.

DOS prompt   An onscreen prompt that indicates that DOS is ready to accept a command but provides no clue as to what command you should type. It looks something like C> or C:\.

download   To copy files from another computer to your computer, usually through a modem. See also *upload*.

DVD (digital versatile disk or digital video disk)   Disks that can store more than seven times as much data as a CD, making them useful for storing full-length movies. DVD drives are designed to handle the discs of the future but are also designed to play discs of the past (CDs).

EDO (Extended Data Output)   A type of DRAM (dynamic RAM) memory that is faster than your average DRAM. Standard DRAM enables the CPU to read one byte of data at a time. EDO DRAM sticks a whole chunk of data in the cache and fetches another chunk while the CPU is reading the first chunk. SDRAM is better, so skip to that term.

EIDE (Enhanced Integrated Drive Electronics)   A type of hard drive that is typically fast and relatively inexpensive. EIDE drives have been popular for years but are being phased out by faster drives.

email   Short for *electronic mail*, email is a system that enables people to send and receive messages from computer to computer. Email is usually available on networks and online information services.

EMS (Expanded Memory Specification)   See *expanded memory*.

executable file   A program file that can run the program. Executable files end in .BAT, .COM, or .EXE.

expanded memory   Additional memory that a computer uses by swapping data into and out of a reserved portion of a computer's standard memory area. With expanded memory, additional memory is added to the computer in the form of memory chips or a memory board. To access this additional memory, an expanded memory manager reserves 64 of the standard 640KB as a swap area. The 64KB represent four pages, each page consisting of 16KB. Pages of data are swapped into and out of this 64KB region from expanded memory at a high speed. Old DOS programs commonly used expanded memory, but Windows and its programs prefer extended memory. See also *extended memory*.

expansion slot   An opening on the motherboard (inside the system unit) that enables you to add devices to the system unit. Expansion slots enable you to add an internal modem, sound card, video accelerator, or other enhancement.

extended memory   Any memory above the standard 640KB that performs the same way as the standard memory. Extended memory is directly available to the processor in your computer, unlike *expanded memory*, in which data must be swapped into and out of the standard memory. Most of your computer's memory is extended memory.

extension   The portion of a file's name that comes after the period. Every filename consists of two parts—the base name (before the period) and an extension (after the period). The filename can be up to eight characters in DOS and Windows 3.x (up to 255 characters in Windows 95 and later). The extension (which is optional) can be up to three characters.

FAT32   A fairly recent hard disk innovation that divides large hard disk drives into small storage units so that the drive wastes less space. If you think of your hard disk as a parking lot, Fat32 paints the lines closer together so that it can fit more cars. See also *file allocation table*.

field   A blank in a database record, into which you can enter a piece of information (for example, a telephone number, ZIP code, or a person's last name).

file   A collection of information stored as a single unit on a floppy or hard disk. Files always have a filename to identify them.

file allocation table (FAT)   A map on every disk that tells the operating system where the files on the disk are stored. It's a little like a classroom seating chart for files.

File Transfer Protocol (FTP)   A set of rules that govern the exchange of files between two computers on the Internet. To copy a file from the Internet, you need a special program that can handle FTP file transfers.

fixed disk drive   A disk drive that has a nonremovable disk, as opposed to floppy drives, in which you can insert and remove disks.

floppy disk   A wafer encased in plastic that stores magnetic data (the facts and figures you enter and save). Floppy disks are the disks that you insert in your computer's floppy disk drive (located on the front of the computer).

folder   The Windows name for a directory, a division of a hard disk or CD-ROM that stores a group of related files. See also *directory*.

font   Any set of characters of the same *typeface* (design) and *type size* (measured in points). For example, Times Roman 12-point is a font: Times Roman is the typeface, and 12-point is the size. (There are 72 points in an inch.)

format (disk)   To prepare a disk for storing data. Formatting creates a map on the disk that tells the operating system how the disk is structured. The operating system uses this map to keep track of where files are stored. Formatting also flags bad tracks or sectors (storage areas) on the disk, to prevent the drive from attempting to store data on defective areas.

format (document)   To establish the physical layout of a document, including page size, margins, running heads, line spacing, text alignment, graphics placement, and so on.

FTP   See *File Transfer Protocol*.

function keys   The 10 or 12 F keys on the left side of the keyboard or 12 F keys at the top of the keyboard (some keyboards have both). F keys are numbered F1, F2, F3, and so on, and you can use them to enter specified commands in a program.

geek   1. An obsessive computer user who sacrifices food, sleep, and other pleasantries of life to spend more time at the keyboard. 2. A carnival performer whose act usually includes biting off the head of a live snake or chicken.

gigabyte   A thousand megabytes. See *megabyte*.

graphical user interface (GUI, pronounced "GOO-ey")   A type of program interface that uses graphical elements, such as icons, to represent commands, files, and (in some cases) other programs. The most famous GUI is Microsoft Windows.

hard disk   A disk drive that comes complete with a nonremovable disk. It acts as a giant floppy disk drive and usually sits inside your computer.

Hayes-compatible   A term to describe a modem that uses the Hayes command set for communicating with other modems over the phone lines. Hayes-compatible modems usually are preferred over other modems because most modems and telecommunications software are designed to be Hayes-compatible.

HTML Short for *Hypertext Markup Language*, the code used to create documents for the World Wide Web. These codes tell the Web browser how to display the text (titles, headings, lists, and so on), insert anchors that link this document to other documents, and control character formatting (by making it bold or italic).

icon A graphic image onscreen that represents another object, such as a file on a disk.

infrared A type of port, normally found on notebooks, which enables cable-free connections. You can then set your notebook in front of your printer (if the printer has an infrared port, too) and print, or connect your notebook to your desktop PC or network without a cable. Infrared ports work like TV and VCR remote controls, and you have to point one infrared device right at the other one to get it to work.

insertion point A blinking vertical line used in most Windows word processors to indicate the place where any characters that you type are inserted. An insertion point is the equivalent of a *cursor*.

integrated program A program that combines the features of several programs, such as a word processor, spreadsheet, database, and communications program.

interactive A user-controlled program, document, or game. Interactive programs commonly display onscreen *prompts* asking the user for input so that they can decide how to carry out a particular task. These programs are popular in education, enabling children to follow their natural curiosity to solve problems and gather information.

interface A link between two objects, such as a computer and a modem. The link between a computer and a person is called a *user interface* and refers to the way a person communicates with the computer.

Internet A group of computers all over the world that are connected to each other. Using your computer and a modem, you can connect to these other computers and tap their resources. You can view pictures, listen to sounds, watch video clips, play games, chat with other people, and even shop.

IRC Short for Internet relay chat, this is the most popular way to chat with others on the Internet. With an IRC client (chat program), you connect to an IRC server, where you are presented with a list of available chat rooms. You can enter a room and then start exchanging messages with others in the room.

ISDN (Integrated Services Digital Network) ISDN is a system that enables your computer, using a special ISDN modem, to perform digital data transfers over special phone lines. Non-ISDN modems use analog signals, which are designed to carry voices, not data. ISDN connections can transfer data at a rate of up to 128Kbs, compared to about 56Kbps for the fastest analog modems.

keyboard   The main input device for most computers. You use the keyboard to type and to enter commands.

kilobyte (KB)   A unit for measuring the amount of data. A kilobyte is equivalent to 1,024 bytes (each byte is a character).

laptop   A small computer that's light enough to carry. Notebook computers and subnotebooks are even lighter.

load   To read data or program instructions from disk and place them in the computer's memory, where the computer can use the data or instructions. You usually load a program before you use it or load a file before you edit it.

macro   A recorded set of instructions for a frequently used or complex task. In most programs, you create a macro by telling the program to record your actions. You then name the macro or assign to it a keystroke combination. You can replay the macro at any time by selecting its name or by pressing the keystroke combination that you assigned to it.

megabyte   A standard unit used to measure the storage capacity of a disk and the amount of computer memory. A megabyte is 1,048,576 bytes (1,000KB). This is roughly equivalent to 500 pages of double-spaced text. Megabyte is commonly abbreviated as M, MB, or Mbyte.

memory   An electronic storage area inside the computer, used to temporarily store data or program instructions when the computer is using them. The computer's memory is erased when the power to the computer is turned off. Also referred to as *RAM*.

menu   A list of commands or instructions displayed onscreen. Menus organize commands and make a program easier to use.

MHz (megahertz)   Pronounced "mega-hurts," the unit used to measure the speed at which computer parts work. For example, a Pentium II 300MHz processor is faster than a Pentium II 233MHz processor. You should, however, compare speeds only between comparable devices. For example, if one device transmits 32 bits of data per clock cycle at 75MHz, and another device transmits only 16 bits of data per clock cycle at 150MHz, the second device isn't any faster overall.

microprocessor   Sometimes called the central processing unit (CPU) or processor, this chip is the computer's brain; it does all the calculations for the computer.

MMX   This acronym doesn't stand for anything. MMX is a new multimedia technology, developed by Intel, that enables your computer's CPU (processor) to take on more of the workload for handling multimedia files. This enables your computer to play media files faster and more smoothly.

modem   An acronym for MOdulator/DEModulator. A modem is a piece of hardware that enables a computer to send and receive data through an ordinary telephone line.

monitor   A television-like screen on which the computer displays information.

motherboard   The big printed circuit board inside the system unit into which everything else plugs.

mouse   A hand-held device that you move across the desktop to move an arrow, called a *mouse pointer*, across the screen. Used instead of the keyboard to select and move items (such as text or graphics), execute commands, and perform other tasks.

MS-DOS (Microsoft disk operating system)   See *DOS*.

multitasking   The process of performing two computer tasks at the same time. For example, you can be printing a document from your word processor while checking your email in Prodigy. One of the primary advantages of Windows is that it enables you to multitask.

network computer   A network computer (or NC) is a streamlined version of a standard PC, which relies on a network server or on Internet servers for most of its computing power. A typical network computer has a monitor, keyboard, mouse, processor, and memory but no hard drive or CD-ROM drive. Programs are stored on a central network computer. Although NCs cannot replace PCs, NCs are excellent for corporations because they require little maintenance and support.

newsgroup   An Internet bulletin board for users who share common interests. There are thousands of newsgroups, ranging from body art to pets (to body art with pets). Newsgroups let you post messages and read messages from other users.

notebook   A portable computer that weighs between 4 and 8 pounds.

online   Connected, turned on, and ready to accept information. Used most often in reference to a printer or modem.

pane   A portion of a window. Most programs display panes, so you can view two different parts of a document at the same time.

parallel port   A connector used to plug a device, usually a printer, into the computer. Transferring data through a parallel port is much faster than through a serial port, but parallel cables can carry data reliably only 15 to 20 feet.

partition   A section of a disk drive that's assigned a letter. A hard disk drive can be divided (or *partitioned*) into one or more drives, which your computer refers to as drive C, drive D, drive E, and so on. The actual hard disk drive is called the *physical* drive, and each partition is called a *logical* drive; however, these terms don't matter much—the drives still look like letters to you.

patch   A set of program instructions designed to fix a programming bug or add capabilities to a program. On the Internet, you can often download patches for programs to update the program.

path   The route that the computer travels from the root directory to any subdirectories when locating a file.

PC card   An expansion card that's about the size of a credit card, though thicker, and slides into a slot on the side of the notebook computer. PC cards enable you to quickly install RAM or a hard disk drive, modem, CD-ROM drive, network card, or game port, without having to open the notebook computer. See also *PCMCIA*.

PCI (Peripheral Component Interconnect)   A bus standard that effectively doubles or quadruples the amount of data that can travel around the highway system inside your computer. See also *bus*.

PCMCIA (Personal Computer Memory Card International Association)   An organization that has set standards for notebook computer expansion cards. See also *PC card*.

Pentium   The most popular CPU for PCs is manufactured by Intel. During the writing of this book, the Pentium II was the latest, greatest chip, offering speedy performance and support of MMX technology. You may also encounter an older Pentium, called Pentium (the original), Pentium Pro (a step up from the Pentium), or Pentium MMX (Pentium with enhanced multimedia features). A Pentium II is essentially a Pentium Pro with built-in MMX support.

peripheral   A device that's attached to the computer but is not essential for the basic operation of the computer. The system unit is the central part of the computer. Any devices attached to the system unit are considered *peripheral*, including a printer, modem, or joystick. Some manufacturers consider the monitor and keyboard to be peripheral, too.

pixel   A dot of light that appears on the computer screen. A collection of pixels forms characters and images on the screen.

PnP   Short for plug-and-play, PnP enables you to install expansion cards in your computer without having to set special switches. You plug it in, and it works.

port replicator   A slimmed down version of a docking station. See also *docking station*.

ports   The receptacles at the back of the computer. They get their name from the ports where ships pick up and deliver cargo. In this case, the ports enable information to enter and leave the system unit.

PPP (Point-to-Point Protocol)   A language that computers use to talk to one another. What's important is that when you choose an Internet service provider, you get the right connection—SLIP or PPP.

program   A group of instructions that tells the computer what to do. Typical programs are word processors, spreadsheets, databases, and games.

prompt   A computer's way of asking for more information. The computer basically looks at you and says, "Tell me something." In other words, the computer is *prompting* you or *prodding* you for information or a command.

protocol   A group of communications settings that control the transfer of data between two computers.

pull-down menu   A menu that appears at the top of the screen, listing various options. The menu is not visible until you select it from the menu bar. The menu then drops down, covering a small part of the screen.

random-access memory (RAM)   Where your computer stores data and programs temporarily. RAM is measured in kilobytes and megabytes. In general, more RAM means that you can run more powerful programs and more programs at once. Also called *memory*.

record   Used by databases to denote a unit of related information contained in one or more fields, such as an individual's name, address, and phone number.

ROM BIOS   See *BIOS*.

scanner   A device that converts images, such as photographs or printed text, into an electronic format that a computer can use. Many stores use a special type of scanner to read bar code labels into the cash register.

Screen Tip   See *ToolTip*.

scroll   To move text up and down or right and left on a computer screen.

SCSI (Small Computer System Interface)   Pronounced "scuzzy," SCSI provides speedier data transfer rates than are available through standard serial or parallel ports and enables you to connect several devices to the same port. Although SCSI makes it much easier to add SCSI compatible devices to your computer, USB offers greater flexibility.

SDRAM (synchronous dynamic RAM)   A type of RAM (memory) that is twice as fast as EDO DRAM because it synchronizes itself with the CPU. Although fast (operating at speeds of 100MHz), SDRAM has trouble keeping up with newer processors, which run at speeds of 300MHz. Look for even faster memory chips, such as RDRAM and SLDRAM.

server   Of two computers, the computer that's serving the other computer. On the Internet or on a network, your computer is the *client*, and the computer to which you're connected is the *server*.

service provider   The company that you pay in order to connect to its computer and get on the Internet.

shareware   Computer programs that you can initially use for free and then must pay for if you decide to continue using them. Many programmers start marketing their programs as shareware, relying on the honesty and goodwill of computer users for their income. That's why most of these programmers have day jobs.

software   Any instructions that tell your computer (the hardware) what to do. There are two types of software: operating system software and application software. *Operating system software* (such as Windows) gets your computer up and running. *Application software* enables you to do something useful, such as type a letter or chase lemmings.

spreadsheet   A program used for keeping schedules and calculating numeric results. Common spreadsheets include Lotus 1-2-3, Microsoft Excel, and Quattro Pro.

status bar   The area at the bottom of a program window that shows you what's going on as you work. A status bar may show the page and line number where the insertion point is positioned and indicate whether you are typing in overstrike or insert mode.

style   A collection of specifications for formatting text. A style may include information for the font, size, style, margins, and spacing. Applying a style to text automatically formats the text according to the style's specifications.

taskbar   A fancy name for the button bar at the bottom of the Windows desktop.

TCP/IP (Transmission Control Protocol/Internet Protocol)   A set of rules that govern the transfer of data over the Internet. To do anything on the Internet, you need a TCP/IP program. This program connects your computer to your service provider's computer, which is part of the Internet. You can then run other programs that enable you to do fun stuff such as browse the World Wide Web. Windows Dial-Up Networking is the only TCP/IP program that you need.

TFT (thin film transistor)   A technology used to improve the resolution on flat-panel displays, like those used on notebook computers.

toolbar   A strip of buttons typically displayed near the top of a program window, below the menu bar. The toolbar contains buttons that you can click to enter common commands, enabling you to bypass the menu system.

ToolTip   A small text box that displays the name of a button when you rest the mouse pointer on the button. ToolTips help you figure out what a button does, when you cannot figure it out from the picture.

touchpad   A pointing device commonly found on laptop computers that enables you to move the mouse pointer by running your finger over the pad.

trackball   A device, often used with laptop computers, which works like an upside-down mouse. It requires less desk space than a mouse because instead of moving it around the desk to move the pointer onscreen, you roll it in place to move the pointer.

transfer rate   A measure of how much information a device (usually a disk drive) can transfer from the disk to your computer's memory in a second. A good transfer rate is in the range of 500 to 600KB per second. The higher the number, the faster the drive.

uninterruptible power supply (UPS)   A battery-powered device that protects against power spikes and power outages. If the power goes out, the UPS continues supplying power to the computer so that you can continue working or can safely turn off your computer without losing data.

upload   To send data to another computer, usually through a modem and a telephone line or through a network connection.

URL (uniform resource locator)   An address for an Internet site. The Web uses URLs to specify the addresses of the various servers on the Internet and the documents on each server. For example, the URL for the Whitehouse server is **http://www.whitehouse.gov**. The **http** stands for Hypertext Transfer Protocol, which means this is a Web document; **www** stands for World Wide Web; **whitehouse** stands for Whitehouse; and **gov** stands for government.

USB (Universal Serial Bus)   The ultimate in plug-and-play technology. USB enables you to install devices without turning off your computer or using a screwdriver. You plug the component into the USB port, and it works. USB enables you to connect up to 127 devices to a single port. You can daisy-chain the devices with cables up to 5 meters long. *Daisy-chain* means that you can plug one device into the system unit, another device into the first device, and so on, until you have completely filled your office with add-ons.

Usenet (User's Network)   A collection of computers that is responsible for managing the flow of messages posted in newsgroups. See also *newsgroup*.

virtual memory   Disk storage that is treated as RAM (memory). Windows 95 can use disk space as virtual memory.

virus   A program that attaches itself to other files on a floppy or hard disk, duplicates itself without the user's knowledge, and may cause the computer to do strange and sometimes destructive things. The virus attacks the computer by erasing files from the hard disk or by formatting the disk.

Web   See *World Wide Web*.

Web browser   A program that enables you to navigate the World Wide Web (the most popular feature of the Internet). The World Wide Web consists of documents (pages) that may contain text, graphics, sound clips, video clips, and other items. A Web browser pulls the pages into your computer (using a modem or network connection) and displays them on your screen. See also *World Wide Web*.

wild card   Any character that takes the place of another character or a group of characters. In DOS, you can use two wild card characters: a question mark (?) and an asterisk (*). The question mark stands in for a single character. The asterisk stands in for a group of characters.

Windows   A way of displaying information in different parts of the screen. Often used as a nickname for Microsoft Windows.

word processor   A program that enables you to enter, edit, format, and print text.

word wrap   A feature that automatically moves a word to the next line if the word won't fit at the end of the current line.

World Wide Web   A part of the Internet that consists of multimedia documents that are interconnected by links. To move from one document to another, you click a link, which may appear as highlighted text or as a small picture or icon. The Web contains text, sound, and video clips, pictures, catalogues, and much, much more. See also *Web browser*.

write-protect   To prevent a computer from adding or modifying data stored on a disk.

Index

full system backups
(Windows 98 Backup
Wizard), 357-358
function keys, 20

G

game cards, installing, 319
Game Controllers icon
(Windows 95 Control
Panel), 67
game ports
desktop machines, 298
notebooks, 299
Games program group
(Windows 95 Accessories
menu), 44
gaming (joysticks), 8, 26,
77
grammar checking (editing
documents), 128
graphics
clip art, 142
adding to pages,
143-144
Internet sources, 143
libraries, 143
program sources, 142
text wrap options,
144
file formats, 149
moving, 148
paint programs
object-oriented
graphics, 147
Paint, 146
PaintBrush, 146
pixels, 147
working with shapes,
147
presentations, 145
35mm slide shows,
145

audience handouts,
145
builds, 145
onscreen slide shows,
145
overhead transparen-
cies, 145
transitions, 145
program text boxes
(entering information),
109
resizing, 148
text as WordArt, 149
graphics cards, *see* video,
display cards
graphics tablets (buying
tips), 302
gutter margins, 133

H

handling floppy disks, 34
handouts (presentations),
145
hanging indents (paragraph
formatting), 134
hard disk drives, 5, 30, 38
browsing contents (My
Computer), 49
cleaning, 352
copying files to floppy
disks, 172
deleting unnecessary
files, 78
desktop machines, 297
logical, 31
maintenance, 324-325
notebooks, 298
optimizing (speeding
up), 325
partitioning, 31
physical, 31

repairing
Disk Defragmenter,
327-328
doubling space,
328-330
ScanDisk, 326
saving space (removing
fonts), 137
software requirements,
77-78
upgrading, 316-317
hardware
companies (Web sites),
377-379
Internet access require-
ments, 226
keyboards, troubleshoot-
ing, 370-371
modems, 198, 208
fax modems, 203
flash ROM, 202
Hayes-compatibility,
198
installing, 204
internal vs. external,
198
ISDN and cable, 201
PC satellite dishes,
202
PCMCIA, 199
Plug-and-Play issues,
203
settings, 205-206
speed, 199-200
troubleshooting, 209,
368
V.34bis standard, 200
V.42bis standard, 200
video support, 203
voice support, 203
multimedia (sound
cards), 226

405

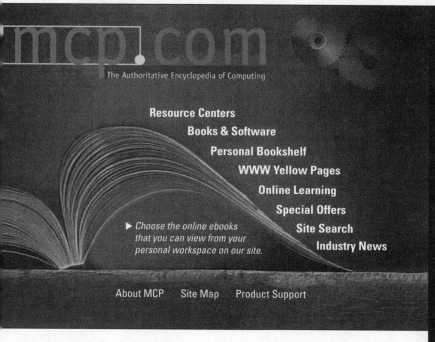